FUCHSIAS

FUCHSIAS

GERDA MANTHEY

Translated by
DAVID CHRISTIE

Technical Editor:
LEO BOULLEMIER

CHRISTOPHER HELM
A & C Black · London

TIMBER PRESS
Portland, Oregon

German edition published 1987 by
Eugen Ulmer GmbH & Co., Stuttgart, Germany

Translation © 1990 Christopher Helm Ltd

First published in Great Britain in 1990 by
Christopher Helm (Publishers) Ltd, Imperial House,
21–25 North Street, Bromley, Kent BR1 1SD

ISBN 0-7136-8001-6

A CIP catalogue record for this book is available from the
British Library.

First published in North America in 1990 by
Timber Press, Inc.
9999 S.W. Wilshire
Portland, Oregon, 97225, U.S.A.

ISBN 0-88192-187-4

Typeset by Rowland Phototypesetting Ltd,
Bury St Edmunds, Suffolk
Printed by Passavia GmbH, Passau, Germany
Bound in Great Britain

CONTENTS

PICTURE ACKNOWLEDGEMENTS

The drawings were produced by Mrs Cornelia Frank of Stuttgart, from sketches supplied by the author.

BIERMANN, H. J.: pages 22, 74, 118 (lower left), 122 (left), 123 (lower right), 126 (top right), 148, 171 (right).

BÖGEMANN, L.: 27, 31 (lower left).

BURDA GmbH, Offenburg: 62, 107.

FELBINGER, A.: 18, 59, 75, 79.

GRUSEN-SELLINK, M.: 66.

HECHT, H.: 78 (right), 110 (left), 127 (top right), 140 (bottom).

HEINKE, M.: 30 (bottom).

NOWINSKI, J.: 58 (right, 110 (lower right).

PREISSEL, H. G.: 67.

SEIBOLD, H.: 71.

SPRINGER, W.: 127 (bottom).

THIEME, E.: 127 (top left).

VAN DER POST, J. W.: 11, 14, 15 (bottom), 30 (top), 31 (top left), 58 (left), 106 (bottom), 111, 119 (right), 122 (right), 126 (bottom), 140 (top left), 141 (top), 144 (right), 145 (top), 152 (right), 156 (all three), 157 (top left, top right and centre), 160 (top and lower left), 181 (bottom), 185 (all three), 188 (top left and top right).

WEIHRAUCH, H.: 15 (top), 19, 70, 106 (top), 118 (top and lower right), 119 (left), 123 (top and lower left), 126 (top left), 140 (top right), 141 (centre and bottom), 144 (left), 145 (bottom), 149 (top and lower right), 152 (left), 153 (both), 157 (bottom), 160 (lower left), 171 (left), 175 (both), 180 (both), 181 (top).

WETTERWALD, M.-F.: 63, 78 (left), 188 (lower left).

CHAPTER ONE

THE DISCOVERY OF THE FUCHSIA

How poor our gardens would be today had not explorers with investigative minds and a wide botanical knowledge embarked upon long and fatiguing travels in earlier centuries in order to bring new, unknown plants to Europe.

At the start of the long history of cultivation of the fuchsia, however, there stands one man whom in the final analysis we must thank for today's splendour: Father Charles Plumier. Born in Marseilles on 20 April 1646, at the age of 16 he entered the 'Order of Minims', a strict Order that itself has passed into history. Initially he studied mathematics, but in Rome soon changed over to botany. From then on his whole passion was devoted to plants.

Having returned to France, he got to know the botanist Tournefort and, at this time, his first great herbarium came into being. On behalf of Louis XIV, Plumier made three great exploratory expeditions to South America in the final decade of the seventeenth century: in 1689, 1693 and 1695. The third journey took him to Brazil and to the islands of Guadeloupe, Martinique and Santo Domingo. In Santo Domingo he discovered a delicate flowering shrub which in his book *Nova Plantarum Americanum Genera*, published in Paris in 1703, he described as *Fuchsia triphylla flore coccinea*—in other words, three-leaved fuchsia with red flowers.

Besides this, the first fuchsia he discovered, Plumier describes and illustrates in his book a further 219 new American plants belonging to 106 genera. All of them he named after famous botanists.

When Charles Plumier was about to undertake a fourth journey in 1704 with the aim of identifying quinine trees in Peru, he fell ill just before embarkation and died on 20 November 1704 in Cadiz at the age of 59.

Even today, more than 280 years after his death, we still remember Plumier as the discoverer of the fuchsia. His importance as a botanist, however, has never been properly appreciated. He was after all the first to describe and name many hundreds of American plant species, yet, because he lived before Linnaeus published his work *Species Plantarum*, he is not regarded today as an authority in this field. Many names which he gave to various plant genera were taken over by Linnaeus and are still in fact used today: for example, *Bauhinia*, *Dioscorea*, *Fuchsia*, *Gesneria*, *Lobelia* and *Matthiola*.

His life's work was so phenomenal that we might ask ourselves when he ever could have found time for his religious order duties. Besides three large works that he published, he left behind 6,000 drawings, 4,300 of which depict plants, 22 volumes of manuscripts in the Royal Library, and nine volumes of manuscripts in the Library of the Royal Gardens (presumably in France). Not even half of this material, however, was ever published, and if it was at all then only as rather inaccurate renderings in books by other botanists. In memory of his friend Plumier, the botanist Tournefort named a plant genus *Plumeria*; this includes, among others, the magnificently flowering tropical frangipan trees.

As already mentioned, Charles Plumier followed the practice of his time and gave the newly discovered plant the name of a famous botanist. *Fuchsia* he named after Leonard Fuchs (1501–1566), who from 1535 until his death worked as Professor of Medicine at the University of Tübingen in southern West Germany and had become renowned through his book *De historia stirpium*.

Only a year later, in 1543, a German translation appeared in Basel of the 'New Herbal, in which not only is the complete history, that is names, appearance, place and time of growing, nature, vigour and effect of the majority of the herbs as grown in Teutonic and other lands, described with the best diligence, but also roots, stems, leaves, flowers, seeds, fruits and in all the complete form and character of all of these accurately and artistically portrayed and copied in such a way the like of which has never before been seen to come to light'.

This work, decorated with 518, in part very attractive wood-engravings, was frequently reprinted and translated; a further facsimile edition appeared in 1958. Leonard Fuchs is one of the fathers of botany. His work also contains the first list of botanical terms published in his German homeland.

Plumier appears not to have brought any seeds of *Fuchsia triphylla* back to Europe from his journey, for not until 1731 are further references to *Fuchsia triphylla* found, in Miller's *Gardener's Dictionary*. From seeds which Dr William Houston had collected in the years 1728 to 1732, Miller raised the first plants of *F. triphylla* in the Chelsea Physic Garden—at any rate it is highly likely that they were *F. triphylla*.

Carl von Linné (Linnaeus), the Swedish botanist and founder of the binomial system of nomenclature, took over Plumier's description and drawing of *F. triphylla coccinea* in his work *Species Plantarum*, but he named it *F. triphylla* in accordance with his own system.

In 1975, in *Gardeners Chronicle*, volume 87, J. Coutts gave an account of the first authentic fuchsia illustration, which R. P. L. Feuillé had published in the

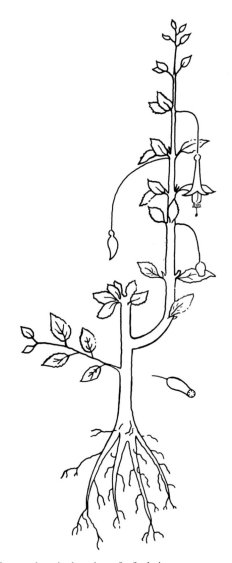

The first authentic drawing of a fuchsia.

Memorial tablet for Leonard Fuchs at his birthplace in Wemding, near Nördlingen in southern Germany (from a drawing by Professor A. E. Förster, Bonn-Bad Godesberg).

Journal des Observations Botaniques under the name of 'Thilco' (Chilean for fuchsia).

In the period from 1768 to 1840 more and more new fuchsia species were discovered and with splendid regularity brought to England. The larger nurseries even manned their own expeditions in order to bring new plant species back to England. Thus the firm of Veitch & Son of Exeter, Devon, sent William Lobb to South America, and from 1836 to 1843 the German botanist K. T. Hartweg made collections in Central America on behalf of the Royal Horticultural Society.

In these years the following species among others were brought to Europe:

Fuchsias can be combined effectively with other plants, as this illustration of the fuchsia display in Amsterdam in 1980 shows.

1796: *F. lycioides* to Kew;

1824: *F. arborescens*, imported from Mexico by Bullock and distributed by the Sloan Street Nursery;

1825: *F. excorticata*, the seeds of which were collected in New Zealand by Richardson and sown out in Colville's Nursery;

1828: *F. thymifolia*, to St Petersburg and England;

1829: *F. microphylla*, to St Petersburg and England;

1830: *F. fulgens*, distributed by James Lee of Hammersmith;

1840: *F. corymbiflora*;

1842: *F. splendens*, whose seeds were collected by Hartweg;

1843–4: *F. apetala, F. decussata* and *F. serratifolia* (today known as *F. denticulata*), imported by William Lobb.

Although the description of the first fuchsia had been known through Charles Plumier since 1703, not until 1873 was it possible to locate the exact site of discovery in Santo Domingo, in what is today the Dominican Republic. In that year Thomas Hogg rediscovered *F. triphylla flore coccinea*, by collecting seed in Haiti (Hispaniola) to send home to America. Subsequently grown plants from this seed were received in Britain from New York by Henderson's nursery of St John's Wood, London; they were identified by Kew Botanical Gardens in 1882.

3

CHAPTER TWO

HISTORY OF CULTIVATION

With the increasing spread of natural forms of fuchsias, the first attempts by gardeners to cross the species with each other soon began. The earliest records come from the year 1832 and relate to hybrids which the gardener Bunney of Stratford had produced using *F. magellanica* (*F. coccinea*) as one parent. In the same year Dennis of Chelsea brought out *F.* 'Globosa'; here, too, *F. magellanica* is assumed as the parent plant.

In 1839 *F.* 'Standishii', one of the first hybrids from *F. fulgens* × *F. magellanica*, was created. *F. boliviana*, *F. corymbiflora*, *F. regia*, *F. cordifolia*, *F. denticulata* and *F. splendens* were likewise used by various growers as parent plants of this first generation of fuchsia types.

A real breakthrough with completely new results was achieved in 1840, when the first fuchsia with white tube and sepals and purple-blue corolla was developed by John Gulliver, the gardener of a country parson in Herstmonceux in Sussex. The firm of Cripps in Tunbridge Wells brought this sensational novelty on to the market in 1842, under the name of 'Venus Victrix'. Even today in some collections 'Venus Victrix' is still carefully protected as something to treasure. For more than a hundred years up to the present day it has been used for cross-breeding. James Travis of Preston for example raised the cultivars 'Silverdale', 'Hawkshead' and 'Little Langdale' from *F. magellanica* var. *moliniae* × 'Venus Victrix' and, using 'Venus Victrix' as mother plant, 'The Tarns'. 'Venus Victrix' is also the mother of Alf Thornley's 'Dorothea Flower'.

In the previous century fuchsia species had already fascinated people, and now, with the introduction of ever newer and ever more beautiful hybrids, they began to sense what possibilities this genus held, what a wealth of forms and colours these elegant foreigners would yet reveal. A veritable triumphant advance of fuchsias began. Many eminent gardeners in England meanwhile occupied themselves with the cultivation of new fuchsia hybrids. Names such as Banks, Bull, Epps, Harrison, Lye, Salter, Standish,

Story, Rundle, Veitch and Youell are still in good repute even today. Many of the cultivars grown by them in those days are still esteemed and cultivated. Others have unfortunately been lost, among them perhaps similar 'gems' to the hybrid 'Mrs W. Rundle', which luckily has survived.

In 1848 Story succeeded in growing the first fuchsias with a white corolla and a double flower. At about the same time the first fuchsias with striped flowers such as 'Striata Perfecta' or 'Bland's New Striped' emerged.

The trademark of James Lye, who raised a series of excellent fuchsias from about 1871 onwards, was the cream-coloured waxen tube and sepals. Among those still being cultivated are 'Lye's Unique', 'Amy Lye' and 'Beauty of Swanley'.

The triumphant advance of the fuchsias was by no means restricted to England, even though it may appear so from the account so far presented.

In 1844, the Frenchman Felix M. Porcher, President of the Horticultural Society at Orléans, brought out the first book to deal exclusively and comprehensively with fuchsias: *Le Fuchsia, son Histoire and sa Culture*. In this he describes as many as 300 species and varieties. In 1848, in the second edition, there are already 520 cultivars and types. Of those described there, some are still being cultivated, for instance 'Queen Victoria' (Smith 1843), of which Porcher writes that it created a sensation; or 'Carnea', the description of which exactly fits the plants still in existence today. 'Petit' is still grown even today, as is 'Hebe' (Stokes 1848), still sought after and a cherished favourite, with its elegant, dainty, white and reddish-violet flowers. The name 'Hebe' was also given by other growers to their plants, but these are apparently no longer available.

In the 1852 catalogue of the Bass & Brown nursery at Sudbury, Suffolk, 'Tom Thumb' appears for the first time. This description also agrees precisely with today's plants ('Tom Thumb', Baudinat 1850). As *F. pumila* (1821) is also described in the same catalogue, these two plants cannot be identical as is often asserted today.

'Dominyana' (Dominy 1852), thought to be a hybrid of *F. spectabilis* × *F. serratifolia* (but is in fact *F. macrostigma* × *F. denticulata*), created a great sensation with its dark leaves and its brilliant red trumpet-shaped flowers. At the time it was extolled as 'profuse in flowers'.

As already mentioned, the first plants of seeds of *F. triphylla* reached Kew Gardens through Thomas Hogg in 1882, although the firm of Henderson of St John's Wood had earlier grown plants from the same source.

In 1895, the first British *triphylla* hybrid came into being, with *F. triphylla* 'Superba' (*F. triphylla* × *F. boliviana*) at Veitch's in Exeter. ('Rubin' raised by L. Vieweg in Quedlinburg, Germany in 1893 was the first of all the *triphylla* hybrids, crossing *F. triphylla* with *F. boliviana*.)

From then on things quietened down in England so far as fuchsias were concerned. Almost the entire development took place during the time of Queen Victoria (1837–1901). It is therefore small wonder if the 'old-fashioned', honest and simple charm of fuchsias—especially if they are cultivated as large crown shrubs—so appeals to the fuchsia-lover of today. They remind people of the 'good old days'.

In parallel with the developments in England, there were also gardeners in Germany and France who were engrossed in fuchsias. The wave of enthusiasm reached Germany early. In the *Deutschen Magazin für Garten und Blumenkunde* (German Gardening and Horticultural Magazine), issue 1 of 1848, we find a detailed account of the recently imported *F. serratifolia* (Ruiz and Pavon.) (syn. *F. denticulata*) and of *F. macrantha* (Hooker). The introduction is so delightful that it is worth repeating it here.

> To eulogise the fuchsia is surely superfluous, for it commends itself at first sight.
>
> Simply the oldest species, the *F. coccinea* (Aiton) has always been a welcome shrub, yet the goodwill of flower-lovers towards the same has increased all the more as ever newer and more beautiful sorts were discovered and were created through artificial pollination. We believed that we possessed the most beautiful thing after we obtained the dainty 'Venus Victrix' and the magnificent *F. corymbiflora*, yet this was by no means the supreme climax for every year we get newer and more beautiful ones, indeed we learn through travellers that the more

interesting species are still to be awaited from their homelands. That this assertion is a fact is demonstrated to us by the introduction of the *serratifolia* [*denticulata*] and *macrantha*.'

In 1855, an article appeared in the German Gardening and Horticultural Magazine at Stuttgart on the creation of a new German fuchsia type 'Glory von Neisse' at Rother's in Neisse. The unnamed author concludes with the following recommendation:

> Herr Gottlob Pfitzer, market-gardener in Stuttgart, Kriegbergstr. 38, by the Friedrich's Gate, has acquired from Herr Rother the sole possession of this novelty, being so far the only one of its kind among the German produce, and opened a subscription for this which is executed next spring, as soon as the necessary number of subscribers is gathered; and therefore the honoured buyers will do well to send in their subscriptions forthwith, as the early timing of dispatch depends on this. One specimen costs 1 fl 30 Kr. With a subscription for three specimens a fourth is added free of charge.
>
> Besides this most recent issue Herr Gottlob Pfitzer possesses the best-known varieties, including the new English one with white corolla and the like . . .

In those days, then, people subscribed for new types of fuchsia as they do today for instance for very expensive books.

Now, the 'Glory von Neisse' has not, so far as is known, outlasted the past 135 years. The descendants of that Gottlob Pfitzer, however, are to the present day keen to pass on good new plants to fanciers.

That plant novelties then, as now, had their price is shown from a further article in the same issue of the gardening magazine:

> Messrs Henderson & Son, Wellington Nursery, St John's Wood, London, this spring announced a number of new fuchsias which they have in exclusive possession and are putting on the market. The most outstanding of these are some beautiful red ones with snow-white corolla, as well as some with striped corolla and one ('Prince Albert') with glorious dark blue corolla. The latter they purchased from E. Banks, Esq., the rest from W. Story, Esq., at the considerable price of 100 guineas. Story is the grower of the first scarlet-red fuchsia with snow-white corolla.

Part of the fuchsia display in Amstel Park, Amsterdam, in 1978.

The cultivars brought on to the market by Messrs Henderson are the following:

'Queen Victoria' (Story) .... 3 crowns 15
'Prince Albert' (Banks) .... 3 crowns 15
'Mrs Story' (Story) .... 3 crowns 15
'Ranunculaeflora' (Story) .... 7 crowns
'Perugino' (Story) .... 3 crowns 15
'Empress Eugenie' (Story) .... 3 crowns 15
'Water Nymph' (Story) .... 3 crowns 15

A total of nine varieties is dispensed at 28 silver crowns. With the commercial spirit of the German gardeners it is not to be doubted that these novel-ties will be available to us in the shortest time possible at considerably cheaper prices.

The gardening magazine of 1855 was devoted almost exclusively to the fuchsia and contained a further article of particular interest, on the rather difficult to cultivate 'Dominyana':

Although the cultivation of fuchsias is in general a very easy and well-known one, there are neverthe-less many species and varieties which are difficult to bring to flower, and yet it is often a small matter to remove this difficulty. As the 'Dominyana' is derived from a species which is one of the more difficult yet was improved through the very profusely flowering male parent species, nevertheless a mistake could be made by many a less experienced person, and for that reason we here give the information on cultivation as imparted by Mr Van Houtte in his valuable 'Flore des Serres'. On this he says:

'To cultivate this hybrid successfully, one proceeds in the following way: The cuttings are kept in a mixture of sand and leaf mould in a sealed, moderately warm closet. In strong sunshine they must be shaded over the midday period, and after 4–5 days be allowed fresh air for a few minutes in the morning. When the cuttings have rooted, they are transplanted individually into pots in the same earth mixture. We prefer this compost to any other because it is particularly suited for winter cultivation and guarantees the young plants a good growth.

After potting out, the plants are still kept in a closet for such a length of time until they have completely rooted. The plants are now placed in a warm and shady place in the orangery, and later gradually acclimatised to the open air by carefully allowing fresh air flow towards them through the ventilation devices. This treatment is given them up to January, from which time the heat is very gradually increased from 4 to 8 degrees Reamur [the old German temperature scale] up to 12 to 14 degrees. With the onset of spring weather the temperature must be reduced at night by about 5 degrees to avoid too luxuriant a growth, and likewise the over-great humidity of the air must be reduced by frequent ventilation. Now they are put nearer the light, but protected from too strong a midday sun.

When growth is luxuriant they are transplanted every 5 to 6 weeks, but in so doing care must be taken that the transplanting is made not with damp but with drier clods of earth. After transplanting they must be kept for several days in a close atmosphere and watered until taking root again. When the plants have reached a certain size, then on further transplanting an additional part of rotten cow manure is added to the sand and the leaf mould. For more uniform moisture control of the earth clod and for the promotion of growth of the upper roots, a layer of moss can beneficially be laid on the soil, which at the same time prevents water-logging of the earth when sprinkling. The best

'City of Pacifica' (upper), 'Alison Ewart' (lower).

water when sprinkling is, as for all other plants, rainwater. The size of the pots when transplanting must be commensurate with the growth capacity. During the vegetative period it is good if a quantity of sheep or cow manure is added to the water every week. The main shoot on each plant must be tied to a stick, the side shoots treated with care and only rampant and proliferate shoots removed. With this treatment one may be assured of a brilliant success.'

A further important grower of this time, the second half of the last century, was Johann Nepomuk Twrdy (1806–1883) from Brno in Moravia. In his article 'Fuchsias of German Cultivation' (in the German Magazine for Flowers and Gardening, issue 14, Stuttgart 1861), he reports on new varieties from this year. His advice on growing, too, is still worth reading, and anybody who takes note of it today is well advised:

The augmentation in the perfection of, and going hand in hand with this the passion for, fuchsias, these such precious and lovely plants for growing in pots as well as the garden, occasioned me to carry out pollination experiments, and I had the pleasure of obtaining seedlings which can compete with the most beautiful foreign ones. As the varieties with double corolla still meet with more approval from flower-lovers than those with a single one, I therefore gave my special attention to the same . . .

By 'customarily good cultivation' it is meant that one uses neither special boosting agent nor artificial forcing method, that one is also not content, however, with planting out the young plants that one obtains in the second-best earth and small pots, or in some place outdoors without being selective at all, but that one chooses a vigorously productive soil and appropriate pots for the same. Over-large pots are not necessary, but all the more so an appropriate transplanting from smaller to suitably larger ones as soon as the pot is completely filled with roots hence the plant no longer finds sufficient food for luxuriant growth and for the most complete possible development of its numerous flower buds.

When planting out outdoors, too, various things must be taken into consideration:

Firstly the soil, which should not be too loamy and heavy but light and productive, for the fuchsia is a forest plant in the wild state and as such enjoys a very humus-rich soil which has been created from dead vegetable matter, and partly also from animal remains, over thousands of years in the primeval forests. Where the soil in a garden seems too heavy and insufficiently fertile for fuchsia-growing, it must be helped along by improving it with light compost and manure.

Secondly the position. This is best a semi-shaded one, protected from the midday sun. The full sun in a very hot place should where possible be avoided, because here the flowers acquire neither the size nor the coloration as in a sheltered spot, particularly pale or white sorts, which in the sun always acquire a red, sometimes very dirty tinge. Also, the green of the leaves is not so intense and lush in the sun as in the shade.

Thirdly the specimens. Quite small specimens, especially of new cultivars whose growth and habitat are not yet known, should never be planted out in the open straightaway. With varieties which by nature have a luxuriant tall growth it does work better, but those which keep low and tend to spread their branches horizontally can never present their flowers handsomely if they grow to maturity so low down. Varieties of this kind, which after all can also have their advantages with regard to their flowers, should always be raised with care beforehand in pots up to an adequate height and only then be planted out. With arrangements it is all the more necessary to get to know the growth of the individual varieties beforehand, because otherwise the whole group could easily acquire a poor appearance if by chance weakly and sparsely growing varieties come to be standing in the middle and more luxuriantly growing ones on the outside.

If these few suggestions are given again here, then this is done purely and simply in the interests of fuchsia-growing in general. How often do we have to listen to beginners that this or that variety has turned out quite differently from the way the description or illustration portrayed it. Indeed, it seems that an enthusiast orders a variety he has seen in particular exuberance and is of the opinion that a newly purchased young plant, sometimes coming straight from the propagation house, must flower just as perfectly as the full-grown specimen. As a result it makes no difference to him whether it is exposed to the burning midday sun on the windowsill or the balcony parapet, whether it stands in deep shadow like a forest plant or whether he has tended the fuchsia properly until it has gained strength and is capable of perfect bloom.

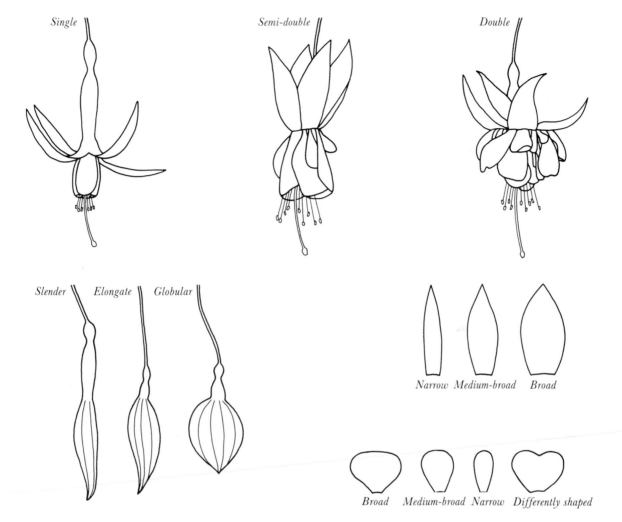

Single   *Semi-double*   *Double*

Slender *Elongate* *Globular*

Narrow Medium-broad Broad

Broad *Medium-broad* *Narrow* *Differently shaped*

Flower types (top), flower-bud types (centre, left), sepals and petals (centre, right). The flower of a fuchsia with details on flower dimensions (bottom, right).

The fuchsias are one of the plant genera 'which demand nothing less than a complex cultivation method; yet the little that is absolutely necessary for their perfection should not be set aside if one wishes to be assured of a good success'.

In Porcher's 4th edition of *Le Fuchsia, son Histoire et sa Culture*, published in 1874, six German fuchsia-growers are mentioned: Koch, Twrdy, Zaubitz, Wilkens, Weinrich and Pfitzer. Later they are joined by further such familiar names as Klein, Eggebrecht, Kiese, Köhler, Teupel, Hartnauer, Rademacher, Mahnke, Schadendorff and finally Bonstedt and Rehnelt.

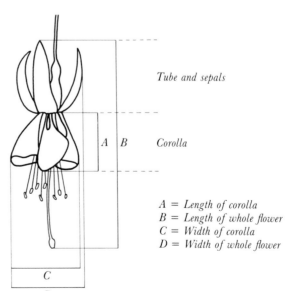

Tube and sepals

A *B* *Corolla*

A = Length of corolla
B = Length of whole flower
C = Width of corolla
D = Width of whole flower

C

D

Few plants flower as profusely and enduringly as fuchsias; here the cultivar is 'Lena'.

Meanwhile, in France, Lemoine in Nancy and Rozain-Boucharlat in Lyon had also started on fuchsia-growing on a large scale. In the course of 80 years more than 400 of their own particular cultivars were brought on to the market by Lemoine and his son. 'Emile de Wildeman' (known in England as 'Fascination'), 'Dollarprinzessin' ('Dollar Princess'), 'André le Nostre', 'Abbé Farges' and many more are still to be found in the collections today and are even offered in the catalogues of nurserymen.

The best-known cultivar from Rozain-Boucharlat is the versatile, robust 'Marinka'.

Other French growers of this period were Crousse, Baudinat, Dubus, Salter and Meillez.

Of the Belgian growers Cornelissen, de Coene, Verschaffelt and Delbaeve, Cornelissen has made a name for himself through his outstanding variety with red tube and sepals and white corolla. His 'Madame Cornelissen' is to be found in many gardens as a good, cold-climate, sun-tolerant cultivar.

The nineteenth century was nearing its end when once again a high point occurred in the history of the development of fuchsias.

Carl Bonstedt (1866–1953), director of the botanical garden at Göttingen in Germany, endowed the fuchsia world with his *triphylla* hybrids, also called

Fuchsias in a container as an eye-catcher: left 'Checkerboard', bottom centre 'Swingtime', next to it 'Gesäuseperle'.

cluster-flower fuchsias, a completely novel group of plants. They were all characterised by erect growth and beautiful dark leaves and had elegant long flowers in shades of bright orange and red. 'Mary' (1894) originated from *F. triphylla* × *F. corymbiflora*. Later, Bonstedt also worked with *F. fulgens* × *F. corymbiflora* and their hybrids. The novelties which sprung up at rapid intervals in the ensuing years, up to about 1906, were all brought on to the market by his friend Bornemann. 'Göttingen', 'Koralle', 'Traudchen Bonstedt' and 'Gartenmeister Bonstedt' can still often be admired as border plants in parks in full sunshine.

In April 1901, in the magazine *Garden World*, Friedrich Rehnelt, garden supervisor at Giessen near Frankfurt, reported on his new fuchsia 'Andenken an Heinrich Henkel' (*F. corymbiflora* × 'Magnifica'). Very much later, in 1928, the garden supervisor Hartnauer raised his well-known cultivar 'Leverkusen' from seedlings of this new *triphylla* hybrid in the works garden of Bayer Leverkusen. It does, however, carry its typical *triphylla* flowers in the leaf axils like most fuchsia hybrids, and not at the end of the young branches in racemes.

Beautiful new varieties still appeared now and then, such as:

'Gruss aus dem Bodethal' (Sattler & Bethge, Quedlinburg 1894),
'Alice Hoffmann' (Kiese 1901),
'Vielliebchen' ('Charming' × *F. magellanica* 'Gracilis', Wolf, Köthen 1911),
'Neue Welt' (Mahnke, Niederschönhausen 1912),
'Hilde Rademacher' (Rademacher, Mühlheim 1925),
'Saarpfalz' (Köhler, Bexbach 1926).

With the start of the First World War things became markedly quieter on the fuchsia front. Throughout Europe, the horticultural businesses saw it as their chief duty to help towards feeding the people. Ornamental plants had to give way to the growing of fruit and vegetables; coal as a matter of priority was used for purposes other than the heating of greenhouses. After the war the people of Europe still had other concerns for many a long year. In the meantime fuchsias—apparently—fell into total oblivion. Some collections, however, predominantly those in botanic gardens, must have survived these troublesome war and post-war years, for many of the fuchsia varieties known at that time are again widespread today.

The sweeping passion for fuchsias which had lasted a whole century in Europe was for the time being extinguished. The spark that was to rekindle it, however, had already been lit. This time the impetus came from North America, or to be more exact from California. In the mild, humid coastal climate of that region fuchsias thrive superbly as garden shrubs. The relatively equable temperatures both in summer and in winter enable fuchsias to flower almost without a break throughout the entire year and thus to be able to display their full beauty. Only to give them an attractive shape are they pruned a little in December.

What could be more reasonable, then, than the wish to make the joy in these beautiful plants available to many people.

In 1929 several particularly keen fuchsia-lovers came together and founded the American Fuchsia Society (AFS). This, the first fuchsia society in the world, was called upon to initiate a new development. A 'fuchsia renaissance' had begun. True to their motto, to further the development of fuchsias, and with American thoroughness, the members set to work.

As early as the summer of 1930 a delegation of three members travelled to England to collect information and fuchsia plants. In order to guard against losses on the long journey, two shipments were made of the 51 European fuchsia types selected. One went to the University of California, and the other, with the same 51 plants, to a famous nursery, George Budgen of Berkeley Horticultural Nursery, California.

Forty-eight of these new fuchsias survived the long voyage, were propagated and were made available to the members of the AFS. Monthly bulletins and very informative books on fuchsias were published. The most important was *A Check List of Fuchsias* by Dr E. O. Essig, an attempt to describe the fuchsia species and varieties—over 1,900 of them—known at that time. It appeared in April 1936. In the foreword to this list Dr Essig particularly thanks Dr Alexander Steffen of Pillnitz, near Dresden, who had contributed a large amount of information on European fuchsia types.

In 1937 the first breeding result with the new fuchsias imported from Europe was declared. Dr Lagen brought out 'Cascade' ('Rolla' × 'Amy Lye'). This was the beginning of a new era of fuchsia-breeding. Ever new fuchsias with bigger and bigger flowers appeared, often of brand-new shapes and of a breathtaking diversity of colour. Some of the early American growers, with their varieties, are listed here:

Brand: 'Joyce', 'Errol', 'San Leandro'
Evans and Reeves: 'Claire Evans', 'Mrs Lovell Swisher'
Garson: 'RAF', 'Winston Churchill'
Hazard & Hazard: 'Chang', 'Flash', 'Other Fellow'
Haag: 'Jack Ackland', 'White Spider', 'Golden Dawn'
Hodges: 'Citation', 'Miss California', 'Purple Sage'
Martin: 'Blue Pearl', 'Lady Beth', 'Sophisticated Lady'
Munkner: 'Curtain Call', 'Golden Glow', 'Torch'
Niederholzer: 'Lucky Strike', 'Bubble Hanger', 'Treasure'
Nelson: 'Rufus' (The Red), 'Gay Fandango'
Schmidt: 'Crown Jewel', 'Carioca'
Tiret: 'Swingtime', 'Sweet Leilani', 'Angela Leslie'
Waltz: 'Flirtation Waltz', 'Royal Velvet', 'The Aristocrat'
Walker & Jones: 'Checkerboard', 'Mission Bells', 'South Gate'
Reiter: 'Falling Star', 'Flying Cloud', 'Mantilla', 'Fanfare'

The scarcely conceivable wealth of new fuchsia varieties very soon brought the AFS new responsibilities. The International Association for Horticultural Science appointed the AFS to register all new varieties in the world. The name of the grower, the parent plants from which the new plant originated, colour and shape of the flowers, the style of growth and other interesting details are accurately recorded and published annually in the March bulletin of the AFS. Above all, however, the registration office makes sure that two different cultivars are not by chance given the same name, something which was unfortunately often the case in the last century and has led to confusion.

With so much activity by the American society —numerous new fuchsias had already come across the Atlantic—it was virtually inevitable that the wave of enthusiasm carried back to Europe. The British were the first to take up fuchsias again. In 1938 a society was formed in London which was later given the name British Fuchsia Society (BFS). Even though the outbreak of the Second World War was not exactly conducive to its development in the early stages, attempts were still made to maintain contact with the members through the publication of year-books. With the end of the war an astonishing development then set in. Before long fuchsias had regained their earlier popularity. Fuchsia nurseries, spread throughout Britain, sprung up like mushrooms and imported brand-new American cultivars into Britain. The BFS, which in the meantime has grown to more than 6,000 members, issues a very informative year-book and periodical publications with advice on growing in which the members also exchange their practical experiences with fuchsias.

One of the early, very active members of the BFS was a retired gardener, W. P. Wood. He spent many years cultivating particularly hardy fuchsias. In this case we must, of course, understand hardiness as it applies in the relatively mild winter climate of England. Some of his varieties, however, have proven themselves to be thoroughly hardy even in gardens of countries such as Germany, for example 'Margaret' (Wood 1943, *F. magellanica* var. *molinae* × 'Heritage'). Unfortunately he was not able to complete his important work: he died suddenly in July 1953. Many of his breeding results are to be found detailed in his book *A Fuchsia Survey* (1950).

Today so many growers in England are very successfully occupied in creating new forms of fuchsia that only occasionally are the very new American varieties found in the catalogues.

Many of the new British fuchsias are even better suited to the sadly often very cool and damp summers. Unlike the Californian growers, who have raised mostly fuchsias with a pendulous growth and large to very large flowers, the British place the emphasis of their work on the raising of upright-growing fuchsias with flowers that are not very full, are rain-resistant and are borne well visible above the leaves. These plants are therefore especially suited for planting out in balcony boxes and in garden borders, whereas the large-flowered 'Californians', in order to bring them to their full beauty, can be used better in the greenhouse, under the shelter of roof projections, on balconies or roofed terraces.

The Dutch also discovered the beauty of fuchsias relatively early on. In 1965 the 'Nederlandse Kring van Fuchsia-Vrienden' (Dutch Circle of Fuchsia-Lovers) was established. Milestones in the systematic efforts to popularise fuchsias were displays at two-year intervals at Zwolle, The Hague, Utrecht, Leiden and Amsterdam. Six issues per year of *Fuchsiana* are published for the members and these report on the work of the 'Circle'. Each issue is accompanied by a colour print of a fuchsia for collecting.

In honour of the first president, Mevrouw Meursing, the woman who carried out vital work for the 'Circle' in its early years, in 1968 the Englishman G. Hopgood named a fuchsia cultivar 'Mieke Meursing'.

The Dutch growers, van Wieringen with the very good cultivars 'Kwintet', 'Boerhaave' and 'Sweetheart', and in more recent years especially, H. J. de Graaff of Lisse with his quite exceptional varieties 'Machu Picchu', 'Medusa', 'First Kiss' and 'Tour Eiffel' (1977 and 1978), have likewise enriched the whole assortment of fuchsias.

In Germany there has probably always been a great affection for fuchsias, although it thrived in a more concealed fashion. Not until the 1960s were the first attempts undertaken, by Wolansky in Trappenkamp, to set up a circle of fuchsia-lovers through circulars and collective ordering of fuchsias from England.

At the same time the firm of Töpperwein in Ortenburg also began to bring new cultivars of American fuchsias into the nurseries through re-importing and propagation. The Töpperwein company deserves the very highest praise for this action, for the fuchsia collections of German nurseries from north to south consisted of the same, at most five or six, cultivars.

The cultivar 'Beacon' (Bull, England, 1871), which has undoubtedly had its quality put to the test for more than 100 years, is even today still the most propagated and best-selling fuchsia in Germany, although in the meantime there are many available with equally good attributes but much more attractive colours.

In 1974 the German fuchsia-fanciers joined up with a society of long standing, the German Dahlia and Gladioli Society. Under the new name of the German Dahlia, Fuchsia and Gladioli Society, with headquarters in Landau/Pfalz, the society has successfully endeavoured to help fuchsias to regain their popularity in the country. It assists the fancier in the creation of new varieties and is always prepared to give advice. In many regions distributed throughout that country, and also in Austria and Switzerland, local circles have been formed which meet for talks and exchange plants and experiences. The first two fuchsia shows in Bad Neuenahr (1978) and at the National Horticultural Exhibition in Bonn (1979) brought great success to the exhibitors.

A long-standing member, Herr Karl Nutzinger, Director of the Admont/Steiermark Horticultural Institute in Austria, brought many beautiful new fuchsias from his own cultivation on to the market. With his quite exceptionally beautiful cultivar 'Elfriede Ott' he has raised a lasting monument to

'Red Ribbon'.

himself among fuchsia-fanciers. On 5 September 1981 a long-cherished wish of many fuchsia-lovers was fulfilled. On that day, in the palm gardens of Frankfurt, the first German botanical society that was concerned exclusively with fuchsias was founded: the German Fuchsia Society. The quarterly *Fuchsienkurier* (Fuchsia Courier), regular shows and meetings of regional local circles should foster the spread of fuchsias.

CHAPTER THREE

SECTIONS AND SPECIES

Fuchsias occupy the following position in the plant kingdom, represented by the example of *Fuchsia microphylla* var. *aprica* (after Engler, *Catalogue of the Plant Families*):

Division: Angiospermae
Class: Dicotyledonae (two seed-leaves)
Subclass: Archichlamydeae (free-petalled)
Order: Myrtiflorae (myrtle plants)
Family: Onagraceae (candle plants)
Genus: *Fuchsia* (fuchsia)
Section: *Encliandra*
Species: *microphylla*
Variety: *aprica*

In December 1943, Professor Philip A. Munz, Botanist at the University of California, published his monograph 'A Revision of the Genus *Fuchsia*, Onagraceae' (California Academy of Sciences, vol. XXV). He divided the 100 species of fuchsia known up to that time into seven sections.

Changes in Munz's book have in the meantime been published. The section *Fuchsia* (previously described by Munz as *Eufuchsia*), by far the largest of the present nine sections, was revised by Dr Paul E. Berry in 1982. It now contains 61 species, described in the *Annals of the Missouri Botanical Garden*, vol. 69, no. 1, 1982.

The section *Schufia* and the new sections *Ellobium* and *Jimenezia*, all native to Mexico and Central America, were revised by Dr Dennis E. Breedlove, Dr Paul E. Berry and Professor Peter Raven. The results have likewise been published in the above-mentioned *Annals*.

Munz is further considered as the authority for the sections *Quelusia*, *Kierschlegeria* and *Hemsleyella*. New results of systematic studies, however, have been completed with 'Systematic Revision of *Fuchsia* Section *Quelusia*' by Dr P. E. Berry in 1989 and 'Systematics of the Apetelous Fuchsias of South America *Fuchsia* Section *Hemsleyella*' in 1985, both of which are described in the *Annals of the Missouri Botanical Garden*, 42-213-251, 1985 and vol. 76, no. 2, 1989.

The New Zealand fuchsias of the section *Skinnera* have been revised by H. H. Allen and published in the work *Flora of New Zealand* (published by R. E. Owen, New Zealand, 1961).

Equally, Munz can no longer be regarded as the authority for the fuchsias in the section *Encliandra* since Dr Dennis E. Breedlove brought out his book *The Systematics of Fuchsia Section* Encliandra *(Onagraceae)* (University of California Press 1969).

The genus *Fuchsia* belongs to the candle plants family, as do our native willowherbs (*Epilobium*) or other evening primroses (*Oenothera*), and the summer flowers *Clarkia* and *Godetia*.

The fuchsias probably have their true home in the Andes in Peru. From here they spread northwards to Venezuela and across the Central America bridge to Mexico. To the south they spread as far as Tierra del Fuego at the Strait of Magellan, and westwards across the Pacific Ocean to New Zealand and Tahiti. Apart from an enclave in the Oregon Mountains west of Rio de Janeiro, they do not appear to have spread eastwards naturally before they reached Europe by human hand.

Forms of *F. magellanica* are today naturalised everywhere along the west coast of the British Isles, from Cornwall to Scotland and in Ireland, as hedges and bushes.

The natural range extends over a distance of almost 10,000 km. It reaches from north Mexico through Guatemala, Honduras, El Salvador, Costa Rica, Panama, Colombia, Venezuela, Ecuador, Brazil, Bolivia, Peru, Chile and Argentina to Tierra del Fuego and harbours a multitude of species and varieties. By way of contrast, the New Zealand species of the section *Skinnera*, which have moved a particularly long distance, display typical characteristics.

Although fuchsias come from tropical regions, they are certainly not tropical plants in the true sense.

The natural habitats of Fuchsias.

North America

Haiti
Santo Domingo

South America

Tahiti

New Zealand

They grow chiefly in higher mountain regions in or on the edge of rainforest. Only in the southernmost parts of their range do they forsake the mountains and find the living conditions that are still to their liking on slopes and in the valleys.

Botanic gardens and private collectors cultivate and maintain a whole number of species which are often of exotic beauty. The interest in them is constantly increasing; as many as 56 of the 100 or so fuchsia species so far recognised are in cultivation either in Britain, Holland or in California.

Section Quelusia

The species which are quite obviously recognisable as fuchsias belong in this first section. e.g. *F. magellanica*

and *F. regia*. Professor Munz also includes here most cultivars, as *F. hybrida*.

Fuchsias in this section have a tube which is not longer than the sepals. The anthers on long filaments project far outside the corolla. Also characteristic of this section are the red tube and sepals and the blue or purple corolla. Only in this section do we find the deep purple-blue colour.

As previously mentioned, this section was revised by Dr P. E. Berry in 1989.

Section Fuchsia (Eufuchsia)

This is the largest section, comprising 61 species. According to the rules of modern nomenclature,

Quelusia

This section was revised by Dr Paul Berry in 1982 with both additions and deletions:
alpestris
bracelinae
brevilobis (newly described species by Berry)
campos-postoi
coccinea
glazioviana
hatsebachii (newly described species by Berry)
magellanica
regia
and three subspecies:
regia subsp. *regia*
regia subsp. *serrae*
regia subsp. *reitzii*

though, it had to be renamed as section Fuchsia because it contains the type species (*F. triphylla*). All species in this section have a very long tube and small short sepals. The colour range is restricted to various shades of red, which are often set off with green. Some grow as shrubs, others are climbing plants or epiphytes. The leaves are usually in whorls of three.

Quite a few species are in cultivation, including *F. boliviana*, *F. denticulata*, *F. gehrigeri*, *F. magdalenae*, *F. sanctae-rosae*, *F. triphylla*, *F. venusta* and *F. wurdackii*.

Section *Kierschlegeria*

This section boasts only one species. The short spikes that remain on the plant as remnants of the midrib

Fuchsia

(previously known as Eufuchsia)
This section was revised by Dr Paul Berry in 1985, with both additions and deletions:
abrupta
ampliata
andrei
austromontana
ayavacensis
boliviana
canescens
caucana
ceracea
cinerea
cochabambana

confertifolia	*hirtella*	*putumayensis*
coriacifolia	*lehmannii*	*rivularis*
corollata	*llewelynii*	*sanctae-rosae*
corymbiflora	*loxensis*	*sanmartina*
crassistipula	*macropetala*	*scabriuscula*
cuatrescasasii	*macrophylla*	*scherffiana*
decussata	*macrostigma*	*sessilifolia*
denticulata	*magdalenae*	*simplicicaulis*
(syn. *serratifolia*)	*mathewsii*	*steyermarkii*
dependens	*nigricans*	*sylvatica*
ferreyrae	*orientalis*	*tincta*
fontinalis	*ovalis*	*triphylla*
furfuracea	*pallescens*	*vargasiana*
gehrigeri	*petiolaris*	*venusta*
glaberrima	*pilosa*	*verrucosa*
harlingii	*polyantha*	*vulcanica*
hartwegii	*pringsheimii*	*wurdackii*

North America

South America

Tahiti

New Zealand

Kierschlegeria
lycioides

when the leaf has fallen are characteristic. The single species is *F. lycioides*, which was found in the Atacama Desert in Chile. There it must remain leafless for most of the year and bear the small pink flowers at the ends of the branches. *F. lycioides*—in pure form—appears not to be in cultivation. What is sold and cultivated today under this name is a hybrid of *F. magellanica*.

Section Skinnera

This section comprises the species which have their natural home in Tahiti and New Zealand. Among the four recognised species, not only the tallest tree of this genus but also a prostrate species only 5 cm high are

to be found. Others are shrubs or climbing plants.

F. procumbens, the prostrate species, has a yellow tube with brown sepals and no petals. The flowers are carried upright and the fruits are very decorative; when fully ripe, the latter look like little plums. This species is a fairly hardy one, even in central Europe, and charming when used as a cushion plant in a rock garden. The species described by Munz as *F. kirkii* is the male form of *F. procumbens*.

In its homeland *F. excorticata* is a tree growing up to 10 m tall with brown bark which often peels away from the trunk in strips. The long flowers are initially green and yellow and later change colour to brownish and violet.

F. perscandens is a climber with similar flowers to those of *F. excorticata*.

F. × colensoi is an untidily growing shrub and a

naturally evolved hybrid between the two previously described species.

New Zealand fuchsias have heterostylous flowers in which species with long styles have narrower flowers. The filaments differ in length and are sometimes almost enclosed. The varying length of the pistils can be explained by the heterostyly morphology. There are flowers with long, medium-length and short pistil. In the long-pistilled type the flower pollen is rudimentary and sits on very short filaments, thus making the flower functional as a female one. In the form with a medium-long pistil the filaments are longer, but still always shorter than the pistil. The long-pistilled form produces more fruits than other forms. Perhaps the species is currently in the process of evolving, and the long-pistilled form is gradually developing into a female flower and the short-pistilled form, which presents more pollen, into a male form.

Section *Hemsleyella*

The species in this section are indigenous to the same areas as the species in the section *Fuchsia*. Characteristic are flowers without petals (*F. apetala*) and the tendency to shed the leaves when the flowers appear. There seemed to be no fuchsias of this section in cultivation until recently. *F. inflata* is now in cultivation.

As previously mentioned, this section was revised by Dr P. E. Berry in 1989.

Fuchsia perscandens

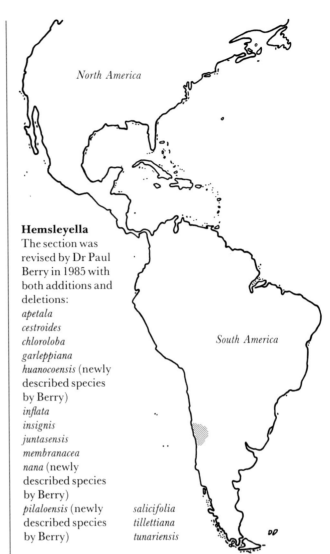

Hemsleyella
The section was revised by Dr Paul Berry in 1985 with both additions and deletions:
apetala
cestroides
chloroloba
garleppiana
huanocoensis (newly described species by Berry)
inflata
insignis
juntasensis
membranacea
nana (newly described species by Berry)
pilaloensis (newly described species by Berry)
salicifolia
tillettiana
tunariensis

Section *Schufia*

In contrast to Munz, who placed only one species in this section, today two species are assigned to the section *Schufia*. *F. arborescens* has small flowers in panicles, like lilac (hence *F. syringaeflora*, lilac fuchsia). The leaves are entire and shiny, the flowers pink and hermaphrodite. The species produces many fruits. On the 6-m tall trees there are many fruit buds and flowers present simultaneously. Occurs in central Mexico.

F. paniculata has small, more purple-coloured flowers in loose panicles. The leaves are slightly dentate at the margins. The species is dioecious, i.e. there are male and female plants. It produces few seeds. Occurs in south Mexico and Panama.

Ellobium
decidua
fulgens
splendens

Jimenezia
jimenezii

Schufia
arborescens
paniculata

Encliandra
microphylla
subsp. *microphylla*
subsp. *hidalgensis*
subsp. *quercetorum*
subsp. *aprica*
subsp. *hemsleyana*
thymifolia
subsp. *thymifolia*
subsp. *minimiflora*
encliandra
subsp. *encliandra*
subsp. *tetradactyla*
obconica
parviflora
ravenii
× *bacillaris*

Section Encliandra (syn. Breviflora)

The species in this section form small shrubs with small, often fern-like leaves and very small white, pink or red flowers which sit individually in the leaf-axils. Munz described 16 species, of which four species and a natural hybrid were left after the revision of Dr Breedlove. In 1969, two further species in this group were newly described by Dr Breedlove.

In the section *Encliandra*, which is indigenous to Mexico and Central America, each species exists in two forms. The flower of one form is female and produces no fertile pollen. This form is always smaller than the second form, which, depending on the species, has either male or complete flowers. The species in the section *Encliandra* are fertilised by hummingbirds, but frequently also by various insects, in Europe by bees. As a consequence of this, there are in cultivation a large number of hybrids between species which in the wild never occur together in the same region. John O. Wright of Reading has investigated all *Encliandra* forms which he came upon in specialist nurseries and botanic gardens and, as a result, has come to the following findings: almost all currently cultivated plants in the section *Encliandra* are hybrids, originating from *F.* × *bacillaris*, which is itself a hybrid developed in 1830 between *F. microphylla* ssp. *microphylla* and *F. thymifolia* ssp. *thymifolia*.

Particular botanical species

F. boliviana Carrière 1876

This species was, as its name suggests, discovered in Bolivia, at an altitude of 2,000–3,000 m. It is one of the racemose fuchsias, which flower particularly profusely and for a long period. The long flowers are uniformly coral-red. As the leaves are pale green, the many-flowered clusters stand out particularly well against the foliage. Unfortunately the species is very susceptible to frost. In a greenhouse with low heat, planted out freely, it quickly grows into large bushes. This variety produces many fleshy, cylindrical, pale green fruits, which on ripening are almost blackish-violet and, together with the brilliant flowers, lend the plant especial ornament.

F. boliviana var. luxurians Ruiz and Pavon 1802

This variety, from Peru, is often to be found under the erroneous name of *F. corymbiflora*. A strongly growing species which unfortunately grows untidily and does not branch well. Raised as a climber in the greenhouse, one can counter this deficiency a little. It is also particularly effective there. The long flowers, appearing in terminal clusters, are uniformly red and with the long, slender tube and the tiny (2 cm) recurved sepals produce a very elegant effect. *F. boliviana* and its varieties can be identified by the raised sepals. In *F. corymbiflora* the sepals are horizontal. The very big leaves are oval-elongate, pointed and entire, with reddish petioles and leaf veins.

F. boliviana var. luxurians 'Alba' Bentham

In many books, Courcelles, a French gardener, is named as the one who introduced this fuchsia to Europe (1850). This cultivar of *F. boliviana* var. *luxurians* originated in the wild and differs from the phylogenetic species in its pure white tube and the pale green leaves without any red veining. It resembles the species in habit and like it flowers particularly profusely on two-year-old wood. Frequent pinching produces many flower shoots. In the adornment of the long brilliant flower clusters and the decorative, initially pale green and later dark red fruits the plant is breathtakingly beautiful. It is a profuse and reliable winter bloomer in the greenhouse. When overwintered in frost-free conditions it demands no more in terms of cultivation than fuchsia hybrids.

F. denticulata Ruiz and Pavon 1802
(syn. *F. serratifolia*)

For the fancier this is one of the most beautiful wild species. Its home is in Peru and Bolivia. The foliage is glossy dark green on the upperside and pale green on the underside. The flowers are well formed with an extra long tube. Dark pink at the base, becoming paler towards the sepals. The green tips of the sepals are particularly bright in contrast to the red corolla. *F. denticulata* is a parent of the beautiful 'Fanfare'.

F. excorticata Forster 1776

Grows to 10 m tall in its natural state in New Zealand. It is typified by the light brown bark, which peels away from the trunk in long strips. The leaves are 3–7 cm long, dark green on the upperside and silvery on the underside. The characteristic flowers, with the tube first constricted and then thickened, are initially green and later purple with blue pollen. Grows untidily in cultivation.

F. fulgens De Candolle 1828

This Mexican species has very big, grey-green, pilose, opposite leaves about 10–20 cm long. Blooms at the end of the shoots in many-flowered clusters, tube 10 cm long, red-lead colour, sepals with green tips, corolla short, scarlet-red. The root extension of *F. fulgens* is tuberous and expanded. The long, cylindrical, somewhat tuberculate berries are glossy pale green.

F. gehrigeri Munz 1930

This species of the section *Fuchsia* comes from west Venezuela in the border region between Venezuela and Colombia, where it grows in cloud-forest areas at 2,200–3,100 m altitude. Upright shrub with flexible branches, 2 m tall or as a liana climbing to 5 m. The dull green foliage is velutinous, the hairs particularly dense along the leaf veins with reddish, denticulate leaf margins. The leaves are long and narrow, 3.5–12 cm long and 1.5–5 cm broad, in whorls of three. The flowers are produced both in the leaf-axil and at the end of the stalk. The red tube is funnel-shaped, 50 mm long. The red sepals are often hairy, 13–21 mm long, corolla scarlet-red. The fruit is pear-shaped, dark purple with large seeds, 15 mm long.

F. magdalenae Munz 1932

This species belongs to the section *Fuchsia*. It comes from northeast Colombia, in the cloud-forest at 2,000–3,500 m altitude. The shrubs of 2–5 m in height

with exfoliating bark climb by means of other woody plants. The leaves are in whorls of three, more rarely of four, and are 8.5 cm long, 4–6 cm broad, glossy, slightly ciliate at the margins. The flowers are produced singly or in pairs in the leaf-axils and are of firm substance, orange-red with a long tube, 42–60 mm, and short sepals. The fruit is purple, elliptical, 20–24 mm long and 10–12 mm thick. The species is tetraploid, n = 22.

F. magdalenae is synonymous with *F. lampadaria* (Wright 1978).

F. microphylla var. *aprica* Humbold, Bonpland and Kunth 1823
Belongs to the section *Encliandra* (syn. *Breviflora*). Its home is in Mexico. Delicate, fern-like foliage, the branches are at right angles to the main stem. Flowers are very small, red, produced in the leaf-axils. The species develops two forms, one with a functional stamen and the other has no stamen and has smaller flowers.

F. sanctae-rosae Kuntze 1892
This species, indigenous to Bolivia and Peru, is vigorous, with verticillate, glossy green leaves. The relatively small flowers grow singly in the leaf-axils. The tube is orange-red, the short sepals and the corolla slightly paler orange. Delicate; reacts to irregularities in cultivation by shedding its leaves. Do not overwinter below 10°C.

F. sessilifolia Bentham 1841–3
Small shrub with narrow, lanceolate leaves. Flowers in clusters of few blooms at the end of the shoot, 2–3 cm long, tube salmon-orange, very thin, sepals and corolla yellowish-green. The home of this species is in Colombia.

F. simplicicaulis Ruiz and Pavon 1802
This plant grows up to 2 m tall in cultivation. The leaves are narrow, lanceolate and glossy dark green. The flowers, which appear in thick clusters at the end of the shoot, are 6–7 cm long and wine-red. Tube long and thin, small corolla. It originates from Peru.

F. splendens Zuccarini 1832
Robust, well-branched shrub with grey-green, heart-shaped, downy, pinnate leaves. The axillary flowers have a compressed, pale red tube; sepals and corolla are short and yellowish-green with enclosed stamen. Good winter flowerer in a moderately warm greenhouse. Natural locations Mexico and Costa Rica.

Fuchsia arborescens (above); *Fuchsia boliviana* (below).

Fuchsia boliviana var. *luxurians* 'Alba' (above);
Fuchsia excorticata (below).

F. thymifolia var. *thymifolia* Humbold, Bonpland and Kunth 1823

Fern-like, delicate foliage. The tiny axillary flowers are initially white, later reddish. Under a magnifying glass the characteristic buds with the four diverging tips are easily recognised. Comes from central Mexico.

F. vargasiana Munz ex Vargas 1936

This new species, which belongs to the section *Fuchsia* (*Eufuchsia*), was discovered at an altitude of 2,350 m in the forests of the Ceja between Yanamaygo and Rio Tambomayo. It resembles *F. tincta* and was earlier confused with this species, to which it is also very closely related. The essential difference consists in the length of the perianth and a few other characteristics. It creates a shrub 1.5 m tall. Described in 'Ecological and Taxonomic Notes' by Professor C. V. Calderon, University of Cuzco.

Any fuchsia-lover who has not yet done so can only be recommended to include some of these botanical species in his or her collection. They are something quite special and have a charm all of their own. Many species flower in winter and in the spring, when only a few other flowering plants are available in the small greenhouse or winter garden.

If we bear in mind their origins and adjust our cultivation measures to them, these species are no more difficult to keep than fuchsia hybrids. The species which originate for example from the cool highlands of Mexico need a definite rest period in November–December. Their water requirements are then only minimal.

Other species, such as those from the frost-free coastal stretch of Chile, do not require such a pronounced rest period and must therefore be kept moister. A study of the climatic conditions of the region from which the species come provides the best pointers for successful cultivation.

Many species are often much too strong-growing as pot plants in the greenhouse. If they are planted through the summer in sheltered spots in the garden, they become more compact and branch out better. Taken up in the autumn and placed carefully in large pots, as one also does with chrysanthemums, they give pleasure for many months with their singularly beautiful flowers. Raised also as standards, many are easier to keep in shape.

Recently discovered species

F. caucana Berry 1979 sp. nov.
Section *Fuchsia*

This species was discovered in south Colombia on the eastern slope of the Central Cordillera at 2,700–3,600 m altitude. These are sparsely branched shrubs, 0.5–2 m tall, with dark green, velutinous, oval-lanceolate leaves 10 cm long and 4 cm broad. The flowers with long tube and short sepals, pink and purple, grow in the upper leaf-axils. The corolla appears darker, red and purple.

F. ceracea Berry 1978 sp. nov.
Section *Fuchsia*
Homeland Peru, at 2,500–2,850 m altitude. The species is very rare and grows as a liana with flexible branches. Leaves are oval-lanceolate, glossy, unusually waxy, 8–15 cm long and 4–6 cm broad, opposite or in whorls of four. The flowers are at the end of the shoots, have an extremely long funnel-shaped tube 10–30 cm long, short sepals lavender-coloured to bright pink with comparatively small red to purple corolla.

F. cinerea Berry 1978 sp. nov.
Section *Fuchsia*
This upright to overhanging shrub of 2–5 m was discovered on the Colombian border with Ecuador quite close to villages at 3,100–3,250 m altitude. Leaves in whorls of three or four, narrowly elliptical, 2–7 cm long and 1–3 cm broad. Flowers are axillary, pendant, tube orange, funnel-shaped, 42–50 mm long, sepals orange with green tips, short corolla reddish-orange.

F. cochabambana Berry 1966 sp. nov.
Section *Fuchsia*
Scattered occurrence in cloud-forest of Bolivia at altitudes of 2,500–3,100 m. The shrubs of 0.5–1.5 m height have elliptic-lanceolate leaves, 3–12 cm long and 1–5 cm broad, green to purple, which stand in whorls of three or four. Flowers are produced in the axils as well as in thick clusters at the ends of the branches. The tube is narrow and funnel-shaped, 45–58 mm in length, very firm, and the pointed 16–18 mm long sepals are orange-red, the short corolla likewise.

F. coriacifolia Berry 1963–5 sp. nov.
Section *Fuchsia*
Occurs rarely in central Peru. Sparsely branched shrubs, 1–2 m tall, with dark green leaves opposite or in whorls of three, 3–6 cm long and 1–2.5 cm broad. Flowers in loose clusters at the end of the shoots. Tube firm and narrow, funnel-shaped, 52–58 mm long, sepals firm, 17–19 mm long, corolla 11–12 mm long. The flower is uniformly pink.

F. crassistipula Berry 1979 sp. now.
Section *Fuchsia*
Locations in central Colombia in cloud-forest at 2,600–3,000 m. Semi-upright to prostrate shrub, 1–3 m tall. The leaves are in whorls of four or five, glossy dark green, 6–16 cm long and 2.5–7 cm broad, with red veins. Flowers abundant in terminal clusters. The tube is funnel-shaped, 32–48 mm long, scarlet and pink, as also are the lanceolate 10–14 mm long sepals. Corolla dark red and purple. A particularity of this species is the firm, persistent stipules.

F. ferreyrae Berry 1978 sp. nov.
Section *Fuchsia*
The species occurs in central Peru at 2,600–3,150 m altitude. Upright or prostrate-climbing, 1–3 m tall. Leaves in whorls of three or four, rarely opposite, elliptic to obovate, velutinous dark green, 2–8 cm long and 1–3 cm broad, with serrate margins. The axillary flowers, particularly at the end of the shoot, are uniform dark red to violet. The funnel-shaped tube is 22–28 mm long, the sepals 14–16 mm.

F. orientalis Berry 1935 sp. nov.
Section *Fuchsia*
Occurs in very misty forests of Ecuador at 1,200–2,600 m altitude. Upright shrub 1–2 m tall. Leaves opposite, more rarely in whorls of three, narrow, oval, 6–21 cm long and 2.5–6 cm broad, entire, tube funnel-shaped, 12–21 mm long, the lanceolate sepals 6–8 mm long are orange-red to scarlet-red, the short corolla red; inflorescence in long, terminal clusters.

F. sanmartina Berry 1965 sp. nov.
Section *Fuchsia*
Occurs at San Martin, Peru, at 2,800–3,600 m altitude. It is a creeping shrub of 1.5–3 m, or as a liana up to 10 m tall. Leaves opposite or in whorls of three, 5–15 cm long and 1.5–6 cm broad, almost entire. The uniformly red flowers are in clusters at the end of the shoot and are very long, 55–85 mm.

F. steyermarkii Berry 1943 sp. nov.
Section *Fuchsia*
Occurs on the eastern slopes of the Andes in the south of Ecuador at 1,800–2,000 m altitude. Densely hairy, many-branched shrub about 2 m tall with copper-coloured bark. The opposite leaves are 20–70 mm long and 2–3 cm broad. Tube narrow, funnel-shaped, 33–37 mm long, scarlet-red, sepals 13–15 mm long, red, the corolla somewhat paler.

CHAPTER FOUR

CULTIVATION

Site requirements

From the origin of fuchsias it follows that success in fuchsia cultivation is in part dependent on the careful choice of position for the plants. Fuchsias occur in their natural state in Central and South America in temperate regions at altitudes of 1,500 to 3,500 m. There they grow in humus-rich forest soil, which guarantees excellent drainage. In these native locations, the humidity is high, and light and sun are filtered through the tall trees. It is thus necessary to create similar living conditions for these fuchsias in cultivation, too.

Balconies or patios on the eastern side of the house are ideal. Here the plants have the full benefit of several hours' morning sun, but are protected from the rays of the scorching midday sun. West-facing or northwest-facing sides are the second-best answer. Small front gardens or narrow plant borders under roof projections (the latter often difficult to use in any other way) on these sides of the house are also eminently suitable positions for fuchsias. The milder sun of the afternoon is sufficient to produce good growth and profuse flowering. South-facing sites are really out of the question, although a fuchsia-lover with a little flair, though also at greater expense, could still create tolerable conditions for his or her plants. Here we might think of shade-giving blinds or trellis frames with fast-growing dense climbing plants, e.g. scarlet runners (*Phaseolus coccineus*) or imperial bindweed (*Pharbitis nil*). The required air humidity can be created by frequent sprinkling of the plants and by spraying the surrounding area with the watering-can. Care of fuchsias grown in a south-facing position becomes somewhat easier if the gardener restricts himself exclusively to *triphylla* hybrids, which are generally better able to tolerate sun. The principle applies in general for fuchsias as for all other plants: the more ideal the position, the more simple the cultivation.

Soils and composts

The choice of soil and composts is again based on the natural habitat of fuchsias in the forests of South America. Therefore it can be concluded that the soil in which fuchsias will prosper best must be light and very, very porous like a forest floor: light so as to ensure good drainage, for accumulation of water is detrimental; porous because many air-filled pores in the soil promote good root growth, and more haustoria (small root hairs) mean a better absorption of nutrients. In addition, the forest floor has a very high humus content, which is constantly replenished by the leaves and needles which fall annually. Humus encourages the micro-organisms and bacteria without which a soil is lifeless.

The pH value should be around 6.5–7, thus in the slightly acid to neutral range. Anybody who grows only a few fuchsias and does not need a lot of soil can use the easily obtainable clean and tidy bags of peat based soilless composts or loam based composts. When requirements are greater, though, they are relatively expensive. All pure peat based composts unfortunately have the disadvantage that they become too dry, and absorb water so powerfully that the sucking strength of the plant is no longer sufficient to draw the vital water from the compost. Peat growing composts must therefore never dry out completely. If this does happen at any time, however, they can be moistened again only with difficulty. The water from the can runs through at the sides of the pot and the soil ball remains dry. Some producers of peat based composts meanwhile add to their products a certain proportion of loam in order to improve the wetting capacity.

On the other hand, some mixtures with a content of garden soil or loam have the advantage that they

—possess better water-retaining capacity and thereby do not dry out so quickly,

—balance out fluctuations in pH value better,

—are better able to cushion against excessive salt concentration through fertilisers and watering.

A standard mixture tested over many years consists of

7 parts medium loam
3 parts sphagnum peat
2 parts washed sand, or grit, graded up to 3–4 mm

by bulk and not by weight.

The compost with a high leaf content is produced without the customary use of calcium cyanamide. It must be well matured, thus at least two to three years old. Loamy garden soil has good water-retaining properties. As to peat, the coarse-fibred type in bales is preferable. The sand can be bought in builders' merchants' stores. It can be either lime-free river sand or washed lime-free coarse sand (grain 0–3 mm).

To this standard mixture, if it is to be used for potting or repotting, the following base fertiliser should be added at the rate of 100 g per litre of compost:

2 parts hoof and horn 3 mm grist
2 parts superphosphate of lime
1 part sulphate of potash

to which 20 g of limestone or chalk is added.

The analysis of this fertiliser is 5.1 per cent nitrogen, 7.2 per cent phosphates and 9.7 per cent potash.

SLOW-RELEASE FERTILISERS

For the planting of window boxes and tubs in May, together with baskets in late March and early April, the comparatively new fertilisers are now widely used, especially by nurserymen, saving both time and energy. The rate of fertiliser released is governed by the soil temperature and is only operative around 21°C. The advantage is that one application will last the whole growing season. The most popular slow-release fertilisers are Osmocote NPK 18-11.10, a coated granular fertiliser released over six to nine months, Osmocote NPK 14.14.14, best for fuchsias, which has a controlled short-term release of three to four months, and the very latest, Osmocote Plus NPK 15.10.12 + 2MgO, trace elements released over five to six months.

Once the slow-release fertiliser is added, the soil should be used as soon as possible. Lengthy storage would free nutrients before they could be of benefit to the plants. In extreme cases the salt content would become too high and harm the plants. On the other hand, the standard mixture is storable only with organic ingredients.

But how does a fuchsia-lover who lives in the city and grows his plants on the balcony get hold of good soil? If he prefers a natural compost, he can make use of any soil that is thrown up on lawns and grassy areas by moles in the spring. In the right place he can find a light, loamy-sandy-humus soil, which should not, however, be used on its own but as a component of a soil mixture. This mole-hill soil, since it is brought up from the root area, is almost totally free of weed seeds.

Anyone not wishing to mix their own compost should use the commercial soilless composts marketed under various proprietary brand names. These are now almost universally used, together with plastic pots. Should a loam-based compost be referred, good John Innes composts made up to the correct formula and right ingredients are still obtainable and are particularly suitable for the old clay pots.

The best ingredients, often hard to obtain, would be wasted, however, if the mixture was not prepared carefully. To begin with everything must be measured out. The soil should on no account be worked when wet but only when slightly moist. Peat on the other hand must not be worked as dry as when it comes out of the bale but must be dampened, preferably the day before. First, all the organic fertilisers are mixed with the dry sand. Then soil is spread as a bottom layer on the most level floor possible or in a large tub. The peat is spread out on top of this and finally the sand-and-fertiliser mixture is added on top. The whole lot must be turned over at least three times so that all constituent parts are equally distributed in the mixture.

Composts for fuchsia-sowing or for the propagation of cuttings are described in the respective sections.

Feeding

Few fuchsia-lovers will have concerned themselves in a scientific way with the mode of action of individual organic or inorganic fertilisers. In an age of chemistry this is not really necessary in view of the various ready-made preparations available. Some basic knowledge of the plant nutrients that are indispensable for the optimal success of a plant should, however, be available, especially if one wishes to obtain healthy plants with a good structure, robust foliage, and the wealth of flowers so typical of fuchsias. Plants in pots and containers, especially if they are kept under glass or on roofed terraces, are at a disadvantage compared with those which are growing freely out in the open. The root system is confined to a relatively small receptacle and consequently the nutrients, which were initially present in abundance in the compost, are quickly exhausted. Owing to the large water requirements of fuchsias, some of the nutrients are also regularly washed out unused. In short, fuchsias are totally dependent on us for their nourishment. With any plant one can very soon tell whether care is taken seriously or whether everything is more or less left to fancy or to chance.

We are often advised by fuchsia experts to supply the plants with a nitrogenous fertiliser during the early period of growth and to change over to a high dosage of potash with the beginning of bud or flower. Although this advice is correct in principle, it does in fact tell only half the story. The great importance of the pH value of the compost should once again be clearly emphasised. It is the basic prerequisite for any well-balanced and effective fertilising. If the pH value is not correctly adjusted, the plant cannot make good use of the fertiliser regularly provided. pH values that are too low or too high lead to various nutrients being locked up in the composts so that they are no longer available to the plant. At the same time substances are dissolved which—in high concentration—can harm the plants. At the generally accepted pH value for fuchsias of 6.5–7, the plants can make maximum good use of the nutrients offered.

The first step in an optimal nutritional programme is to find out the pH value of the compost. Low-priced pH gauges can be obtained in specialist garden centres. These are easy-to-use measuring instruments. The number of free hydrogen ions is measured and expressed in degrees of concentration from 0 to 14. The mean value of 7 is defined as neutral. All values below this are in the acidic, i.e. lime-deficient, range and all those above it in the alkaline, i.e. calcareous, range.

If the compost, on testing, is too acid, thus below pH 6.5, lime must be added in order to achieve the desired value. If the compost is too alkaline, in other words exceeding a top value of pH 7, no addition of lime is made and more peat is added.

For the beginner it is difficult to take in the many reciprocal possibilities of interaction between individual nutrients and pH value. For the specialist they are the subject of a comprehensive study. True, it is quite possible, with a little aptitude and with the help of the well-balanced ready-made fertilisers available in shops, to raise good fuchsias. Yet no sooner do the plants start to become sickly, the leaves turn yellow or the buds fall off than we wonder why this is so. For this reason a little has to be said about the most important nutrients.

The plant nutrients that are necessary for healthy growth are usually divided into macro-nutrients and micro-nutrients. Macro-nutrients are needed in larger quantities. These include nitrogen (N), phosphorus (P), sulphur (S), potassium (K), calcium (Ca) and magnesium (Mg). Micro-nutrients, also known as trace elements, are used only in minute quantities, but are indispensable for the plants' good growth. These include iron (Fe), manganese (Mn), copper (Cu), zinc (Zn), molybdenum (Mo) and boron (B).

THE BASIC NUTRIENTS

Nitrogen (N)

Nitrogen is essential for vegetative growth, in other words for the formation of healthy foliage and strong branches and stems.

It must be available to the fuchsias in sufficient amounts throughout the vegetative period. That is why it is wrong to stop giving nitrogen feed altogether when, at the time of bud or flower, increased potash fertiliser has to be given. With a deficiency of nitrogen, first of all the lower leaves turn yellow and fall; the process then continues upwards. Too high an input of nitrogen on the other hand leads to enlargement of the plant cells, which as a result accumulate more water and grow soft. This makes the plants more prone to possible diseases and late in the year, in unsheltered positions, also to early frosts.

Phosphorus (P)

Phosphorus is important as a check on the nitrogen. It promotes in particular the root growth of young plants and has an influence on the development of flowers and fruits. It is used in the form of superphosphate or bone-meal with 25 per cent phosphorus.

Potassium (K)

Potash plays a very big part in plant life, especially in photosynthesis and the building-up of chlorophyll. It compensates for the action of N and P. Potassium is important for the creation of strong plants, increases the resistance to diseases and improves the colours of fuchsia flowers. It speeds up the ripening of the wood, and the fuchsias therefore overwinter better. In fuchsias, overfeeding with potash over a lengthy period of time leads to magnesium deficiency and can completely block the action of the nitrogen. Although present in the compost, it is not available to the plants. They become woody prematurely and growth is stunted.

TRACE ELEMENTS

These nutrients are required only in minute amounts. The garden, mole-hill or field soil worked into the composts contains sufficient of them. Lack of micro-nutrients, however, gives rise in fuchsias to clear deficiency symptoms, which are most obvious in leaf discoloration.

Iron deficiency, also known as chlorosis, is caused by an excess of phosphorus or lime. It can be recognised by the greenish-yellow discoloration of the upper leaves. The leaf veins and the leaf margins remain green. Remedy: sulphate of iron in the concentration indicated.

Molybdenum deficiency also gives rise to leaf discoloration and comes about if the compost is too acid. The leaves look as if they are mottled with variously coloured spots. Remedy: make sure of the correct pH value.

Magnesium deficiency. The leaves show chlorotic, yellow zones or develop necroses, i.e. a part of the leaf tissue, mostly the tips or margins, becomes brown and withers. Remedy: magnesium sulphate (Epsom Salts), 1 large tablespoon per 10 litres of water.

Boron. With boron deficiency, the leaves often curl up in the shape of small boats. Vegetative points and entire shoot tips die off.

Manganese. Manganese deficiency is recognised by the fact that the larger leaf veins are edged with broad green bands. The leaves themselves are pale green between the veins and lighter at the margins.

Zinc. With zinc deficiency, the internodes, the spaces between leaves at the tips of the shoots, are unusually and conspicuously shortened. The leaves develop as small chlorotic rosettes.

It appears that the discoloration of the leaves is very similar in the various deficiency symptoms. A correct diagnosis is difficult to make. While iron or magnesium deficiency can appear separately and the remedy accordingly be put into action, deficiency symptoms with the trace elements boron, manganese and zinc can be checked with a liquid fertiliser that contains these elements (note the instructions for use). The deficiencies are quickly and effectively corrected with foliar feeding. If one uses exclusively the slow-release fertiliser Osmocote for basic feeding, trace elements must be given in addition, e.g. 50–100 g of sulphate of iron per cubic metre of compost.

FREQUENCY, QUANTITY, FERTILISER

Fuchsias on the one hand draw heavily on nutrients but on the other are susceptible to salt, especially as freshly rooted cuttings and as young plants. A well-rooted larger plant by contrast can hardly be overfed. With feeding, the result depends on the experience and the powers of observation of the gardener, but perhaps even more so on the carefulness and regularity in the application. Some basic rules are to be noted.

— Never feed a dry plant; if necessary first water and then allow the release of nutrients to follow.
— Never feed a sickly plant. The feed would lead to its complete collapse. In this case the reasons for the disease must first be found out and remedied.
— Rooted cuttings and young plants, until they are in 10-cm pots, manage with the organic base fertiliser present in the compost. Should this not be satisfactory at any time, it is better to help it along with a foliar feed in weak concentration than to feed into the not yet fully rooted-out pot. The young roots themselves are particularly susceptible to salt and must not be damaged.
— Once the plant is in its final pot and the roots have filled this, regular feeding with liquid fertiliser begins. In old English books on fuchsias the easy-to-remember piece of advice 'weekly-weakly' can be found. The correct concentration is half the amount indicated by the fertiliser manufacturer. If one gets into the habit of one particular day in the week as 'feeding day', then the all-important regularity is also ensured.

For the period of the plant's development up to the final pinching out, and until the fuchsias have attained the desired shape and size, a fertiliser with high nitrogen content, i.e. one with a ratio of something like 30:10:10, is chosen.

When the first rudimentary buds appear, a fertiliser with high potash content (8:12:16) is used. Any good fertiliser of approximately this composition fulfils the purpose.

FOLIAR FEEDING

Fuchsias easily assimilate liquid fertilisers through their leaves. This is helpful when bringing on cuttings or young plants. Young roots are particularly susceptible to salt and also to too much moisture in the pot. To help the plants in this early stage to grow efficiently, give them a foliar feed using a hand spray. To 1 litre of water, add 2 g of a highly nitrogenous fertiliser and thoroughly cover the plants with this, although not in the blazing sun otherwise leaf spots and burning could be the outcome. Algal preparations, applied as a foliar feed, also have an invigorative effect. Whenever fuchsias do not develop satisfactorily, or if the development of a plant has to be stimulated, e.g. when raising standards or other decorative forms in which a speedy growth is particularly important, foliar feeding is helpful.

Among Dutch fuchsia-lovers with magnificently flowering plants, the 'mysterious' substance UDK was often recommended as a particularly effective fertiliser. By this was meant the urine of pregnant cows. On analysis, the structure was found to be 6:0:15, in other words little nitrogen, no phosphate, but a high content of potassium and hormones, which gives rise to profuse flowering. Anybody with rural connections should try out this 'fertiliser' in heavily diluted form.

The slow-release fertilisers with a long-lasting effect of several months, which have been available for a few years, offer enormous advantages not only to the professional gardener but also to the fuchsia-fancier who is not able to devote too much time to his or her hobby. The extremely important regular supply of nutrients is thus ensured. The granules bonded to synthetic material are easily dispersed in the compost. They contain all major nutrients, which are gradually released in the soil in a form assimilable by the plants. Soil temperature and humidity, bacterial activity and pH value release the nutrients according to the respective demands of the plants. Periods of deficiency with the familiarly distressing consequences, such as unsatisfactory growth, buds which do not open or are dropped altogether, may not appear at all at the outset. Nutrients which are released only when the plant really needs them can also therefore make sure that no damage is caused by over-feeding. The nutrient supply in the plant containers is not washed out with watering and so lasts even longer.

Bear in mind of course that the fertiliser reserve in the compost is exhausted after about two to three months. From this point on, supplementary fertilising—preferably with a liquid feed—must then be done again. As any feeding is suspended about the end of August to mid September in order to promote a good maturing of the plants, which means better overwintering, this period does not last long. Finally, note that organic fertilisers in the compost are at the same time also a source of humus and therefore particularly beneficial. Their action, however, is very dependent on the outdoor temperature. In cool summers, when the temperature remains below 20–25°C for a lengthy period, they cannot develop their full effect. In this case it is better to change to the inorganic liquid fertilisers to tide over the cool period.

Nutrient provision and flower development

(after Dr Helmut Burghardt)

Feeding experiments* with fuchsias have revealed that a proper provision of nutrients—besides the other growth factors during the summer—promotes flower and number of flowers quite considerably: a fact which must be of interest not only to the fuchsia enthusiast but also to the commercial gardener. This all the more so as the fuchsia enjoys great popularity as a pot plant, balcony-box plant and border plant, and in ornamental-plant cultivation represents a substantial economic factor.

The results of the tests clearly show that the base fertiliser largely serves the vegetative growth of the plant and that only a supplementary fertiliser—

*The detailed report on tests by Dr Helmut Burghardt appeared in a special issue of *Gartenwelt* 62 (13), 267–8, published by Paul Parey, Hamburg and Berlin, 1962.

which would in any case seem advisable, if only to avoid over-high single doses of necessary nutrients —is able to produce optimal flowering results. Of course the other growth factors during the summer also promote flower development, compared with the spring generally, although independently of these the number of flowers increases quite noticeably with increasing doses of nutrients. Plants which received a maximum possible dose of fertiliser developed more than three times the number of flowers compared with those that were not fertilised.

An essential requirement for a worthwhile cultivation of fuchsias is thus an adequate provision of nutrients, which at the present total of 4–5 g of a highly nutritive multi-nutrient fertiliser per pot may well not yet have reached its maximum.

CHAPTER FIVE

CARE

Watering, grooming, pests

The care of fuchsias, whether bought as young plants or raised from cuttings, is not particularly costly. It does, however, call for some attention and some time. This begins with watering.

A plant with so much foliage has substantial water requirements because the leaves constantly transpire a great deal of water. On the other hand a continuously wet soil is extremely harmful to the fuchsia roots. They rot and can no longer fulfil their function of assimilating water and nutrients. Most fuchsias probably die from wet and thus 'cold feet': they are watered to death. Particularly susceptible are newly potted-on plants, which have not yet completely filled the new soil in the now larger pot. In this case one should water heavily once and hold off the next watering until the plant has become almost dry.

Never allow fuchsias to dry out completely, although this danger is not so great because lack of water can immediately be recognised from the leaves. They lose their firm freshness, become dull and soft, and 'flap about'. In extreme cases a fuchsia that has become completely dry sheds leaves, buds and flowers. The ideal situation would be a soil that is always uniformly slightly moist. In days when only clay pots were used, the gardener tapped on the pot with his knuckles: if there was a dull sound, there was still enough moisture; if it gave a ringing sound, urgent watering was needed. This practice can no longer be used with today's plastic pots. Instead we tell the plants' needs directly with rather well-trained powers of observation.

On hot summer days, especially if it is also windy, watering can often be done twice, morning and evening. On such days the plants are kept cool through additional spraying or light sprinkling of the leaves and surrounding area, although this tried and tested means also has disadvantages with plants in full flower. The flowers of the light, pastel-coloured and white cultivars then acquire unsightly brown spots.

If, despite such scrupulousness, a blunder should still have crept in and the danger exists of losing a fuchsia, there is only one way left to save it. Take the plant out of its pot and remove all the old soil, as well as all ailing roots and leaves. Larger plants are drastically cut back. Then repot with fresh, light soil in the smallest pot possible. Water carefully, or instead of this spray well. With a little luck the fuchsia will soon put forth new shoots and new leaves. To assist the recovery process, the sick plants can be put in a polythene bag in order to speed up regeneration through higher air humidity.

An important part of the care is the continuing removal of the withered flowers and of the production of seed pods. If the fuchsias are spared the development of these seed pods, they can concentrate their energy to form brand-new flowers. Yellow and damaged leaves should also be cleared away. Now and then during the course of the summer, shoots that have grown too long or those that threaten to break under the weight of their big and accordingly heavy flowers must be given a support to which they are carefully tied.

Great attention must be paid at all times to pests. Apart from the green aphids which are very visible at the ends of shoots, most pests are concealed on the undersides of the leaves. As often as time allows, the plants should be checked and the appropriate measures taken immediately so that heavy infestation with its disastrous consequences is avoided. Simply spraying the undersides of leaves with plain clear water often prevents infestation by the dreaded 'red spider', which likes hot, dry conditions. Details of control measures are given in Chapter 6.

Overwintering

Most fuchsias which are reared every year by gardeners live to see only one summer. In the months from May to October they adorn window seats, balconies, patios, garden borders and churchyards and with their profusion of flower provide so much pleasure that one might think that that is enough. We enjoy the beauty for as long as it lasts, and then have nothing more to do with the plants.

Many people do not know that fuchsias belong to the group of deciduous woody plants, which in the natural state in their homeland put forth new shoots every spring, as for example forsythias or lilacs do in temperate climates. The decisive difference, though, is that winter temperatures in central and northwest Europe are far too low for most fuchsias. They must therefore be brought indoors, away from the frost, over the winter. Admittedly it does require a little consideration to find suitable accommodation. A real fuchsia-lover who has raised his own plants would not be able to bring himself simply to throw them away in the autumn, especially since he knows that fuchsias become more lovely from year to year. Many cultivars do not attain their optimal beauty until the second and third years, and with every succeeding year the fullness of flower increases.

As deciduous plants, fuchsias need a rest period in winter during which they gather new strength for the coming season. Although they cannot get this rest period under natural conditions in the open, that is not to say that the only alternative is simply to stow them away and forget them for the rest of the winter; when necessary water should be given so that the soil in the pots and boxes is slightly moist and does not dry out completely.

One must also keep an eye on the temperature in the wintering quarters. It should not rise above about 5–7°C. At these temperatures the plants will get a proper rest. In too warm a situation the production of new shoots would very soon begin again and a rest period would be out of the question. Because the light in winter is not sufficient for healthy shooting, the developing new shoots are pale and unrestrained and undermine the plant to no good purpose. They must therefore be removed. If the room is cool enough, the fuchsias could even be allowed to stand in complete darkness for the period from November to February.

PREPARATIONS FOR OVERWINTERING

To facilitate storage, the following needs to be done, although how far to go in this depends on the individual circumstances in the winter accommodation.

First, all branches that are frail, broken or have grown in the centre of the plant, especially the un-ripened, still soft parts of the plant which would rot anyway, are cut. So as not to bring in any germs or diseases or any pests through the winter, all remaining leaves and flowers are removed. These are not simply pulled off but are cut off carefully with a pair of scissors in order not to wound the bark. The greatest danger to plants in winter accommodation, namely the growth of *Botrytis* (grey mould) on fallen leaves and flowers, is thereby dispelled. These mould fungi also spread quickly to the main stem and branches of fuchsias, and this often means the death of the plant.

VARIOUS WINTERING QUARTERS

The temperate greenhouse

The owner of a greenhouse has no problem with overwintering. The greenhouse is first thoroughly cleaned, preferably with soda-water. When all plants are stowed away, everything—plants and greenhouse—is sprayed once more with an insecticide as a precautionary measure, the thermostat is set at 5–7°C, and the winter can begin. Frequent ventilation in mild, frost-free weather keeps the plants healthy.

The cold greenhouse

Here, because there will not or cannot be any heating, the plants in their pots must once more be thoroughly watered beforehand and dug as deep as possible into the soil beds. Then the whole lot is covered over with a thick layer of peat, old potting soil or leaves. In periods of frost the plants should in addition be protected with polythene, thick layers of newspaper, old sacks or blankets. In mild periods the additional protection must be removed, however, so that the plants do not suffocate. Here, too, the moistness of the pots should be checked every couple of weeks. If the greenhouse is covered on the inside with polythene, then a lot of cold air is kept out.

Cold frames

For overwintering in the cold frame, the plants are prepared as previously described. They can then be taken out of the pots and the fine hair roots removed from the soil ball. The plants are arranged on their side close together, either in or out of their pots, in the frame. The spaces in between are filled up with the smaller plants. As a preventive measure, the plants should in this case, too, be sprayed with a fungicide, e.g. Benlate, against *Botrytis*. The frame is filled to the edge with moist peat, or alternatively with dry chestnut, beech or walnut leaves.

Finally, the close-fitting windows are laid on. On top of the moisture present in the frame, which one tries to reduce through ventilation in mild, frost-free weather, on no account should any rain be able to penetrate. In severe, persistent periods of frost, mats, sacks, polystyrene sheets, boards or similar materials are again placed over. In extremely cold winters, one can fill up all around the frame with peat or leaves.

Earth pits

This method was much used in earlier days but then was forgotten for a while. All non-hardy plants such as geraniums and oleanders, small pomegranate trees and also fuchsias were placed in a durably cut, firm pit supported with boards in the ground. Gardens are seldom so large nowadays that we could plan a permanently installed pit. But a pit—it can also be an elongated trench—at least 60 cm deep could be set up.

The measurements are determined by the size and the number of the existing plants. As dry a place as possible should be sought as a location. In regions with a high water table this fact should be included in one's considerations, for the winter could be very rainy. The fuchsias are again cleared of leaves and flowers, taken out of the pots and the soil balls shaken out. With this method of overwintering the labelling must be particularly durable and waterproof. A list of the stored plants should also be made.

A layer of moist peat or dry leaves is placed on to the floor of the pit. Then right at the bottom come the heavy plants and the spaces in between are again filled with smaller plants. No more than three layers of plants, however, should be stored one upon the other. To finish, everything is filled up again with fairly dry peat or leaves. Straw is not suitable for this purpose. It would decompose too quickly owing to soil humidity. This results in high temperatures, as we know from the preparing of compost. For the same reason, no leaves which decompose quickly must be used either. Chestnut, beech and walnut leaves are best suited. Peat has the great advantage of being sterile and of being capable of being used again in the spring in all sorts of ways in the garden. This is covered over with a couple of light boards or a frame covered with fine wire mesh in order to stop the sides of the pit crumbling. A large piece of PVC sheeting keeps rain and snow away from the plants. The earth previously dug out is finally laid on the top. No frost will now be able to do any damage to the plants.

Other frost-free places

Non-hardy plants have always been brought into cellars, spare bedrooms or frost-free garages and other storage rooms over the winter. Generally applicable rules, however, are difficult to draw up: local factors are too variable. If a room is bright and slightly warmed, naturally more frequent watering is required than in a dark cellar, which perhaps has the ideal temperature of 5–6°C but no light and in which the bare plants can hardly volatilise water. In today's houses, almost invariably centrally heated, the real problem lies rather in keeping the temperature low enough so that the plants do not put forth shoots prematurely. Here one will have to ventilate as often as possible in frost-free weather.

Finally, the three main requirements once again:

Overwinter in a frost-free place
Do not allow drying-out
Protect against *Botrytis*

Treatment in spring

After a rest period of about three months, as a rule from November to the end of January, the fuchsias are again exposed to brighter and warmer conditions in February, but 7–10°C is sufficient first of all. In regions with long harsh winters, March is early enough. To speed up the new shooting process and to soften up the hard, old wood a little, the plants are sprayed twice daily with lukewarm water. The bottom of the pot should be kept regularly slightly moist. The dormant eyes will soon expand and the tips of the shoots reveal the first small green leaves.

PRUNING

As already described, fuchsias belong to the group of deciduous woody plants. Flowers appear only on the young, one-year-old shoots. If the fuchsia is able to put forth shoots without being controlled, in spring it will carry on growing at exactly where it has stopped in the autumn. Only the tips will carry on growing and the lower, woody part of the plant remains bare. Of course, only relatively few flowers develop in proportion to the size of the plant.

Pruning back is therefore necessary. It stimulates the lower, dormant eyes to put forth new shoots, the plant is rejuvenated and brought back into an attractive shape. How far one prunes back varies from one cultivar to another. Young plants are pruned in a different way from one ones of several years. There are even some forms which do not like being pruned back at all. These are better renewed each year from autumn cuttings.

Young, year-old plants are cut back to two eyes of the wood grown the previous summer. Eyes or joints, also known as nodes, are the slightly thickened spots on the branches where the leaves were situated in the previous year. These are the places where the new shoots always emerge.

In older plants, pruning back to the old wood is often a must if a well-shaped plant, with foliage from top to bottom, is the desired aim. In this case, of course, it takes longer for the new shoots to emerge.

Pruning is done with a sharp pair of secateurs. The wood must not be bruised. A bit of the old wood should always be left above the earmarked eyes. If the branch is about 0.5 cm thick, then the cut is also made 0.5 cm above the eye. Bigger shoots are dealt with accordingly. Thin, spindly shoots, as well as any growing inwards or crossing other branches, are removed altogether. Through observation of various cultivars and with experience it soon becomes clear what kind of pruning produces the best results. It is also important to know that some cultivars by their nature put forth shoots only very late. They remain dormant a long time, but soon make up lost ground through fortified growth.

Pendent plants are cut above the eye that is pointing downwards directly above the edge of the pot. This way the new, tender shoots cannot rub on the edge of the pot. With standards really drastic mea-

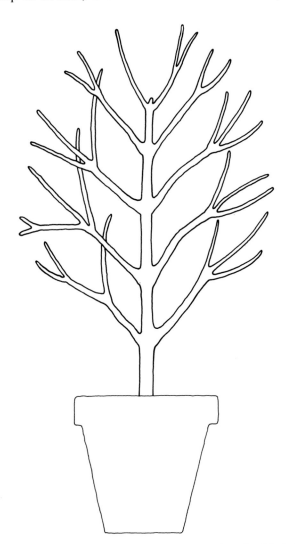
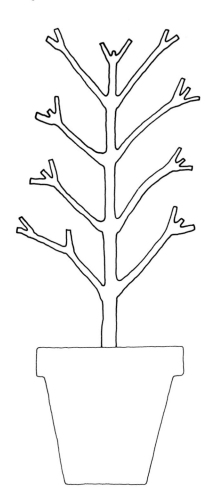

A bush-trained fuchsia before and after pruning.

sures are called for and they should be cut right back every year. A head that is bare on the inside and completely woody is not a pretty sight. It can generally be said that robust, strongly growing cultivars can always be pruned right back.

REPOTTING

After pruning, the fuchsias must be replanted in fresh soil. Because of their substantial nutrient requirements the old soil is completely exhausted. Pots and containers are also so crammed with old, dead roots that the new roots would not be able to find any more room to develop.

On the subject of 'repotting' there are two differing opinions. One recommends potting in new soil immediately after pruning on the grounds that this limits the shock which the plants suffer through pruning and repotting to one single occasion. In the second, rather more 'gentle' method, the plants are allowed two to three weeks to recover from pruning and to develop new shooting growth; only then is potting in new soil carried out. As much as possible of the old soil ball and the brown, dead roots is carefully removed. Any newly formed white shoots already present must not, however, be damaged. The plant is placed in the smallest possible pot with fresh soil. The point of this is that the new roots should quickly fill the small pot again. This way the above-ground growth, the forming of a large number of young shoots, gets underway again more quickly. If at this point, however, we use a pot that is too big, the plant will strive to fill this with roots first and the production of shoots would be delayed.

One should also be aware that soil that is not yet filled with roots tends to become sour in an oversized pot. Toxins can be created which harm the plant. Newly potted plants—this is particularly important —must therefore be watered only very carefully and sparingly. Otherwise most plants are already lost at this point. If the pot soil is always kept slightly damp, however, and the visible parts of the plant above the surface are sprayed frequently, then new roots very quickly develop and the danger period is past. Once the small pot is filled with roots, the plant, with soil ball intact, is then potted on as circumstances demand.

Each new shoot, when it has formed two pairs of leaves, is gently nipped off at the tip. With thumb and index finger, or with a small pair of scissors, the tip of the shoot is removed. The more often this 'pinching' is done, the more shoots the plant acquires—and of course correspondingly more flowers as well.

CHAPTER SIX

DISEASES AND PESTS

Well-looked-after and well-fed fuchsias will with any luck rarely suffer from diseases. Nevertheless, their resistance is reduced in large monocultures, as also happens with other plant genera. Under artificial conditions, isolated from the ecological and biological protection which fuchsias enjoy in the natural state, diseases can appear, and attack by pests increases as well. What is more, there is the human tendency to preserve feeble plants by any means possible, whereas in the wild the weak plants are eliminated by continual selection and only the healthy, strong plants are able to survive. The few natural enemies of animal pests, e.g. ichneumon flies or ladybirds, are often themselves eradicated when control measures are taken. Today there are, fortunately, institutes which rear and sell ichneumon flies and ladybirds of various species in large numbers. Their use, however, is worthwhile only in large cultivations under glass.

Much has already been written about the way of handling plant-protective agents and the dangers that lie ahead when they are used irresponsibly. Many protective agents are more dangerous than others, but all are toxic and the necessary warnings are always given in this matter. The very best plant protection, however, is always good cultivation. Fuchsias which are given the proper care at the right time and are fed correctly are healthy, resistant and not particularly prone to diseases and pests.

Fungal diseases

GREY MOULD (*Botrytis cinerea*)

This fungal disease usually appears in the winter and early spring months when the air humidity in the greenhouse or in the overwintering quarters is extremely high. Often emanating from fallen leaves or flowers, brownish-black mouldy areas form on the stalks near the soil and these cause entire branch sections to die off. If the infestation is further advanced, the grey mat of fungus can be seen even with the naked eye. The *Botrytis* spores are always present and await favourable conditions to be able to germinate. Hence, corresponding preventive measures follow.

—do not place plants too close together,
—ventilate well so that no stale air accrues,
—water sparingly, preferably early in the day, so that the leaves have dried again in the evening,
—meticulous tidiness: immediately remove and destroy every leaf shed.

Plant-protective agents:

—benomyl (Benlate),
—carbendazim (garden fungicide),
—or other agents, in the respective concentration indicated.

Liquid plant-protective agents, if required, are likewise recommended early in the day.

As white and pastel-coloured fuchsias are particularly susceptible, they should be protected by spraying with a systemic fungicide.

FUCHSIA RUST

This rust fungus (*Pucciniastrum epilobii* f. sp. *palustris*) has been known in the scientific literature since 1918 and is widespread on fuchsias in America and England. In recent years it has also entered cultivations elsewhere, e.g. in Germany, and can, if not recognised in time, cause great damage.

The rusts are all specialised parasites on specific plant species. All belong to the group of fungi that change hosts and have a very complicated developmental cycle of several stages. The fuchsia rust thus spreads to fuchsias from willowherbs (*Epilobium*). For this reason willowherbs should not be tolerated in the vicinity of fuchsias.

The rust first attacks the lower leaves of the plant. Groups of yellow-brown to rust-red spores are discovered on the undersides of the leaves. A little later brown-grey round spots can also be seen on the uppersides. When the spores are mature, they are transferred to neighbouring healthy plants with the slightest movement and by every current of air. Even if a fully grown plant—with well-timed control—is not severely damaged, any help for cuttings and young plants often comes too late. Preventive measures:

—avoid overcrowding plants,
—reduce high humidity, particularly in low temperatures, by watering sparingly and ventilating frequently,
—absolute tidiness in cultivation: carefully gather up fallen leaves and burn them immediately.

Plant-protective agents:

—Nimrod T systemic,
—Plantvax 75 systemic (for use by commercial growers only),
—Dithane 945

Spray carefully twice at an interval of eight days, especially the undersides of the leaves and also the surface of the soil. Following this the treatment is repeated several times at intervals of 14 days. In order to break the cycle, the willowherbs which often grow wild in the neighbourhood of gardens must be removed.

ROOT ROT

Fuchsias which are standing in a good, porous compost, are properly looked after and are watered with care should not have to suffer from root rot. And yet sometimes a plant droops its leaves as it were overnight, although the soil is moist. This disease, however, has certainly not arrived as suddenly as it seems. If the 'patient' is taken out of its pot, then a black, completely rotten root system is discovered; no fibrous roots exist any more. The plant must have died of thirst in the moist pot.

Root rot is caused by various soil fungi, e.g. *Phytophthora*, *Thielaviopsis basicola*, *Fusarium*, *Verticillium* or *Rhizoctonia*. Preventive measures:

—promote the development of a good root system through proper care,
—create good drainage,
—never allow fuchsias to stand in water for longer than 30 minutes; pay attention to this especially when using outer pots,
—never let the root ball dry out completely.

Once a plant has become completely dry, the fine fibrous roots die off first. If one subsequently waters very heavily in order to rectify the omission, the cycle of disaster is already established. The plants can no longer take up the water, the soil remains too wet, the rest of the roots rot and the fungi begin their work of destruction.

At the very start of this process the plant could still be saved by treatment with a fungicide. Unfortunately, when the damage is noticed it is already too late. Now the only thing that can be done is to cut the diseased plant right back, remove all soil, carefully wash out the roots and cut away the rotted roots. If the plants are then planted with fresh soil in the smallest pot possible, they can form new roots and slowly recover. To assist the growing of roots, the 'patient' is placed in a sealed polythene bag. If the root rot has not already attacked the stem structure of the fuchsia, it may still be possible to take cuttings which will root again. Otherwise the plant must be destroyed.

Pests

APHIDS (many species)

Of the many different species of aphid that exist, fuchsias are attacked mainly by the peach-potato aphid (*Myzus persicae*). Unlike other aphids, these are fairly active and do not form dense colonies. Like the whitefly, aphids also secrete sticky honeydew. If the black sooty moulds frequently establish themselves, the plants soon become unsightly. Leaf respiration is impeded and the leaves suffer from lack of light. Aphids, by their sucking activity, deprive the plants of their sap. Leaf deformities and leaf-curl result and the leaves turn yellow. For control, the less toxic pyrethrum sprays, and derris, malathion or HCH, are sufficient.

RED SPIDER MITES

The pest known as 'red spider' (*Tetranychus urticae*) is a tiny mite barely visible to the naked eye. It is generally not discovered until one becomes aware of the white-yellowish leaf spots. The mites, which breed rapidly, live on the undersides of the leaves, pierce the leaf tissue and suck out the cell contents. Seen through a magnifying glass, the undersides of the leaves look as if they are sprinkled with red pepper. On hot, dry summer days the mites breed particularly rapidly. In a heavy infestation the undersides of the leaves are often coated with a dense web. Remedies should be sought as quickly as possible, before young plants die through the heavy loss of foliage.

In the greenhouse, the first thing to do is try to lower the temperature by keeping the benches and gangways moist. Water and dampness are not appreciated by the mites. In old books the advice is given to spray every single pot from beneath with a sharp jet of water. But who can find the time for this? Fuchsias growing wild in the open in hot situations with a dry atmosphere can also be attacked by red spider mites.

Plant-protective agents:

—malathion,
—pirimiphos-methyl (Sybol 2),
—dimethoate.

It is recommended that all spraying be repeated at seven-day intervals. As the red spider mite very soon develops resistance to specific chemicals, the remedies must be changed frequently. Spraying should not be carried out in very high temperatures and too dry an atmosphere.

WHITEFLY

Seen under a magnifying glass, the whitefly (*Trialeurodes vaporariorum*) looks like a small white moth, barely more than 1 mm long. A fully grown female whitefly lives for about 30–40 days and in this period lays up to 500 eggs. The eggs are yellowish at first, and later almost black. Under favourable conditions the whole developmental cycle from egg to full-grown animal lasts about five weeks. Several generations can be expected. If the host plant, in this case the fuchsia, is particularly well fed, then the development of the whitefly is also speeded up.

The larvae and the adult insects not only suck out the sap from the leaves but also secrete sticky honeydew, on which sooty mould fungi soon establish themselves. In heavy infections the leaves soon turn black and can no longer assimilate. The first signs of whitefly attack are rolled-up leaf tips, especially on young shoots. If the plants are moved in any way, swarms of the insects fly up. In America, experiments have shown that whiteflies are attracted by patches of bright yellow colour. Yellow cards were therefore smeared with motor oil and hung up in the greenhouses. The startled whiteflies always landed on the yellow cards and were left sticking to the film of oil. With heavy attacks this method is certainly worth copying.

Among the whiteflies there are various species specialising on particular plant groups. The species which lives on brassicas and various weeds (e.g. cabbage white fly) does not attack fuchsias.

Plant-protective agents: The whitefly very quickly becomes immune to insecticides. The agents used should therefore be changed constantly. Pyrethrum preparations, and applications of bioresmethin, diazinon, dimethoate, malathion and HCH, are effective. In particular, the undersides of the leaves must be sprayed until they are dripping wet.

CAPSID BUGS

Capsid or leaf bugs are represented by many species in the garden and in the wild. They can be recognised by their shield-shaped wing-case. On fuchsias, the two species *Lygus ruguli pennis* and *Lygus* (*Lygocoris*) *pabulinus* in particular cause great damage. The first species is greenish with a black head, the second uniformly green. Both are about 6 mm long. They overwinter as adult insects in fallen leaves or in long grass, and two generations are produced in one summer. The first generation appears about the end of May and the second towards the end of August. Leaf bugs suck at the young, succulent tips of the shoots and deprive the plants of their cell sap. In so doing they pierce the leaves as if with fine pinpricks and at the same time secrete a substance which makes the young tissue atrophy and causes the growing points to become deformed. As a result the buds that have already formed also die off, so that it is six to eight weeks before new shoots with new flowers develop in the places where the plant has been attacked. When the damage is noticed, it is unfortunately already too late. It is worth taking some preventive action.

Plant-protective agents: Before the plants are brought outdoors after the frosts are over, one should spray or water with a systemic agent such as Tumblebug as a preventive. These agents remain active in the sapstream of fuchsias for about 14–21 days.

LEAF HOPPERS (*Zygina pallidifrons*)

These, too, are small green or brown, slender, boat-shaped insects which live predominantly on the undersides of the leaves. If the plants are handled they jump up, hence the name leaf hoppers. Leaf hoppers suck at the leaves, and as a result of this fine white spots appear. In heavy infestations the leaf margins turn brown and the leaves drop. In the wild frog hoppers may also sometimes be found on fuchsias but these cause little damage. Control of both species is achieved with pyrethrum preparations, or malathion, at weekly intervals.

WEEVILS

The black vine weevil (*Otiorrhynchus sulcatus*) with its advanced trunk-like masticators is a nocturnal beetle that is only rarely seen. It is blackish-grey and about 10 mm long. In late spring the beetle eats semicircular holes in the leaves of fuchsias.

The really serious damage, however, is caused by the larvae. They feed on the roots, so that the entire root system is soon destroyed. If fuchsias do not put

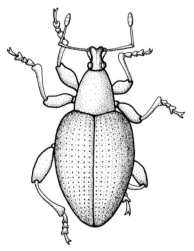

The vine weevil (*Otiorrhynchus sulcatus*) feeds on the fuchsia leaves; its larvae destroy the roots.

forth shoots again after the winter rest, the larvae of the vine weevil are often to be found in the pot. The legless larvae with brown heads are always rolled up in a crescent shape, which distinguishes them from other similar larvae.

Although the beetle has always been present in the garden, where it causes damage to yews, rhododendrons or shrubs, its frequent appearance in ornamental plant cultivations under glass can be traced back to the wide use of peat based composts.

Plant protection: It is best to eradicate the adult beetles in summer and autumn before they lay eggs. For this, Murfume Lindane Smoke Pellets or Fumite HCH cones are effective, or try dusting with Murphy Gamma HCH Dust. If grubs are present, water thoroughly with Gamma HCH diluted as in normal spraying.

FUNGUS FLIES (*Heliothrips* ssp. *Thrips tabaci*)

There are various species of these small black flies, whose larvae attack the plant roots. Species which appear most commonly in the greenhouse are the *Sciara* species. The black fly, only 3 mm long, can reach plague proportions anywhere where a lot of work is done with peat based composts. Because of their black camouflage colour they are very difficult to see on the soil. Typically, once they are disturbed they rise only reluctantly and after flying a few centimetres immediately settle again.

Great damage is done to young, just rooted fuchsias, while older plants are weakened and therefore more easily fall victim to soil-borne fungi.

Plant-protective agents: All spray agents are effective. The spraying must, however, be repeated at intervals of a few days. The larvae are controlled by watering with malathion (0.2%). With a heavy infestation this must be repeated at ten-day intervals.

CATERPILLARS

Damage done to fuchsias by caterpillars is limited. Now and again, however, regular holes are discovered eaten into the leaf from the margin. On closer inspection, the dark, almost black excretions of the caterpillars can also be found on some leaves.

The caterpillar of the elephant hawk-moth (*Deilephila elpenor*) is particularly feared on account of its voraciousness. It is bright green with round red spots on its head that look like eyes. The body is up to 8 cm long, fat, cylindrical and tapers off into a horn.

There are of course chemical control measures against caterpillars, but it is easier to pick off the animals by hand. Anybody frequently finding caterpillars of the above species on his fuchsias should once again look out for *Epilobium* (willowherbs) and other plants of the evening primrose family in the neighbourhood. These moths lay their eggs, which look like a frozen drop of water, on the undersides of the leaves of these plants. For the sake of conserving an uncommon moth, however, it is better to remove the caterpillars to willowherbs growing well away from fuchsias.

WASPS (*Vespula vulgaris*)

Wasps damage fuchsia flowers by biting oval-shaped holes in the tube in order to get at the nectar. They also occasionally bite off stamens and pistils, and even whole petals of the corolla. Such damage to the flowers can be observed especially in late summer. Where wasps are abundant and become a real nuisance, the nests should be sought out and destroyed with derris.

Real control is difficult as the pest is usually a flying visitor. Small mesh or netting over ventilators and doors is the best remedy.

EARWIGS

These pests cause similar damage to the flowers to that caused by wasps. When they appear in large numbers they can be caught using the time-proven method of straw-filled flowerpots.

As earwigs prefer to live among fallen leaves or flowers, make sure that by keeping areas between plants and containers clean there will be no places for them to hide.

Leaf spots

These symptoms can have a great variety of causes. One should first consider whether some mistake has been made in the care of the fuchsias.

The brownish spots which may appear in many cultivars after planting out in mid May to the beginning of June, are alarming but harmless. 'Marinka' and 'Mission Bells' are well known for this, but the phenomenon can also be seen on other, mostly red and blue, cultivars. These fuchsias are particularly susceptible to cool overnight temperatures. When it gets warmer again, the regrown new leaves are perfectly normal once more. Proper burn marks appear if the fuchsias are watered in the hot, sunny hours of the day and the foliage thereby gets wet. In addition, plant-protective agents in too strong a concentration or incompatible agents also cause burns. Warnings are given with preparations which are bottled ready for use in spray cans. When spraying, a minimum distance of 30 cm from the plant must be maintained, otherwise cold damage sets in and the leaves turn black. Leaf spots of a different kind arising from overfeeding or from lack of certain nutrients have already been described in the section on feeding (page 28).

CHAPTER SEVEN

PROPAGATION

Anyone who is intensely preoccupied with plants will always be particularly fascinated by propagation. Watching how a big strong plant grows from a grain of seed or how, from a cutting, a plant emerges which in all respects resembles its 'mother' perfectly, is interesting and exciting. It is always a 'success story' when propagation turns out well.

In this respect the propagation of fuchsias is particularly pleasing because it is simple and unproblematic and nearly always successful. The technique, however, should be mastered. There are three methods of propagating fuchsias:

1. from seeds (generative propagation),
2. from cuttings (vegetative propagation),
3. by grafting (very rarely used).

Seeds

The seed berries (see page 88), which in most fuchsia species and cultivars are produced in large number, are, depending on species and variety, green, reddish or almost black, small and round or narrow and elongated; everything up to thick, almost plum-sized shapes is represented. When the berries on the plant are fully ripened, i.e. succulent, soft and swollen, they are gathered and opened carefully lengthways with a razor-blade. The delicate seed grains are loosened out one by one with a small pointed stick (a toothpick) and dried on blotting paper. Many breeders simply squash the berries with a fork and flush out the seeds with water. This way it is immediately obvious which seeds are capable of germination: these sink to the bottom, while the infertile ones float on the water's surface.

As the seeds quickly lose their germinative capacity, immediate sowing is most likely to lead to success. The seed tray must be washed scrupulously clean. A seed sowing mixture is prepared of

1 part sieved soil
1 part peat
1 part vermiculite or Perlite
1 part sharp sand

The seed tray is filled to about full with this mixture and the surface is made level. So that this light mixture does not become consolidated, it is allowed to draw up water from the bottom. The seeds are now placed out individually on top, about 3 cm apart, covered with a very thin (same thickness as seed) layer of soil using a sieve, and placed in a plastic bag. As fuchsias germinate in the dark, a piece of brown paper is used to cover the top. At 12–16°C the first green tips will appear after three to four weeks. Up to this point the humidity in the closed bag is generally sufficient.

At the first signs of germination, light ventilation is applied: first for half an hour, then longer each day, so as finally to remove the covering altogether when the young seedlings have acclimatised to the dry outside air.

Fuchsia seeds are well known for being 'fickle'. The first seedlings have already developed several leaves when the last seeds are only just beginning to germinate. In this case all seedlings which have grown two pairs of leaves are carefully taken out one by one and pricked into small pots. The tray is then put back into the bag and the continued development of the rest of the seedlings remains to be seen.

Young seedlings are vulnerable and prone to fungal diseases. *Botrytis* in particular but also soil-borne fungi are dangerous. To be on the safe side the sowing mixture should have been treated with an application of Chestnut Compound. If working with valuable seeds from a particular cultivation or cross-breeding, very special care must be taken and the seed tray and the mixture should be sterilised. The following method has proved very effective:
Flat, rectangular pie dishes made of aluminium foil can be purchased at household stores. A few drainage

holes are made in the bottom with a pair of closed scissors. Then the previously described mixture is put in until the tray is half full and the tray is heated in an oven for two hours at 200–225°C. If the tray thus sterilised is in addition placed in boiling water until it has drawn up all the water it can, all harmful fungi should really be killed off. After cooling, sowing proceeds as described above. Naturally, sterilised soil must also be used for sieving over the seeds and the PVC bag should likewise be new and sterile. All this is admittedly a bit of an effort, though one can now be assured that the seedlings have been given the best possible start. All plants which originate from seeds are thereafter treated as cutting plants, and with good care develop so quickly that they will flower in the next summer.

Cuttings

If one has the necessary space requirements at one's disposal, e.g. a greenhouse or a glassed structure, propagation from cuttings can be practised through-out the year; perhaps with the exception of the two darkest months of November and December, when vegetative growth seems to be at a standstill. The best time for propagation from cuttings, however, is the early spring. The overwintered plants are back in brighter conditions again and are potted in fresh soil. They put forth new shoots, so good material for cuttings is available in abundance. This early in the season, in March–April, no buds have yet developed and every strong shoot is usable for cuttings.

The cutting should be healthily and strongly de-veloped, still tender and thus not woody, and free of pests and diseases. Only then can it be guaranteed that good plants will also result. The cutting can be taken when the new shoot of the parent plant contains four pairs of leaves, i.e. it is removed below the third pair of leaves. The lowest pair of leaves is left in position on the plant. The latter, which was raised to a particular shape in the previous year, does not lose this shape and can form new lateral shoots from the two remaining eyes. Not much time should elapse between the taking of the cuttings and the actual striking process. Today, cuttings are struck directly into peat based mediums, which are mixed with half peat and half sand or Perlite. Pay attention of course to the pH value, and if necessary add carbonate of lime. After no more than about eight to ten days the

cuttings are given a weak foliar feed. With this method the fuchsia cuttings develop a thick, robust and healthy root system. Single varieties root more quickly than double ones, but nevertheless all cut-tings should have rooted within a fortnight to three weeks, up to 14 days with bottom heat and 3 to 4 weeks without.

POTS, MULTI-POT TRAYS, PROPAGATION BEDS

The size of the containers used for striking naturally depends on the number of cuttings. Cuttings must not touch one another; they must have adequate space in the container. An amateur who makes only a few cuttings can strike them individually in as small and shallow a pot as possible. Clay pots are porous: the air has access on all sides and that speeds up root development. The striking mixture is poured in and lightly firmed down, then watered thoroughly. This should without fail be done before striking.

A hollow is made with a small pointed stick in the centre or around the edge of the pot. Do not simply press the cutting into the soil, for, if the delicate tissue is split or wounded in the process, roots could no longer develop. The cutting is now carefully struck 1–2 cm deep into the small hole and gently firmed in. Obviously each cutting is given a label with the name of the variety or species. It is also helpful to put the striking date on the label as this makes checking easier.

Fuchsia cuttings must be protected from draughts, strong sun and evaporation, but should stand in a bright place. With PVC this is no longer a problem today. The small pot is placed in a plastic bag which reaches 10–15 cm above the pot, so that the bag is not touching the cuttings. In the past, cuttings were rooted under a preserving jar. In principle it is the same thing, whether under glass or under polythene: in both cases the result is that the air is suspended, which prevents evaporation and accelerates rooting.

Multi-pot trays with small 3½-cm to 4-cm pots are well suited for larger propagation units. The rooted cuttings hold the ball together well and transplanting into individual pots takes place without any hitch. In this case, too, it is necessary to use polythene to protect cuttings against evaporation and draughts. Beneath the polythene, which in this case is resting directly on the cuttings, a lot of condensation forms and one should therefore ventilate now and then.

An inverted preserving jar is the simplest form of mini propagator, creating a close humid atmosphere.

Miniature hothouses is a term we might use for propagation trays made of shock-resistant plastic material with a transparent covering hood. They can be purchased in various sizes in horticultural outlets. They have proved outstanding for the fuchsia-fancier with a larger collection of fuchsias and who accordingly has more cuttings to make. A tray with a volume of $60 \times 22 \times 8$ cm will hold a good 30 cuttings. The hood is high enough so that it will not be resting on the cuttings at any point and can easily be removed for ventilation. The narrow shape will fit on to any windowsill in the house, and the warmth from the central heating which is present anyway can be used with autumn propagation or in the early spring. To regulate the temperature, polystyrene sheets can be placed underneath.

SOIL AND AIR TEMPERATURE

Fuchsia cuttings root quickly and easily in a soil temperature of 18–20°C. If for any reason one wishes to speed up the process, one can go to a maximum of 22°C. When covering over, the air temperature must definitely be lower. If roots have successfully developed, this can be seen from the glossy shoot-tips which have become firm and succulent. By carefully lifting up the cutting one can also feel the pull of the roots. The temperature must now be lowered to 15–16°C. The cuttings, which have become very soft and tender owing to the warmth and being covered over, must now be gradually acclimatised again to the cooler outside air. This is achieved by removing

the cover for half an hour on the first day and then for a longer time each day thereafter. This way the young plants become hardened to the conditions.

ROOTING IN WATER

This method of rooting cuttings has long been known to plant-lovers and is still often practised even today. It is interesting to watch closely as the roots develop in a transparent container. The glass is placed on a kitchen windowsill, for the air humidity is generally higher in the kitchen than in other rooms in the house. In most cases the necessary ground temperature also exists in the kitchen. As the cuttings cannot find any food in water, the roots very soon get overlong and become really matted. If one waits too long then planting becomes difficult and the fine root hairs are also slightly damaged. Potting is best done when the roots are 2–3 cm long. With this quick transition from water into a peat based potting compost, the shock suffered from transplanting which can often be witnessed does not occur. Care must be taken as the new roots are extremely brittle and the compost must be open.

ROLLING TECHNIQUE

This reliable and space-saving method enables a larger number of fuchsia cuttings that are semimature or even a little woody to root in autumn in the smallest spaces.

A rectangular piece of polyethylene sheeting is spread in the centre with a thick layer of damp sphagnum moss. Cuttings 7–10 cm, prepared in advance as already described, are positioned with their cut end placed in the moss. The ends with the leaves remain outside the sheet. The lower half of the sheet is then folded over the upper half and the whole is carefully rolled up from one side to the other. Tied up with raffia, the result is thus a small bunch of cuttings. Several of these bundles can easily be placed in a tray, covered with polythene, and in a warm bright spot rooting follows very quickly.

PROPAGATION IN PLASTIC BAGS

This method of propagation is even more simple and produces splendid results. A rectangular, tube-like

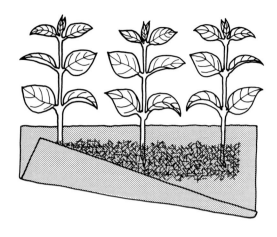

Rolling technique.

in sufficient numbers from the plants, which are often still in full flower. If a variety that one would really like to propagate is already very woody, a single shoot is cut back by one to three eyes; no further, otherwise it takes too long for a new shoot to come from the dormant eyes. The young shoot tips emerge after a short time in the leaf-axils and produce good cuttings.

The shoot tips are already almost ripe in the autumn; the tissue is firmer and no longer so sappy as in spring. In order nevertheless to stimulate these shoots to develop roots quickly, they are dipped in a rooting hormone (e.g. Murphy's rooting powder) before striking. Experts remove as cuttings half-ripe side shoots with a piece of the bark about 1 cm long (termed the 'heel') still attached: i.e. they carefully pull off the cuttings from the other plant. The forming of callus (wound tissue), which must first form at the site of the wound on the cutting and from which the new roots then grow, occurs particularly quickly and strongly in half-ripe cuttings with a small heel. With cuttings of this kind the long-known piece of gardening wisdom is confirmed: that cuttings root more quickly at the edge of clay pots because the porous clay lets more air through to the cut surfaces. Air and moisture ultimately speed up root development.

To this end, a slightly larger clay pot is taken and in the centre of it is placed a clay pot about 2–3 cm smaller and in which the drainage hole has been

plastic bag is completely filled with the propagation medium previously described, which must be uniformly moist. There must be no empty spaces in the bag. The bag is closed up with a piece of strong, durable hemp or sisal cord which is knotted tight. The ends of the cord are not cut off but 20–30 cm must be left hanging. Cuttings can then be inserted all around the bag in small slits, which are cut in the required number and spaced accordingly. The bag is hung up with the remaining ends of the cord in a shady, protected place.

AUTUMN CUTTINGS

As the above shows, fuchsia-fanciers who lack opportunities for overwintering larger plants several years old do not by any means have to forgo maintaining their stock, once they have got it together, by their own propagation. Many fuchsia varieties duly shoot once more in August and September, when the day temperatures are no longer so high and the nights become distinctly cooler. Cuttings can then be taken

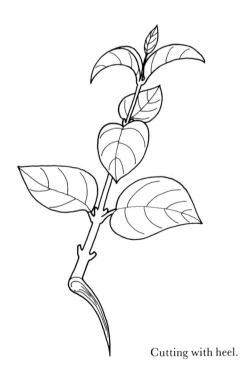

Cutting with heel.

44

sealed. The space left between the two pots is filled with propagation medium and the cuttings are placed around in such a way that they are not touching one another. They are firmed down well, watered from below and put out in a shady place in the open. The air temperature at this time of the year is still warm and perfectly sufficient. The supply of air now takes place from within and from without and has a very positive effect on the fast rooting of the cuttings. If watering is necessary, then the inner pot is simply filled with water. The pores of the smaller pot allow the water only slowly to seep through. A uniform moistness is always ensured.

INTERNODAL AND BASAL CUTTINGS

If, through a bit of good fortune, you perhaps obtain a cutting of the very fuchsia variety you have long been searching for in vain, under no circumstances would you want to take the risk of losing it. Supposing the cutting is a fully grown side shoot with four pairs of leaves and the shoot tip, with a little luck six cuttings can be taken from it and six plants also therefore raised. The risk of loss has already become considerably smaller.

As can be seen from the illustration, first the shoot tip is separated off; this gives the first cutting. Then two internodal cuttings are similarly used. The next cutting is cut in half lengthwise with a razor-blade so that each half possesses one leaf with one dormant bud. The last one, the basal cutting, can equally be used divided or undivided. With the divided cuttings a rooting powder preparation must in all cases be used. Further treatment is as described for spring cuttings.

SPRING CUTTINGS FROM RIPE WOOD

The propagation technique comes in useful with hardy fuchsias of the *magellanica* group when a larger requirement for young plants is to be met, e.g. for planting a fuchsia hedge. The technique is simple, takes hardly any effort and yet produces results.

In autumn, when the first frost has already destroyed the foliage, large branches 25–30 cm long are cut from fully ripened parts of the hardy fuchsias. Any soft shoot tips must be removed. The individual branches are bundled up and tied together with raffia. A small trench about 20 cm deep is dug in a

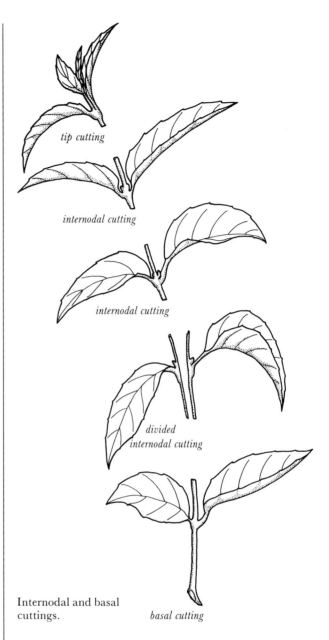

tip cutting

internodal cutting

internodal cutting

divided internodal cutting

basal cutting

Internodal and basal cuttings.

sheltered place in the garden, and the bundle is laid horizontally inside and covered over again with the excavated earth. If the soil is very heavy, it should be made lighter beforehand with sand, peat or polystyrene pellets.

Spraying against fungal attack cannot do any harm. Then cover with leaves or fir brushwood. In normal winter temperatures wound tissue (callus), which is the prerequisite of root formation, forms on the lower points of the cut section up until the spring. When the soil is to be worked again in the spring, the cuttings are removed and inserted individually deep enough into the soil for only one eye to be showing. As soon as it is warmer, the cuttings put forth shoots. In the next year they can then be planted as a hedge with 30–50 cm between them. Even in the first summer, however, one can delight in the plants, which are already flowering profusely. This method of propagating hardy fuchsias is horticulturally the best. The plants become more resistant than those propagated indoors or in a frame.

For professional gardeners who have to propagate slow-growing fuchsia varieties in autumn, it is perhaps interesting to know that fuchsias propagated under short-day conditions develop vegetative shoots. To get plenty of cutting material one should effect a short-day treatment of the mother plants by keeping them in the dark between 17.00 and 07.00 hours each day. The dark period must total at least 13 hours every day. Begin about eight to nine weeks before the planned date for propagation and carry this through until the natural short day arrives. See also page 80.

FURTHER CULTIVATION OF ROOTED CUTTINGS

When the fuchsia cuttings are rooted they must immediately be planted individually in the smallest pots possible. The cutting is carefully lifted out of its container with a fork, without damaging the young roots. The first pots should not be any bigger than 5–7 cm. The pots are filled to about two-thirds full with the potting soil described on page 000. The young cutting is held firmly with one hand in the middle of the pot and more soil is added with the other hand to the point where there is still enough space for watering left at the rim. The soil is not firmed down; the pot is just knocked once or twice against the flat of the hand or potting bench. Do not forget to label. The first watering is not done from above with the watering-can, but the pots are placed in a shallow tray with a little water. This way the compost can slowly draw up all the water it needs from below. The pots are left in this tray for about 24 hours. The slowly evaporating water does the young plants visible good. The next morning they are standing fresh and upright in the pot.

A plant is always only as good as its root system. For this reason, in the following months everything must be done to encourage root development. The small pots are not simply placed on the bare window-sill or the empty greenhouse bench, but on a bed of moist peat 2–3 cm thick. For the greenhouse bench, watering mats made of synthetic material have also been available for some time. These store a great deal of water and transfer it to the plants as required. The peat layer, which is kept constantly moist, works in the same way. It saves a lot of work if not every single pot has to be watered. At the same time the young plants are protected from an excess of water. In addition to this a high air humidity results from the evaporated water from the mat or the peat, and this is essential for the fuchsias.

After four to six weeks, depending on the time of year, the first pot should be completely filled with roots. Take a plant out of its pot and have a look. Potting on now takes place, this time into a 9-cm pot. This is continued until the plant has reached the desired size. The plants repay the effort of repeated transplanting by speedy uninterrupted growth. The root ball must at all costs remain intact when potting on. If it disintegrates, the plant needs much longer to grow in again. This means an undesirable and needless interruption in development. Provided that cleanly washed pots are always used when potting on and the plants have been well watered the previous evening, the plants slide smoothly out of the pot without any trouble.

The next largest pot is made ready with a little soil, the plant is gently inserted and the space left free is filled up with fresh compost. Here, too, the soil is spread out lightly simply by repeatedly knocking the pot and is not firmed down too much, finger pressure only. Air pockets must not develop, though. Freshly potted plants are well watered once and then kept rather dry, i.e. only slightly moist, for a few days.

The following can be said in summary: Do not pot on too quickly, though do not delay too long with this process, either. The roots should not have already grown several times around the inside of the pot, for this leads to premature ripening of the wood and serious retarding of growth and premature flowering. When potting on, also take care that the plants are standing at about the same height in the new pot as they were before. If need be a thin layer of new soil is scattered on top.

Late-summer and autumn cuttings stay healthier during the months when light is poor if they are in the smallest possible pots (7 cm), at most 9 cm for strong-growing varieties. It is important that they are cultivated through at about 10–12°C. Such young plants would not survive a rest period. If all goes well, the fuchsias should be standing in the 15-cm pot in late spring. In this they will spend their first summer and thus their first period of flowering.

For potting and potting on, the compost already described, which contains adequate provision of feed, is always used. Liquid feeding is not started until the plant is in its final pot and this is filled out with roots. At all stages of development, however, from cutting to mature plant, growth can be stimulated by foliar feeding, which is applied in a 0.2 per cent solution with a single-hand aerosol spray. The foliage becomes visibly firmer and the plants altogether invigorated. Suitable agents are fertilisers with a fairly high nitrogenous content (25:10:10).

We may now ask ourselves: why all the effort of constant repotting? Professional gardeners do not even do this. This is explained by the fact that an amateur very rarely has such ideal growing conditions for his plants as a horticultural business does. In the latter case the pots are standing on warm bench beds uniformly heated from beneath. In the big greenhouses the light conditions are also better. Generally, only robust fuchsia varieties are propagated, which by nature possess a strong rooting capacity. The appeal of a private fuchsia collection, however, lies in the very fact of getting difficult varieties to flourish well. As one example among many other 'prima donnas' we could take 'Texas Longhorn', which can be induced only by the 'step-by-step method' to produce a good root system which adequately supports and nourishes the plant in all phases of its development.

A certain restriction on space for roots leads to more profuse flowering, although there are differences in this respect from one variety to another.

Root runners

All hardy fuchsias and also many of the more robust fuchsia hybrids form root runners, i.e. near the mother plant new shoots appear through the soil from the root. If these are carefully detached with the root and placed in pots for further cultivation, new young plants can be obtained without any problem.

CHAPTER EIGHT

USES OF FUCHSIAS

Fuchsias as indoor plants

The days when fuchsias, especially in the country, adorned sitting rooms and country cottages are probably gone for good. With the coming of central heating and the dry atmosphere resulting from this, fuchsias cannot find the living conditions acceptable to them indoors during the period when the heating is on. No matter how adaptable fuchsias may be, they cannot tolerate a dry atmosphere for a lengthy period of time. If the conditions are otherwise favourable, i.e. the heating element is not directly beneath the windowsill, the light is sufficient and bright, and there is no sun blazing in which would damage the foliage through the burning-glass effect of the window pane, then it can be tried. The fuchsia pots are placed into larger outer pots containing moist peat. This way, through evaporation, a micro-climate with sufficient air moisture is created around the plant. Frequent mist-spraying aids this process.

It helps in summer and in early autumn if windows and doors of the house are open and plenty of fresh air gets in. A fuchsia standard in the bright hallway, plants in full flower on the windowsill (not at the south-facing window!), are a lovely sight.

Some cultivars which are particularly well suited for growing indoors are

'Achievement'	'General Monk'
'Chang'	'Gruss aus dem Bodethal'
'Display'	'Mrs Marshall'
'Fascination'	'Swanley Gem'

All have a compact, upright habit, do not grow too big, and flower profusely and for a long period in brilliant colours. The choice of cultivars is critical for success with fuchsias as indoor plants. Those listed above do not even drop their buds and flowers when the surroundings temporarily become warm and dry. Now and then the pots should be placed for a few hours just outside the window or the door in a warm summer rain; there they can recover from the atmosphere in the room.

Fuchsias for balconies and window-boxes

For many people who live in the city, flowers, lovingly cared for in window-boxes, are their only permanent contact with nature. A balcony, even if only a few square metres in size, can well be a paradise and a source of constant pleasure and relaxation.

Modern architecture with its monotonous concrete façades just asks for its rigid lines to be broken up by decoration with greenery and flowers. In front of the pale walls the fuchsias with bright red and blue or red and white flowers stand out particularly well. The long flowering period, which with good care lasts from mid May to the end of October, is more than reward for the little energy expended in the initial planting and the day-to-day care.

Plant boxes of every size, from 40 cm up to 1 m in length, from inexpensive but serviceable plastic moulds up to durable polypropylene boxes, can be obtained in any department store or garden centre. Plastic boxes are easy to transport, but when buying one should make sure that the rim is solidly moulded, in other words not hollow. Nowadays there are ingenious designs which are quite stylish and can hardly be distinguished from wooden boxes. The fastening of the boxes to the window ledge or the balcony parapet is very important. They must be safe and stable so as not to endanger people passing by on the street and for the plants not to be lost with the first strong gust of wind.

On the subject of plant soil—including that sold ready for use in bags—everything has already been said in the chapter on cultivation. It is essential to ensure a satisfactory number of drainage holes in the bottom of the boxes so that no harmful accumulation of moisture can develop. The choice of suitable fuchsia cultivars and attention to the direction the plants face are also very important for a long-lasting success and unmixed pleasure. If the boxes are standing on the windowsill, the cultivars should not be too tall-growing lest they should darken the room behind them too much. If the position is particularly windy, compact-growing varieties with smaller flowers should be selected. Overhanging fuchsias with big flowers would be too easily damaged by the wind.

The effect that one would like to attain with the boxes should also be considered. The greatest possible effect in the smallest space should be achieved, after all. A splendid appearance is given if upright and pendent forms alternate with each other in the boxes. As a window-box, open to the wind and the sun on all sides, dries out relatively quickly, more frequent watering is necessary. In exposed positions, the individual shoots of the plants should from the beginning be carefully tied to stakes and any additional growth, which with good care is inevitable, should also be considered. On hot dry days there is no better benefit for fuchsias than fine mist-spraying with the easy-to-use single-hand sprayers. If the undersides of the leaves are also borne well in mind, then this is the best prevention against pests. Spraying should not be done in blazing sunshine, however, otherwise unsightly leaf spots could appear.

There are few plants which flower unaided even on the northern side of a house quite so profusely as fuchsias. Particularly suitable are the following cultivars:

'Berliner Kind' (Eggebrecht 1882)
One of the good old German cultivars that go on forever. It has a bushy upright growth and is double; sepals salmon-red, corolla pure white.

'Deutsche Perle' (Twrdy 1874)
A good old cultivar, single, with cream-coloured tube and sepals and bright orange-red corolla, which has proved itself in the best manner. Growth is upright and bushy. It flowers particularly profusely and for a long time (see pages 63 and 67).

'Display' (Smith 1881)
Has single flowers of especially handsome shape and is versatile. The sepals are pink; the corolla is expanded and dish-shaped, rather brighter pink.

'Dollar Princess' (Lemoine 1912)
Has small but thickly double red and blue flowers which are present in large numbers on bushy, overhanging, very resistant plants.

'Flash' (Hazard 1930)
Of upright, well-branched growth with small light green leaves, which offset the medium-sized, numerous, uniformly red flowers to particularly good effect.

'Gruss aus dem Bodethal' (Sattler and Bethge 1894) (see page 55)
Also a German cultivar from the last century. The upright growth and the good, spontaneous branching allow the classic flowers with brilliant red sepals and, in the young flower, almost black-blue corolla to stand out conspicuously well. The single flowers are clearly visible at the ends of the branches and should always be at eye-level so that this contrasting play of colours can be admired.

'Mrs Victor Reiter' (Reiter 1940)
Single, the long snow-white, waxy tube with snow-white sepals and the corolla of exquisite red form a strikingly elegant flower. The growth is overhanging and the dark green foliage very healthy and robust.

'Other Fellow' (Hazard 1946)
With bushy, many-branched growth, and a single flower with almost white tube and sepals and delicate salmon-red corolla, is an excellent, neatly elegant cultivar.

These should be seen only as a few suggestions from the large number of fuchsias available for planting in balconies and window-boxes on the north side. Anybody can take his pick of cultivars from the large assortment, according to his own taste. There are indeed many other fuchsias tough enough to flower satisfactorily even in north-facing positions.

For west and east sides of the house, which are ideal for fuchsias, there is an abundance to choose from; all possibilities are open. In windy situations a little attention should be given to the growth shape of the individual cultivars, in other words do not select the very ones which, owing to spiky growth and brittle branches, are particularly prone to breaking. Otherwise virtually anything that is to one's liking can be planted and tried out. Particularly effective are boxes which have in each case been planted with only a single colour combination, e.g. upright and

'Moonraker'

Fuchsias on the patio

A terrace or patio offers still more opportunities for attractive arrangements with fuchsias. The choice of decorative plant containers available today could hardly be bettered. Set up on support walls and side walls of steps, these containers are planted all around with pendent fuchsia varieties. To produce height a strongly growing upright variety is put in the middle. Planted tubs, barrels or vats of this kind become a real showpiece during the course of the summer. Terraces often have a pergola built over on which hanging baskets of every size desired can be hung. Perhaps a stepped flower display can be set up on a sheltered wall, which helps the pots with the delicate white and pastel-coloured fuchsias to produce a distinctive effect. Standards are well protected from wind here and, being at eye-level, are particularly close to.

As everything is mobile the picture can be changed at any time and there are hardly any limits to the imagination.

Because of the loose structure of fuchsia plants and the colours in all their splendour yet subtlety, the architecture of a house is not masked but rather is enhanced. Where there is no pergola, containers with fuchsias can be fixed at differing heights to telescopic poles.

pendent varieties all with red and white flowers. Boxes planted with white cultivars work very well in front of brick walls. If windows or balconies of a house are facing south, only the sun-tolerant *triphylla* hybrids with their dark foliage and brilliant flower clusters are really suitable for planting. They are described in a further section of their own.

When decorating balconies with fuchsias, do not in any way simply be content with the boxes on the parapet. Fuchsias suspended in half-pots and baskets on side and rear walls or freely arranged fuchsia standards transform the small areas into a paradise of flowers. Hanging baskets, too, are picturesque and can accommodate a larger number of fuchsia varieties.

Hardy fuchsias in the garden

Sad to say, people are far too unaware that there is a range of fuchsias that are perfectly hardy even in a

'Swanley Gem'

Fuchsias in a window-box or balcony-box produce a big effect in a small space.

British and central European climate. They can be raised all year round in the open. Once planted they will endure many years in the same position. In the course of a period of growth they form slender, loose shrubs about 1–1.5 m tall, and with their beautiful foliage and rich profusion of flowers are real gems for the garden. Flowering as a rule begins in July and lasts without interruption until the first overnight frosts. Hardy fuchsias thus brighten up the garden at the very time when many other shrubs have long since withered.

The light requirements of these rainforest plants are modest. Shady parts of the garden, e.g. in splen-did older gardens, are often difficult places for plants. If the shade is not too deep and the sun reaches the shrubs for a few hours of the day, even here fuchsias can still find good living conditions and bring fresh invigorating brightness to these parts of the garden. The position must on no account be too close to trees or other woody plants, for fuchsias cannot tolerate pressure on their roots. In such cases they can, however, be planted in larger containers and buried in the ground.

The hardy fuchsias belong mostly to the species *Fuchsia magellanica*, which was introduced to Europe by Lamarck in 1768. As the specific name implies, they come from southern Chile and Argentina, in the mountains and rainforests near the Strait of Magellan. (*F. magellanica* itself can be found at sea level around Tierra del Fuego.) Here they are found at altitudes of up to 3,000 m. Climate and temperature at these altitudes are largely comparable with European winters. This explains their amazing hardiness. This group of fuchsias is versatile and very adaptable. They fit in well in perennial borders or beds with woody plants, and are thoroughly tolerant of full sun if the essential cool 'foot' is provided for with a mulch layer of compost or peat.

Hardy fuchsias of diverse varieties and colours, planted between the large shrubs of once-flowering old roses, ensure colour, once the splendour of the roses is over at the end of July, right up to the frosts.

Anybody travelling in Cornwall or Wales, or in Scotland and Ireland, who has ever seen the long hedgerows and large shrubs of fuchsias adorned all over with delicate, elegant flowers will not forget this enchanting picture. In this privileged and, owing to the influence of the Gulf Stream, mild climate the old wood of the fuchsias only rarely freezes back. In central Europe fuchsias behave as perennials. The visible part of the shrubs, the part above ground, freezes up and dies back. In spring, however, about the beginning of April, the new shoots come forth from the root stock. With good care they quickly reach their customary height again. Just as with the perennials, the diameter of the root stock becomes bigger and bigger and after a few years can be divided up if one wishes to secure new plants.

PLANTING AND CARE

Everything already written on the subject of cultivation and care of fuchsias must also be borne in mind with the hardy group of fuchsias growing in the open.

The hollow for the plant is dug deep and the soil brought to a high humus content with peat, compost or leaf mould. As the shrubs are to endure many years in the same place, organic fertilisers such as hoof and horn, bonemeal, dried cow manure, dried blood or a mixture of these substances (e.g. superphosphate) are mixed in with it. Positions where excess moisture could build up are better avoided. If this is not possible, good drainage must be provided.

Planting is done at the end of May, when the risk of overnight frosts is past. The roots of the young plants should have completely filled pots of at least 10–12 cm and the plants should already possess several healthy shoots. Planted this early, they have time throughout the whole summer to develop a strong, deep-drawing root system. Planting is into a shallow 8–10 cm deep depression which is gradually filled up completely with soil during the course of the summer. This depression at the same time facilitates watering, as it creates a watering space. The ideal, however, is to manage to ensure that the plants have some spare eyes (leaf buds) protected below the soil level. When the plants are well grown in, supplementary feeding can begin. Either the feed is given directly into the water or the practical slow-release fertiliser is used. In the first summer plenty of water should be given every evening in dry weather. It is best to sprinkle over plants and surroundings in order to raise the air humidity.

In late autumn, when the leaves are shed after the first overnight frosts, a layer of dry peat 10–15 cm deep is put over the fuchsias. Leaves from trees that do not rot quickly also give a good protective cover. If one lives in the vicinity of a wood, get hold of some bracken, which is particularly well suited as a covering layer especially as it also contains active substances and minerals which promote a particularly profuse flower production.

Pruning back, to 5–10 cm above the ground, is better not done until spring. The old wood framework gives added winter protection, and the protective cover that has been put over is better left as it is and will not be blown away by the wind. Plants that have been pruned back in autumn are threatened by stem rot in wet winters. In spring, all protective material that has been put on is distributed evenly all around the plant as a mulching cover.

SPECIES VARIANTS

Fuchsia magellanica var. *conica*
Remains a low shrub of about 50 cm. The leaf is pale green and the buds are more roundish; the flowers are red and purple.

Fuchsia magellanica 'Longipenduculata'
This form is recognised by its particularly long, often 8–10 mm, pedicel. Also the flower, with red tube and sepals and mauve-lilac corolla, is longer than in the species.

Fuchsia magellanica var. *magellanica* Lam. (1768)

This fuchsia belongs to the section *Quelusia*. The shrub grows loosely and fairly upright. In Europe it reaches a height of 1–1.5 m. The thin, hairless stalks carry the dainty, oval leaves as opposites or in whorls of three. The leaves are 2–2.5 cm long and slightly dentate. The flowers hang from pedicels which are at most 35 mm long. Tube and sepals are red, the corolla violet-purple. The stamen protrudes beyond the anthers.

Fuchsia magellanica var. *macrostemma* (syn. var. *gracilis*) Ruiz and Pavon (1802)

Forms a dainty shrub with elegantly overhanging branches; 0.8–1 m tall. It is very similar to the previously described form, but has leaves which are longer than 25 mm and often up to 5 cm long. The pedicel also is longer than 4 cm. The flowers appear from July in large numbers, often four together in one leaf-axil.

Fuchsia magellanica var. *molinae* (syn. var. *alba*) Elliot (1930)

For a northwest and central European climate this is the hardiest of all hardy fuchsias. If the winter is not too severe, it puts forth shoots again in the lower section from the previous year's wood. Seedlings are often found scattered around the plant and these can be transplated the next summer. The shrub has a straight upright habit and even in Europe can reach a height of 1.5–2 m. Leaves and branches are uniformly pale green without any red veins. Tube and sepals of the long, slender flowers are almost white, the corolla pale pink. If this lovely fuchsia form is to produce a rich display of flowers, it must be given a position in full sun and must be fed only a little. The poorer the soil, the more plentiful the flowers.

Fuchsia magellanica 'Pumila'

The dwarf of this group grows no higher than 30 cm at most and with its delicate red and blue flowers is well suited as a rock-garden plant. It is hardy, though, only under ideal conditions. It loves to slip its roots underneath a rock or to be sheltered by a thick bolster of other rock-garden plants. Anybody not wishing to lose this treasure should always overwinter a few cuttings indoors.

Fuchsia magellanica tricolor

As the name indicates, this variety has tricoloured foliage. The leaves are variegated greyish-green, yel-lowish and pink and the colours become particularly pronounced in a position in full sun. The height of the plant is 40–60 cm; the flowers are red and blue and appear very late. The two varieties *variegata* and *tricolor* are especially charming as edge planting for fuchsia beds and are also often used in colourful carpet beds.

Fuchsia magellanica variegata

This fuchsia forms a dainty shrub 50–60 cm in height. The green leaves are margined white, spotted and become especially beautiful in colour in a shady position. In the sun, which the plant is able to tolerate remarkably well, the leaves acquire a rosy tinge. The flowers are red and blue and appear relatively late. This variety is planted mainly for its decorative foliage.

Fuchsia procumbens Cunnington (1839)

This fuchsia comes from New Zealand (section *Skinnera*) and is of interest particularly to lovers of rock-gardens. The very small rounded leaves grow on creeping stalks. The yellow flowers stand upright and have stamens with blue pollen. The fruits which adorn the plant as well look like miniature plums.

HYBRIDS

Besides the hardy species and variants so far described, we can also regard some of the early fuchsia hybrids as to a limited extent hardy in a central European climate. Many of them originated right back in the last century and the hybridists often used *Fuchsia magellanica* or variants of it at least as one parent plant for crossing.

The English hybridists Wood and Travis, and in more recent times Cliff Gadsby, continued to work with this older stock and very much enriched the colour range above all. The flowers are no longer exclusively red and purple, there are now also red and white, red and pale blue, pure pink and pure white flowers. These cultivars of limited hardiness have single, semi-double or even double corollas. The breeding results are astonishing and remarkable. The hybrids have forfeited nothing of their relative hardiness, but have gained a great deal in beauty and colour and flower. Compared with the fuchsias of the *magellanica* group, however, the hybrids survive the winter only under very favourable conditions. One can only try out the individual cultivars and attempt

to find a suitable position in the particular garden. As every garden presents its own special mini-climate, generalisations cannot and must not be made. What flourishes well and lasts through the years in one garden may fail altogether in a neighbour's garden a few houses up the road. These fuchsia hybrids are particularly happy in borders against the house or in front of walls and fences which offer a little shelter. The preparation of the ground and care are the same as for the previously described group.

The cultivars described below have been watched for years as to their hardiness, and even survived the harsh winter of 1978/9 well. At that time, though, they were protected from the worst of the cold by a thick layer of snow.

There were, however, some casualties in spring 1980. After some weeks of warm, damp weather all cultivars had put forth shoots splendidly again. Then in May sunny weeks came, with drying east winds and cold nights. At this period the young, tender shoots were partly dried up and partly frost-bitten. How tough these fuchsias really are, however, in spite of the adverse conditions, was to be seen later. Most forms produced further new shoots from the root stock in the course of the summer which did not of course come to fruition. By removing cuttings, however, the cultivars could ultimately be kept alive. For all fuchsia-lovers with no opportunities for over-wintering, these rather hardy fuchsia hybrids have an advantage that is not to be underestimated. An extensive fuchsia collection can be cultivated in the garden with no great problem.

All cultivars described are of upright habit, branch without pruning and bear the beautiful flowers clearly visible at the ends of the shoots. Planted in groups of three, they are particularly decorative and effective.

'Alice Hoffmann' (Kiese 1901, G*)
A charming shrub 40–60 cm tall, with beautiful bronze-green foliage. The delicate flowers are semi-double and very numerous. Tube and sepals light red, corolla white with red veins.

*Initial of country in which breeding originated: A = Austria; B = Belgium; F = France; G = Germany; GB = Great Britain; NL = Netherlands; USA = United States of America.

◁ The plant tub with 'Beacon' on the patio becomes a showpiece during the course of the summer.

'Berliner Kind' (Eggebrecht 1882, G)
This dainty plant reaches 25–30 cm at most. Tube and sepals are brilliant scarlet, the compact double corolla is snow-white. This cultivar is well suited for planting in front of taller ones.

'Beacon' (Bull 1871, GB)
This everlasting, robust cultivar has been able to hold its own among the many fuchsias on offer for more than 100 years. In the open it grows to 60–70 cm. The rather coarse, sturdy foliage is heavily dentate. Tube and sepals are red, the single corolla magenta. The flowers are bell-shaped.

'Jeane' ('Genii') (Reiter 1951, USA)
A garden gem and tolerates a position in full sun. Only in the sun does the golden-yellow foliage on the red stalks light up properly. This many-branched, slightly pendent shrub grows to 60–80 cm. The small, well-shaped single flowers have a red tube and red sepals. When opened the corolla is of the purest blue and only slowly does this change to violet. It is hardy and is the first fuchsia to put forth shoots, as early as the beginning of April.

'Gruss aus dem Bodethal' (Sattler and Bethge 1894, G)
A charming fuchsia cultivar with single, well-shaped flowers of unusual substance and long durability (see page 55). Tube and sepals are enamel-red; the corolla very dark blue, almost black when opened. This unusually beautiful colour combination lasts for days, the corolla later becoming wine-red. The plant

'Gruss aus dem Bodethal'

grows to about 40 cm tall and develops very beautifully. It does, however, need a very sheltered position.

'Hawkshead' (Travis 1962, GB)
Here the hardiness of *F. magellanica* var. *molinae*, which James Tavis crossed with the famous cultivar 'Venus Victrix', comes to light. The mother plant is recognised in the rigid, upright growth of the plant; height 1–1.2 m. The foliage, though, is dark green. The pure white flowers are similar to those of var. *molinae*, but have a characteristic curvature. Thus the name 'Hawkshead' is an appropriate choice. This was the first pure white English-bred hybrid and aroused some excitement. It was registered in America under the no. 1142.

'Ire' (unknown, NL)
A *magellanica* hybrid of great hardiness originating in Ireland in a fuchsia hedge. This cultivar puts forth new shoots early in the year, from about the beginning of April, and the young shoot must therefore still be lightly covered on cold nights with temperatures below zero. From the middle of June the shrub then has a height of 80 cm to 1 m and is literally studded with buds and flowers. The flowers are of the *F. magellanica* type but shorter and the corolla is of a more beautiful blue.
The really remarkable thing, however, which distinguishes 'Ire' from other *magellanica* species or hybrids is the extraordinary branching. While 'Riccartonii' for example branches only in the upper third of the shoots and so most flowers appear only there as well, in 'Ire' branching starts right at the base. Every long shoot produces from all leaf axils short side shoots which all terminate in buds and flowers. The number of flowers on a shrub several years old is incredible. A further plus point is the beautiful, rounded, very thickly foliaged growth shape which results quite naturally from the good branching.

'Lena' (Bunney 1862, GB)
In addition to all its other qualities, this old English fuchsia cultivar is also very hardy. Growth is loose and bushy, the height about 30 cm. The semi-double flowers have a distinctive shape. Tube and sepals are flesh-pink; corolla purple, magenta when faded.

'Madame Cornelissen' (Cornelissen 1860, B)
A very successful old cultivar which, when it appeared 130 years ago, was one of the early, sensational hybrids with white corolla. The shrub grows rigidly upright and strongly; 80 cm to 1 m tall, with dark reddish-green leaves on the red branches. The semi-double, medium-sized red and white flowers stand out particularly well in front of this background. This cultivar, though, flowers rather late.

'Margaret' (Wood 1937, GB)
Strong, upright shrub of 80 cm to 1.2 m. The good hardiness again comes from *F. magellanica* var. *molinae* × 'Heritage'. The flowers are large for a hardy fuchsia and semi-double. The tube and sepals are bright red, and the corolla of an almost pure blue with very little red veining.

'Mephisto' (Reiter 1941, USA)
Grows upright and rather vigorous, the habit originating from the mother plant (*F. lycioides* × 'Mrs W. Rundle'). As an outdoor plant it is excellent, about 60 cm tall. The single, not very big flowers appear continuously in great profusion, in clusters at the ends of the shoots. The flower is uniform scarlet-red and of classic shape.

'Mrs Popple' (Elliot 1899, GB)
A very beautiful, large-flowered, single cultivar with red tube and sepals and blue corolla. Grows to about 70 cm tall and flowers freely and for a long time.

'Mrs W. P. Wood' (Wood 1949, GB)
An F$_2$ seedling of 'Margaret', hybrid of *F. magellanica* var. *molinae* quite clearly shows itself again in the growth, foliage and flower shape. The vigorously upright habit, up to 1 m tall, the pale foliage and the white, slender flowers are suitable for brightening up a sheltered, half-shaded corner of the garden. The prolific flowering and the branching of this cultivar are considerably better than in the species.

'Prosperity' (Gadsby 1970, GB)
A double cultivar with leaves in whorls of three. The flowers have waxy, red tube and sepals of firm substance and the corolla is pale pink with darker veins. This cultivar must be particularly well sheltered. ('Bishop's Bells' × 'Strawberry Delight', AFS no. 1224.)

'Riccartonii' (Young 1830, GB)
This, the most widespread of the hedge fuchsias, is often assigned as a variety of *F. magellanica*, but is a hybrid developed in 1830 in Riccarton near Edin-

burgh, Scotland, from 'Globosa' × *F. macrostemma*. It is quite distinctively strong-growing and hardy and can attain a height of 1.5–2 m. The small leaves are overshot with bronze. The numerous flowers are similar to those of *F. macrostemma* but longer and the buds somewhat rounder.

'Schneekoppe' (Twrdy 1866, G)
Grows in the garden without any pinching into a lovely pyramid about 60 cm tall which catches the eye from a distance. The semi-double, medium-sized flowers are very pretty with red tube and red sepals; the corolla is white with slight red veining. Also one of the still good old fuchsia cultivars.

'Susan Travis' (Travis 1958, GB)
With this beautiful 70–80 cm tall, pure pink cultivar the hybridiser has succeeded in making a breakthrough into a new colour in hardy fuchsias. The strong-growing, well-branched cultivar with many single flowers of beautiful, distinct shape is uniformly deep pink.

'The Tarns' (Travis 1962, GB)
This cultivar has a famous mother, namely 'Venus Victrix', the first fuchsia with white sepals, which appeared in 1840. The bushy plant with dark foliage grows to about 50 cm tall. The flowers are conspicuous through their very long, narrow, almost white sepals. The corolla is violet and the whole flower medium-sized (AFS no. 1148).

'Thompsonii' (Thompson 1840, GB)
Also a cultivar which has *F. magellanica* as a parent, though is not a variant. The shrub reaches a height of 60–80 cm and the flowers are distinctively bright red and violet. In Denmark, large, old specimens which have often been passed on through generations in the family can be seen in many country gardens.

'Tom Thumb' (Baudinat 1850, F)
A delightful dwarf shrub only 30 cm tall (the name is well chosen) and ideal for the rock-garden. The dainty flowers have pinkish-red tube and sepals and a mauve-coloured corolla. Why this fuchsia has so often been confused with *F. pumila* is difficult to understand. The two are very different in appearance. In the fuchsia literature the undoubtedly very stalwart 'Tom Thumb' is even sometimes promoted to 'General'. 'General Tom Thumb', an even older English cultivar (Bass 1848), is described in an English gardening magazine shortly after its introduction as follows: single flower, tube and sepals white with red margin, corolla violet. This latter, however, appears no longer to be in cultivation.

'Vielliebchen' (Wolf 1911, G)
This cultivar's *F. magellanica* origin can be clearly seen ('Charming' × *F. magellanica* var. *macrostemma*). It does not, however, grow so tall as the male parent and the flower shape and colour are also improved. Tube and sepals are brilliant red, corolla blue, height 60–70 cm. In small gardens this fuchsia could well be planted instead of the larger species. The pretty little shrub can find a place anywhere.

In summary, it should once again be emphasised how much everything depends on the position, good preparation of the soil, planting and care in the first years when dealing with the half-hardy fuchsias. Once the fuchsias have grown in properly, they repay the care by flowering for years.

Every ardent fuchsia-lover is also recommended to make a few attempts with other, older cultivars. A very great number of fuchsias will still be happy enough to survive European winters.

An important criterion when choosing half-hardy fuchsias for permanent planting is early shooting. If the new, strong shoots are not at least 10–15 cm long at the end of the April–early May, it is better to abandon the attempt and to pot the plants again. In outdoor conditions such cultivars do not come into flower until very late. For once one no longer gets much out of them, but what is worse is that in such cultivars the wood can no longer ripen sufficiently and they fall victim to the first sharp frosts.

Of interest to lovers of hardy fuchsias is the hybridising of the Tabraham Brothers at St Mary's, the Isles of Scilly. They are very successful in raising new, hardy fuchsia hybrids which have stood the test in the best possible way for years, even in the raw climate of northeast England.

Fuchsias as border plants

Much is written today about fuchsias in connection with a wave of nostalgia. Attributes such as 'old-fashioned charm', 'Victorian enchantment' or 'grandmother's favourite plant' are ascribed to them. In a certain way all that is true. The nostalgic charac-

In this garden fuchsias are the centre of attraction.

ter of the fuchsia is clearly in evidence, e.g. in the highly traditional German spa gardens where extensive border planting has long been common practice and lends a distinctive charm. In this connection, round or oval borders, surrounded by grass, are particularly stylish. This effect can certainly be achieved even in smaller house gardens. As highlight and leading plant, a standard at least 1.5 m tall is placed in the centre of the bed. Several small standards about 80 cm tall are planted around and, since the circumference of the crown makes adequate spacing necessary, the areas in between are filled up with fuchsias about 60 cm tall raised in bush shape. The next circle is formed by rather lower forms 40–50 cm tall, the dwarf forms of slightly overhanging growth follow as edge planting. A border of fuchsias with colourful foliage is also very attractive.

Everything must naturally be co-ordinated in shape and colour and should fit in harmoniously in the garden. With the first attempt it is advisable to use only those cultivars whose growth and flowering characteristics are already well known. If the border could be in a place sheltered from the wind, this would be a particular advantage to the standards. Otherwise only cultivars with very flexible branches can be used so that the crown does not suffer too much damage from the wind. With relatively close planting the smaller standards provide mutual shelter for each other. A border such as this would create an ultimate highlight in any garden and excite much admiration from July until the frosts came.

The scheme must be planned a year in advance. After all, a number of plants is needed which must be raised ready and at one's disposal no later than the end of May, the deadline for planting. Everybody will of course devise a colour arrangement according to his or her own tastes and the realities of the garden. The following arrangement would be a suggestion for the creation of a 'red and white bed':

1 'Swingtime' as tallest standard	(1.5 m)
5 'Checkerboard' as half-standard	(0.8 m)
5 'Schneekoppa' as bush	(0.6 m)
25 'Alice Hoffmann'	(0.5 m)
35 'Berliner Kind'	(0.3 m)

This magnificent *Fuchsia triphylla* type 'Billy Green' comes from the mansion house gardens in Hannover.

All these bright red and white cultivars result in a well-balanced bed with a very good effect from a distance.

One could very nicely imagine planting each side of a sweeping garden path with standards at suitable intervals which are in turn accompanied by colour-balanced bush-shaped fuchsias. To design borders with just the various *triphylla* hybrids would be a fascinating task as well. The more sunny the aspect and the more sheltered the bed, the greater is the success at any rate.

Granted, it is no small effort in autumn to pot all the plants again. The job can, however, be made easier by sinking the larger plants together with their containers into the soil, though they then never attain that full display of flower that freely planted-out specimens produce. It is obviously not true to claim that fuchsias do not form balls and therefore are difficult to transplant. A standard which, when it was being raised, was always potted on only to the next largest pot as per the rules has such a compact root system that replacing in pots takes place with no damage to the plant. If during this procedure some of the thick, old roots come to grief, this does not matter. They would have to be cut, anyway, when repotting in the spring.

The method which is employed in many municipal nurseries and spa nurseries, appears to be a practicable, labour-saving interim solution. In this, the standards and the larger old plants are stood in wire or plastic baskets which enable the fuchsias to root through into the surrounding earth and which can simply be taken up again in the autumn without disturbing the root ball. Anyone who considers that his plants could suffer with direct planting into the soil or who would like to simplify his work can plant in baskets from the beginning. This is advisable in any case with very light, sandy soils.

In the Netherlands the passion for fuchsias is very widespread. The maritime climate is very advantageous for the growing of these humidity-loving plants. Enthusiastic, knowledgeable fuchsia-lovers make fuchsias the leading performers determining the rest of the garden. Much cared-for grass and some choice, exceptional woody plants form the backdrop or the stage on which the fuchsias in every conceivable form play the leading part throughout the summer. Such gardens are usually not very big and are well shielded against the wind from the sea. They have a magic all of their own which is difficult to express in words. One needs to have seen them.

CHAPTER NINE

RAISING ORNAMENTAL SHAPES

Even the wild species of fuchsia in the open country have very variable growth shapes. Bushes of every height, from dwarfs of a few centimetres up to giants several metres tall, can be found beside pronounced climbing plants or prostrate cushions. As parents of the *Fuchsia* hybrids, they have passed on the diversity of habit to today's cultivated fuchsias. In a very simplified way these could be divided into upright-growing fuchsias and pendent fuchsias. Between the extremes every growth shape imaginable exists, from elegantly curved or far-overhanging branches to completely horizontal ones.

Over 100 years ago, fuchsia-gardeners and fuchsia-lovers recognised that the many various growth characteristics could be made use of in order to raise the plants to distinctive, decorative shapes. At that time many people developed such a great artistic ability that their reputation has been passed down to the present day, e.g. James Lye and his son-in-law George Bright. Photos in old fuchsia books show the two of them between their 3-m tall fuchsia pyramids. They are said to have worked for three to four years on these works of art. This does not mean to say, however, that no further artistic ambition should be developed nowadays. Even today, any well-rooted cutting still harbours within itself every possibility for a bit of creative work. We just have to be content with smaller dimensions. The creative aspect, however, makes fuchsia cultivation all the more interesting.

Some ornamental shapes, such as bush, shrub or standard, often called crown shrubs, can be raised without any particular difficulty. Others demand greater skills. Because fuchsias grow quickly with good cultivation, all shapes can be reared to maturity in one or at most two years. That is a relatively small expenditure for the many years of pleasure one can get from them.

Growing always starts off with young, healthy, well-rooted plants of cultivars that are well chosen and suitable for the special purpose. The best-known and particularly attractive shapes that can be raised are bush and shrub, standard, pyramid, pillar, weeping fuchsias in hanging baskets and wall baskets, espaliers, fuchsias as climbing plants and fuchsias as bonsai.

Effective plants by a simple method

It would be regrettable if, because of the following, necessarily detailed description of the raising of different fuchsia shapes for beginners, the impression should be given that everything is very complicated and impossible. Quite the opposite is the case. In practice, if the correct things are done step by step and always at the right time, everything will seem much simpler and sometimes it suddenly becomes quite clear what matters. The more one experiments, the faster one's knowledge increases. Having a go and winning are closely correlated, even in fuchsia cultivation.

Since everybody has been a beginner once and the great uncertainty of the first steps is not forgotten, first of all I shall give a brief description of how to obtain effective, decorative, taller fuchsia plants in a simple way. If we disregard a few cultivars of poor constitution and those fuchsias which by nature form only a low bush, the choice of fuchsias is still very wide.

'Amy Lye'	'Elfriede Ott'
'Belle de Spa'	'Flirtation Waltz'
'Daisy Bell'	'Little Beauty'

are oft-tried favourites for this simple growth shape. While still in the second pot the cutting is given a stake and from now on fastened loosely to it at about every 5 cm. The shoot tips must on no account be damaged. The plant should grow to the normal height in accordance with its variety. That is, all side shoots remain on the plant. It should be in the most open situation possible so that it can develop uniformly on all sides. Every couple of days the pot is turned so that another side is facing the light.

Potting on as and when necessary and frequent foliar feeding enable the plant to make speedy progress. When it is getting on for spring, many fuchsias raised in this way are already 80 cm tall. When the planned height is reached, the top shoot is removed and—importantly—at the same time all side shoots are stopped at two to three pairs of leaves. From this moment on one needs to wait only another six to eight weeks for the flowers. It is amazing how beautiful and big the plants have become in this relatively short time.

Many of these tall but slim fuchsias can be accommodated on a greenhouse bench. Even fuchsias such as 'Fiona', 'La Campanella' and 'Swingtime' which, raised as bushes, demand a lot of room because of their wide-branching growth become modest in this form. This method of growing brings the greatest advantage with pendent varieties with long internodes which, because of their untidy growth, often cause problems. If the shoots are raised in a spiral around the inserted stake or are tied in loosely, then they develop much more in the way of side shoots, and even cultivars with big heavy flowers such as 'Aunt Juliana', 'Pink Marshmallow' and 'Taffeta Bow' will produce as many flowers as one could possibly wish for.

'Mieke Meursing'

Bush and shrub

Most fuchsias are probably raised as bushes or shrubs. With few exceptions this shape can be achieved without any trouble. The beginner should glean his first experiences when growing these shapes. Beautiful bush or shrub forms are used for the planting of balcony boxes, for garden beds or even as pot plants in the greenhouse. As a rule an upright-growing variety is used for these. When the young cutting has formed three pairs of leaves, the centre growing tip with just two to three of the smallest tip leaves is removed.

This stopping stimulates the dormant eyes in the leaf-axils of the remaining pairs of leaves to grow out rapidly. After only a short time the plant has formed four new side shoots in place of one. These four shoots are stopped again when three new pairs of leaves have developed. After a few weeks 16 side shoots exist. Fuchsias usually flower at the tips of the shoots. The buds and flowers come from the upper leaf-axils. The more often stopping is done in this way, the more side shoots the plant develops and the more flowers one can expect. A twice-stopped plant with 16 side shoots is already nicely bushy and in most cases one can let it rest there.

For all that, from the last stop until the appearance of the flowers takes 60 days in single cultivars. 70 days in semi-double cultivars and 80 days for double cultivars. How often stopping is done depends on how early in spring the process was started. When stopping, single buds which often develop early in the year are always removed as well for the benefit of a full flowering later. With an early start and efficient cultivation, up to four stops can be made on many strong-growing cultivars. Generally, however, one should cease at the end of May in order to get a full flowering from mid July. In purely mathematical terms, a fuchsia plant stopped four times, which by then possesses 256 shoots, could at a conservative estimate of four flowers per side shoot come up with 1,024 flowers.

It should not, however, be forgotten that not all fuchsia cultivars react the same way. Sometimes only one eye produces a shoot instead of the expected two and so the arithmetic is no longer correct. It is all a question of cultivar. At fuchsia shows, therefore, we find mostly fuchsias which react positively to stop-

'Deutsche Perle', photographed in the historic gardens of the ▷ Hannover mansion house.

ping. As 'positive' examples, the cultivars 'Mieke Meursing', 'Lena Dalton' and 'Countess of Aberdeen' may be mentioned. In addition there is a whole range of cultivars which are naturally self-branching without having to be stopped even once, e.g. 'Dollar Princess', 'Display' and 'Ringwood Market'.

In many fuchsia cultivars which develop strong, healthy shoots, we might like to think that tying would be unnecessary. If, however, we think of the weight of the flowers which the still supple shoots have to bear in the first year, then it is certainly advisable to support the branches. For this, the practical, plastic-covered wire ties, available in any garden centre, can be used. They can be placed around stake and branch in the shape of a loose spiral and they expand when the shoot becomes stronger; there is no need to fear damage through growing into the wood. Carnation-rings serve the same purpose.

The feature of fuchsias to be naturally self-branching always indicates a particular vitality of the cultivar. Many fuchsias have in addition the further advantage of producing shoots anew from the root ball and by this means creating shrub forms with several shoots in one pot. These natural shrubs are particularly well suited for border planting in the garden. Almost all hardy fuchsias belong in this category. As a rule, with these cultivars of strong growth a single stop, or two, is sufficient to obtain shrubs with an abundance of flowers. Raising bush shapes from cultivars of pendent growth and more supple shoots, which is perfectly possible, necessitates supporting the initially soft shoots with a stake. For this, try to use thin stakes which are as unobtrusive as possible. The basic shape of the bush, once reached, is completely woody at the end of the first season, so it should survive in the second and subsequent years as a structure that is self-supporting.

Standard

The standard is probably, after the bush-trained plant, the favourite and currently also the most sought-after form of presenting a fuchsia. A standard can be raised to a fine height in only one year. It bears its flowers to particular advantage at eye-level.

The strong-growing cultivars which develop a sturdy root system are particularly well suited for cultivation. If an upright-growing type is used, the head becomes big and broad and during the course of

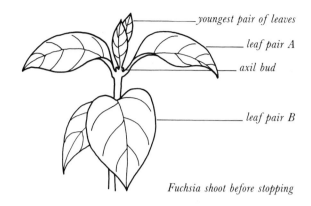

youngest pair of leaves

leaf pair A

axil bud

leaf pair B

Fuchsia shoot before stopping

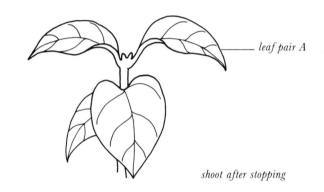

leaf pair A

shoot after stopping

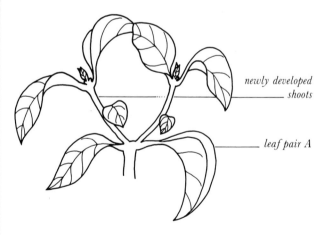

newly developed shoots

leaf pair A

Stopping is important for the shaping of a well-balanced plant.

the year can assume considerable proportions. If one wishes to raise a weeping standard, one of the pendent or lax cultivars should be selected. The finished standard then appears lighter and more open and the head remains narrower because all the shoots are growing downwards.

Although one can begin rearing at any time, cultivation is made much easier if begun in the vegetative phase: in other words at the time when the fuchsias can put all their energy into growth. As we shall read in a later chapter, the fuchsias belong mainly to the 'long-day plants'. That means that they have their vegetative phase, during which only shoots and leaves are developed, in the short-day period, i.e. in autumn, winter and spring. As the days start to get longer, when the fuchsias receive 12–14 hours of daylight, the buds and flowers are formed. With this the fuchsia enters the generative phase, in which fruiting also begins. This phase thus serves the purpose of propagation and the vegetative growth is distinctly curtailed, as is the case in all other plants as well.

If cuttings of the scheduled cultivars rooted in autumn, from about August, are used for raising standards, then the natural short day is exploited for the target to be aimed at, that of getting as tall a stem as possible in the shortest time. But if cuttings from the spring propagation are used, then a great deal of time needs to be spent in preventing the standard from flowering.

The height of standard aimed at depends on how it is to be used later and not least also on the vigour and growing strength of the cultivar selected.

Table standards are raised mainly for decoration indoors and should therefore not exceed a stem height of about 30 cm. It would be good if for this purpose two or three standards were raised at once. They could then be swapped around during the course of the summer. While one is fulfilling its decorative function in its appointed place in the house, the others can be recovering in the open or in the greenhouse from the dry indoor air conditions.

The next size up, the half-standard, should be about 45–75 cm tall. This is the ideal height for the various uses it can be put to in the garden. Half-standards can be used as the focal point in fuchsia borders or alongside pathways, and do not offer such a large surface area to the wind as their larger cousins the full standards (which are at least 75 cm tall). However, one can by all means go even higher. Limits are set only by the vigour of the earmarked cultivar, the skill and perseverance of the gardener and the spot chosen on the sheltered patio; and not least by the space available in the overwintering site, for a standard can reach many years of age. For that matter, it should not be forgotten that during the course of its life a standard grows a little taller with each year. The height of the head or its bulk can of course be regulated by pruning, but the stem length no longer can.

FORMING THE STANDARD

The starting point is again a healthy cutting which should have rooted in August or at the latest September. A whole array of particularly growth-minded fuchsia cultivars bear their leaves as three-leaf opposites, unlike the remainder which have two-leaf opposites. The difference can be seen particularly well by looking down on to the young plants from above. These cultivars accordingly branch in three-fold manner, quickly form a thick head, and later also bear a threefold number of flowers. Some typical representatives of this group of cultivars are

'Barbara'	'Mission Bells'
'Beauty of Exeter'	'Mrs Lovell Swisher'
'Checkerboard'	'Orange van Os'
'Margaret'	'The Doctor'
'Masquerade'	

If, when training the young plant to a bush shape, the tip was stopped at three pairs of leaves, when training to the standard every care must be taken that the tip is never damaged. So that the standard can grow straight and upright, from the start it is provided with a supporting stake and is fixed to this at every 5 cm. Again it is best to use the green wire ties with a plastic sleeve. When in the course of time the stem becomes thicker, the places where it is tied must be checked from time to time to see that they do not on any account get overgrown by the bark. If tying is not done, the young plant like all plants grows towards the light; through this the initially soft stem develops curves, which look unsightly later when the wood is ripe.

Constant attention must now be devoted to the speedy, uninterrupted growth of the fuchsia. Side shoots which develop on the stem are carefully removed shortly after they appear so that all growing energy can be concentrated on the main shoot. The actual leaves that belong to the main stem, however, must always be left in place until they drop by themselves one day after the head has formed. They are the only leaves that are available to the plant for assimilation at this period.

For efficient growth the young standard always needs a larger pot with good, nutritious soil as described in the section of composts. Whenever the white roots have reached the rim of the pot it must be planted in the next pot up. In so doing the ball must remain intact so as not to slow down growth. If the plant is well watered on the day before the rather critical potting on, then this should turn out well.

Continuous potting on not only keeps the standard growing smoothly, it also prevents premature development of flowers which in fuchsias is stimulated by their being restricted to relatively small pots. At this point, however, flower development would, for the time being, stop vertical growth and must therefore be prevented.

Throughout the entire cultivation period the standard is given a weekly foliar feed which is applied with the spray bottle. All liquid fertilisers that are sold can be used in the concentration specified. Towards the end of May, as soon as there is no risk of any more frosts, the standard is placed in a sheltered spot outdoors. The fresh air and the influences of the weather have a general invigorating effect. It is always surprising again to see what tremendous growing energy lies hidden in many a fuchsia which is raised on a single shoot in this way.

(1) 'Checkerboard'

The day when the standard has reached the desired height, the chances are that it is already in the final (for this season) pot, which should have a diameter of about 16 cm for a table standard, 20–22 cm for a half-standard and 24–30 cm for a full standard. With the last potting on a particularly strong stake is provided which is tall enough so that it projects into the head to be formed and can later protect this from being broken by the wind. For the stability of the taller stems, the sturdier and, owing to their own weight, more stable clay pots are preferable. Square plastic containers are also better in this respect than the usual downward-tapering plastic pots.

If one wishes to use the standards for garden ornamentation, and to this end to sink the pots into a bed, then the stake can be stuck a further 10–20 cm through the drainage hole into the ground. This way the standard will stand perfectly steady. This safeguarding of the plants against breaking should be taken seriously, and well before the proud results of one's work over a whole year are seen lying broken up on the ground after a storm. In the first year the head is still comparatively small and pliable. A head several years old, often with a diameter of 1 m, has a considerable weight, especially at times of rain, because of its many, often weighty flowers.

The young standards taken into cultivation in the autumn must in every case grow throughout the winter; they must not undergo a rest period like other, older fuchsias. In the greenhouse this is simple. If one is not available, a bright place must be sought in the house or the living quarters that is not too warm (15–16°C).

One day, when will depend on the intended height of the standard, the time comes when the tip is removed. In general, when the planned stem height is reached, three or four pairs of leaves are allowed to grow over and above this and any side shoots that may have already emerged on these are no longer removed. The head of the standard will be formed from these upper shoots. Stopping in this case too means that only the uppermost two or three small leaves are gently pinched out. Thereafter all dormant eyes of the three or four upper pairs of leaves mentioned should break in the following days and weeks. When these new shoots have formed the third pair of leaves, the tip of each is again removed and the

(2) The full standard is a popular shape in which to present ▷ fuchsias; this example shows 'Deutsche Perle'.

continued process of shaping the head from now on takes place exactly as described in the section on bush and shrub. Basically, a standard is simply a bush on a stem.

One should always try to get a good balance in the proportion of the head size to the stem height. A tiny head on a metre-tall stem is just as disharmonious as a head of 60 cm diameter on a 30-cm tall stem. When raising standards from rigidly upright-growing cultivars, it is often advantageous to bring the lower side shoots of the head carefully into a more horizontal position before they make wood. To do this, carefully guide the shoots slightly downwards using thin raffia which is fastened to the main stem. Or light weights can be hung on the still supple branches; a clothes-peg for instance is practical and easy to attach.

In everything written so far, the starting point has always been robust, strong-growing fuchsia cultivars. Nevertheless, many a person has a special preference for the somewhat less sturdy cultivars and would like to see the perhaps particularly beautiful flowers on a larger plant at eye-level. In earlier times when this was the case, stems of robust cultivars were raised as base plants and in the second year the desired fuchsia cultivar was grafted on to the stem. These techniques, however, demand a great deal of practice and also are successful only when all factors such as light, warmth and timing are ideal. Anybody without a greenhouse will rarely be successful. The site of grafting is always a seat of trouble and is often not able to support larger heads.

From these sorts or from pendent fuchsias with only thin branches it is easier to raise standards which stand on their own feet if they are allowed in the first year to retain not only the leaves but for the time being also the side shoots, which are then cut back to two pairs of leaves in each case. With this method, though, one must allow for a longer period for the stem development, as in this case part of the growing strength goes into the side shoots. The growth so checked is of visible benefit to the stem. The internodes remain shorter and that can only be an advantage.

The sole disadvantages, at least for the perfectionist, lies in the fact that the side shoots must later be removed from the stem with a pair of scissors. The places on the stem where cuts are made always remain visible as unsightly spots.

How many years the standard will bring pleasure depends primarily on the cultivar chosen. 'Checkerboard', 'Royal Purple' or 'Deutsche Perle' standards

can reach 20 years and older. A basic requirement is a good, frost-free overwintering place with temperatures of 4–6°C. The stems must get a real rest in the months November to February. Other cultivars lose their vitality after several years, put forth shoots more and more sparsely in the spring and must then be replaced by young new growth. Some cultivars which are particularly well suited for raising as standards are

'Ambassador'	'Igloo Maid'
'Beauty of Bath'	'Joy Patmore'
'Beauty of Swanley'	'Lena'
'Bon Accord'	'Leonora'
'Brutus'	'Lye's Unique'
'Caroline'	'Mazda'
'Celia Smedley'	'Mrs W. Rundle'
'Claire de Lune'	'Nina Wills'
'Cyril Holmes'	'Other Fellow'
'Earl of Beaconsfield'	'Pink Temptation'
'Falling Stars'	'Rufus'
'Flying Cloud'	'Sleigh Bells'
'Forget-me-not'	"Snowcap"
'Gay Fandango'	'Spring Bells'
'Hidcote Beauty'	'Temptation'
'Hindu Belle'	'Uncle Charlie'

If older standards are in large tubs, it is not necessary to replant every year in completely new soil. It is quite sufficient to remove the upper, spent layer of soil and to replace it with new rich soil, though feeding then requires particular care.

Pyramid

The pyramid is the shape which every ardent fuchsia-lover regards as a challenge to his or her ability and will therefore sooner or later tackle. Only somebody who has a thorough command of fuchsia cultivation from A to Z, and who has had a good look at the cultivars in question, is capable of bringing this particularly effective shape to maximum beauty and perfection. A greenhouse is in this case absolutely essential, for raising to the finished pyramid takes two to three years. In addition one must be endowed with patience and perseverance.

A really well-constructed pyramid should be thickly and uniformly foliaged from top to bottom. Nowhere must any leafless spots be allowed to detract from the harmony of the shape. Only profusely flowering cultivars with strong, upright growth can be considered for training. The cutting with which one begins must have grown straight and be well rooted. At the very beginning it is given a strong support stake so that no curvatures develop in the main stem. The most important point, which should never be lost sight of, is to keep the plant continuously shooting forth. Any interruption in growth, no matter how slight, can lead to failures and disappointments. This means:

The plant must always be potted on to a larger pot at the correct time, with care, without ruining the ball in so doing. Water conservatively, so that at any one time the soil is uniformly moist but no wetness ever accumulates.

The first condition for strong growth is a healthy, well-branched root system. To assist this, at the second or third potting on the long tap-root which usually grows around the ball right at the bottom of the pot is carefully cut away. The roots then develop better and fill the whole pot more evenly. The plant should be given a priority place in the greenhouse where the incidence of light is particularly good but there is shelter from dazzling sun. Regular turning of the pot is important, so that the pyramid does not grow lop-sidedly towards the light.

When the cutting has reached a height of 18–22 cm, the height being determined by the length of the internodes (distance on stalk between two pairs of leaves) which differs in each cultivar, then the first stop is made. Six to eight side shoots will develop from the dormant eyes. The weaker of the two shoots developing at the top is removed after a little time when the more vigorous one can be distinguished. The remaining shoot is now looked upon as the new leader and must again be carefully tied to the stake.

The side shoots emerging below the leader are allowed to grow until they have developed three healthy pairs of leaves, then all are stopped at the same time. The upright-growing leader and the side shoots are never stopped at the same time but alternately. By stopping the side shoots the leader is stimulated to speed up growth, whereas stopping of the leader stimulates a sudden thrust of growth in the side shoots.

At this point one will have to try to bring the lower side shoots carefully into a horizontal position with the help of canes and raffia ties. They will later represent the base of the pyramid. When new shoots develop on these lower side shoots after stopping, no more than two should be left on each shoot. Everything else must be removed because a superabundance of shoots would claim too much of the plant's growing strength and could thereby put a brake on vertical growth.

When the new leader has developed four pairs of leaves, it is again stopped and the strongest of the new shoots emerging at the top is once again selected as the leader. The process is clearly recognisable in the illustration. It is repeated until the pyramid has reached the desired height. If the pyramid is to be uniformly foliaged from the bottom of the pot to the gradually tapering top of the plant—and that is the aim—particular attention must be paid to the lower lateral branches, which determine the lower diameter of the plant and must therefore grow very long.

The fuchsia cultivars which are generally suitable only for the growth shape of a pyramid always grow straight upwards (negatively geotropistic), contrary to the laws of gravity, unlike the pendent fuchsias,

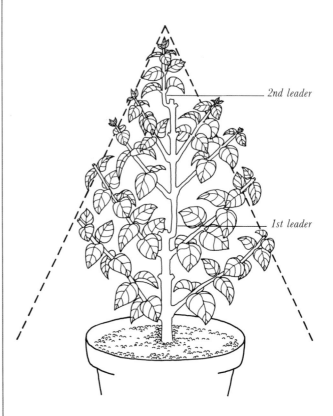

The pyramid, a challenge to the skills of the fuchsia-lover.

'Mrs W. Rundle'

With good cultivation in nutritious soil with weekly foliar feeding the fuchsias grow very quickly. Gardeners or enthusiasts with a greenhouse have the great advantage that they can begin on the growing of a pyramid very early in the year. One-and-a-half years from January up to the summer of the following year are then available for the raising of the pyramid, for even through the winter the plants must be kept growing continuously without a rest period. When the many shoots which have developed in this long period come into flower in the second summer—all flowers appear simultaneously because all shoots were after all always stopped at the same time—then the magnificence of the pyramid will be impressive.

Once the pyramid has filled the large final pot with roots, the masses of leaves and flowers must also be fed adequately. A weekly feed, alternating organic and inorganic fertilisers, has proved successful.

Before the first winter rest and in all subsequent years pyramids should be carefully trimmed and, in so doing, care should always be taken to retain the laboriously trained basic shape. During the actual rest period the pyramids must be given a place lying down in the greenhouse and be regularly turned carefully from one side to the other. This horizontal position gives the lower buds a better chance for breaking out in the spring. The flow of nutrients, which always rises straight up into the upper shoots and causes these to break out first, is thereby diverted.

When the new fuchsia season starts, the plant is placed upright again. By this time the lower shoots have most probably already broken through and there will be hardly any need to trim here. On the other hand, the upper shoots must be cut back drasti-

'Celia Smedley'

which grow horizontally (diageotropistic). Only the cascade types grow positively geotropistically and thereby follow the laws of the earth's gravitation. For this reason the initially supple lower side shoots of the upright-growing cultivars must always be brought carefully into a horizontal position. This way the sap flow and the growing power is directed more into the upright-growing shoots of the plant, where it is also most urgently needed. All devices which are required for this purpose, such as canes and raffia, can be removed later. These shoots, through their own weight and the weight of the flowers, later fall into the horizontal position by themselves.

Many people consider the hanging basket as one of the best ways of presenting fuchsias, here with 'Red Spider'.

cally in order to retain the characteristic pyramid shape. A pyramid can be kept in shape for perhaps three to four years, then it will become bare from the bottom upwards and produce the main shooting only in the upper part. Through skilful cutting, however, the plant can bring many more years of pleasure as a standard.

Cultivars to be recommended are

'Abbé Farges'	'Lord Roberts'
'Achievement'	'Marinka'
'Amelie Aubin'	'Molesworth'

'Brutus'	'Mrs Marshall'
'Cardinal Farges'	'Pink Pearl'
'Cascade'	'Pink Quartet'
'Coachman'	'Royal Purple'
'Constance'	'Santa Cruz'
'Gesäuseperle'	'Sunset'

Pillar

During the heyday of the fuchsia in the last century, the pillar shape, also known as 'cordon', was very popular and could often be seen. In contrast to the pyramid, which gradually narrows from a broader base to the top, a pillar must be of uniform width from bottom to top, from the pot to the top of the plant, foliaged in like manner all around, and in the finished state look like a pillar studded all over with flowers. There are two methods of achieving this. For both, strong-growing upright fuchsia types are again needed.

In the first and older method, one begins with a well-rooted cutting, which is stopped after the third pair of leaves. From the start the cutting must again be supported and tied to a stake at regular distances. The two shoots developing after the removal of the top vegetative point are from this moment on treated differently. The right-hand shoot is raised up as if to a standard. Only the leaves remain on the stem. All side shoots are rubbed out immediately after they appear. The left-hand shoot is raised to a bush shape and all further shoots stopped always after the second pair of leaves. The idea is that the finished pillar in the upper half bears leaves and flowers on a standard, but in the lower half develops into a bush which overgrows the bare stem of the standard. When everything has grown together the impression of a uniform pillar is created.

The person who first developed this idea must have been an outstanding fuchsia expert and good observer. He has outwitted the plant using its own quite special growth characteristics. He has duly recognised the occasionally fatal inclination, which fuchsias have in common with many other woody plants, of naturally developing new shoots only on the upper branch ends. Only through regular cutting back are uniformly foliaged plants arrived at. Now at last it is becoming clear what is to be achieved with this method. Standards as well as bush forms are kept vigorous through annual and drastic pruning and are constantly rejuvenated. The fuchsias raised to pillars can thus be kept in good shape and free-flowering for longer than, say, the pyramid.

Back to the cultivation of the pillar. The two main stems are kept close together by fixing them to the support stake. When the left side has reached the desired height, the right half has already outgrown it a fair bit because it has not been prevented from rapid vertical growth through stopping. As a rule both halves of the plant can be stopped at the same time. Then the shaping of the head begins, as described in the section on standards, and on both halves the uniform pillar shape is raised by continuous stopping

of the new shoots, after the second or third pair of leaves according to the cultivar. The plants must be turned regularly so that no side is disadvantaged through lack of light. No shoot is allowed to grow outside the pillar shape: all must be of the same length. If then, at the end of the shaping and perfecting of a pillar, all existing shoots from top to bottom are stopped, without overlooking a single one, this time irrespective of the pairs of leaves that happen to be present, the flowers will also develop on all shoots at the same time and will accordingly appear in great number.

The second method of training a pillar is more simple and also leads more quickly to the final result. From the outset two cuttings of one cultivar are planted close together in a pot and these are then treated in the manner described for the first method. The plants, although treated and cultivated as one, have two separate root systems. Vigour and growing strength are therefore markedly greater. Especially after the first winter rest, those pillars raised from two plants are more dependable in putting forth new shoots compared with those raised from one plant.

The reason why the method of raising pillar fuchsias from one plant has been described at such length is to be found in the show stipulations of the fuchsia societies. In England, for example, both pillars raised on a single shoot and multiple plants are allowed to enter the competitions as candidates for a prize.

James Lye, the renowned English breeder of the Victorian era, was a great master in the training of pillars and pyramids. Many of his cultivars are therefore well suited for this work with fuchsias. Should things not go smoothly at the first attempt at training them, pillars can always still be used as bushes or standards and no costly hours of spare time are then invested in vain.

Pendent fuchsias in baskets and hanging baskets

Fuchsias in baskets, hanging baskets or similar containers hung on the balcony, in the pergola or in the greenhouse in such a way that the flowers can be seen from below or at eye-level from all sides are very popular. Many fuchsia-lovers consider this as simply the best way of presenting fuchsias. Anyone who has ever been able to see the magnificent cartwheel-sized hanging baskets in full bloom at Wisley, the gardens of the Royal Horticultural Society, or has been to the botanic gardens at Bremen in West Germany, will fully agree with them.

England is a country that holds very firmly to its traditions: that is why the wire baskets padded with spagnum moss are still used for this cultivation. They have the great advantage of having a small net weight. Today the garden-equipment business supplies many very suitable and tasteful containers which can also be suspended by chains.

If one wishes to enjoy a hanging-basket plant throughout the season, it is necessary to begin on the cultivation of the selected fuchsias early in the year. Naturally the trailing or lax cultivars are the most suitable for this purpose. Particularly effective are hanging baskets planted with just one type of cultivar. A container of 30 cm diameter should be provided with at least four plants of the strong-growing cultivars such as 'Fiona', 'Marinka', 'White Spider' and so on. Five plants per basket are used of the less vigorous cultivars such as 'Balkonkönigin', 'Pink Galore' and 'Postiljon'.

The required number of cuttings is pre-cultivated from January in pots. When being transplated into

Basic shape of a fuchsia trained as a pillar, raised from a single plant.

the hanging basket or baskets, they should have filled the pots with roots; the plants should already be stopped several times and have as many shoots as possible.

We often read the recommendation to stop pendent fuchsia cultivars only once and then to let them grow freely. Anyone who has had a lot to do with fuchsias, and knows the varying characteristics of the individual cultivars from personal experience, will not let such simple advice pass in this general form. Only a few cultivars of the pendent species branch out sufficiently in a natural way. 'Marinka', 'President Margaret Slater', 'Swingtime' and 'Temptation' be left to their own resources after the first stopping. Most cultivars, however, often those with the loveliest flowers, have long internodes and bear only few flowers at the ends of the shoots.

The hanging baskets would look skimpy if we were not to stop these fuchsias as often as possible. Only this way can we achieve a large number of flower shoots and a hanging basket that is fully foliaged all around.

Cuttings of fuchsia cultivars such as

'Boerhave'	'Mantilla'
'Bouffant'	'Pink Marshmallow'
'Enchanted'	'Red Jacket'
'Lillibet'	'Taffeta Bow'

are better propagated in autumn in order to have full-flowering plants with many shoots at one's disposal in May.

No matter how many plants one puts in a basket, one of them should always be planted in the centre so as to give the basket a fixed height. A flat planting in which all shoots are hanging only downwards does not look good. As the wind can reach the freely suspended hanging basket of all sides, the danger of drying out is great. For this reason wire baskets can be lined with sphagnum moss and 2–3 cm of the moss is left projecting out at the top, as a watering rim as it were. With many containers a polythene lining also prevents drying out too quickly.

For watering, a small clay pot let into the soil between the individual plants and always kept filled with water is very helpful. Owing to the porosity of the clay pot the plants are kept regularly moist. Many of the containers on sale have a very big drainage hole. This is best blocked up with a cork before watering until the water has soaked the compost well; the cork is then removed and the excess water can drain away. If a hanging basket or basket ever gets completely dried out in hot and dry periods, there is only one solution left. The whole lot is put into a bucket of water until it has all thoroughly drunk its fill. Cautious people allow their hanging plants this rather grandiose recuperative remedy once a week. If a little liquid feed is added to the water, then one operation can be saved.

Half-baskets or wall baskets are containers which are flattened on one side and are already provided with hanging tabs by the manufacturers. They are planted on one side only with trailing fuchsias of a strong-growing type. Hung up on house walls, fences or the rear wall of the balcony, they make a good show.

Espalier

Unfortunately, only rarely do we get to see fuchsias in variously shaped espaliers. Nevertheless, there are many cultivars with very supple branches which can be presented to advantage only in this form. Think of cultivars with a great deal of foliage and large leaves, beneath which the beautiful flowers are often entirely concealed and so are hardly noticed at all.

Wooden or plastic espaliers can be bought complete in every conceivable shape. A rather dextrous fuchsia-lover can also easily nail together a couple of thin battens to make a lattice. Bamboo canes, firmly tied together diagonally with colourless raffia, are a simple way to make a structure. Problems lie rather in anchoring the frames. Once they are completely grown over and the plants are in profuse flower they become really heavy and slightly top-heavy. They must, therefore, either be sunk deep into the soil in larger plant containers or else, if the whole lot is to embellish e.g. a balcony or a patio throughout the summer, be additionally fastened to a wall.

The principle of covering the espalier with fuchsias is simple. One, or better two, plants of a trailing or lax cultivar of the greatest possible vigour, and which develops long side shoots, are taken into cultivation indoors or in the greenhouse very early in the year. Cultivars such as

'Chang'	'South Gate'
'La Neige'	'Swingtime'
'Miss California'	

are particularly well suited for this purpose. Two young fuchsias raised on a single shoot which must not be stopped are, when potting on from the 9-cm pot, placed as close together as possible in a 14-cm pot. When the 14-cm pot is well filled with roots, and the 'double-plant' is then some 50–60 cm tall, it is planted in the final container with the pre-prepared espalier. It is placed close in front of a perpendicular brace and attached loosely to this in several places.

It will now become clear which of the existing side shoots must be attached to the cross brace. The side shoots which would grow into the spaces between are superfluous and are removed close to the main stem. When the main stem has reached the full height of the frame it is stopped. The growing strength of the plant can now flow completely into the side shoots. When these have grown over the horizontal battens of the espalier along their whole length, they, too, are stopped.

Young shoots develop on these horizontally trained shoots after stopping. They break out of almost every eye with great vehemence. On these numerous, short side shoots buds and flowers very soon develop which look like Chinese lanterns strung on a line. Whether it is possible in subsequent years to bring this 'wall of flowers' back to the beauty of the first summer again depends largely on the vitality of the cultivar chosen and on the skilfulness of the cultivator.

After the winter rest espalier fuchsias must be cut back to two eyes on all side shoots. The new shoots are then distributed decoratively on the espalier again.

In the choice of espaliers on which fuchsias can be raised there are absolutely no bounds to the imagination. The versatile growth habits of fuchsias enable a great deal to be done so long as suitable cultivars are selected. 'Berkeley', 'Falling Stars', 'Marinka' and 'Mephisto' can be pleasing in all kinds of ways. Strong wire can be bent into circles, arcs, heart shapes and even into a figure-of-eight. The principle of training is always the same as described for the conventional espaliers.

With round shapes, one can get the plant to grow over quickly by working with two plants and training them upwards, one around to the left and the other around to the right. The thicker and fuller one wishes to get the shape grown over (the wire should nowhere be visible), the more frequently the side shoots must be stopped and all the new growth always attached as unobtrusively as possible to the basic design or to neighbouring branches. Always remember to control and tie on all accretive growth as soon as possible. If side shoots have become too long and are beginning to get woody, it is no longer possible to bend them into the desired shape. In this case plants shaped in such a way are likely to fire the imagination. Anybody who has mustered the necessary patience to create such a work of art will always find admirers and imitators.

Climbing plants in the greenhouse

The heritage of some wild forms of fuchsia, that enables them to grow with respectable strength and with the support of other trees and shrubs from the diffuse light of the forest up towards the light, is still latently present in many of today's fuchsia hybrids. This ability can be used to achieve a lasting pleasure from the fuchsias. A basic requirement, though, is a greenhouse, no matter how small it is.

As climbing plants, strong-growing cultivars can be picked out from the large choice available. Upright-growing, pendent as well as the more horizontal-growing fuchsias are suitable. For example:

'Rose of Castille Improved' or 'Royal Purple' grow upright,
'Daisy Bell' or 'Muriel' are pendent sorts,
'Chang' and 'Hidcote Beauty' represent the horizontal-growing ones.

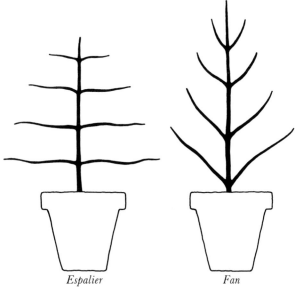

Espalier   *Fan*

Espaliers (left) or fans (right) as trained specimens are only seldom seen.

In this case lasting results depend primarily on the cultivar. Everything from now on is simple and at the same time familiar. A well-rooted young plant, raised on a single stem and not stopped, is planted in a greenhouse bed close to a vertical strut and not too far away from the glass. As this plant is to stand for many years in the same place, the soil in the ground bed must of course be prepared with particular care and be enriched with organic fertilisers or slow-release fertilisers. The earlier in the year this sturdy plant—a good root ball is very important—is available, the longer the pleasure is even in the first season.

Using every means the first shoot is raised up on the lateral support and further on to the roof incline, and secured at suitable distances, according to greenhouse type, either to a plastic-covered washing-line fitted for this particular purpose using ties beneath the clamping-bolts or to wire. With wire, one should use the sheathed types, which do not rust in the high air humidity.

Frequent foliar feeding and removal of the side shoots as when training to a standard allow the plant to grow upwards at an astonishing rate. Undivided attention is to be given to general care. An interruption in growth jeopardises results. If growing strength seems to be waning, it is quite permissible to clip the leader shoot and to train up the strongest of the two new shoots that develop. An impeccable stem is not so very important.

From the moment the plant has grown on to the roof incline the side shoots are no longer removed. They should certainly flower in the very first summer. Side shoots can, however, always be stopped after two or three pairs of leaves. This way the number of flowers increases considerably. Many fuchsia-lovers will agree that the special beauty of the single flower in shape and colour seen from below or at eye-level is a unique experience. The climbing fuchsia flowers freely almost throughout the year. Irrespective of all the influences of the weather, sheltered from cold and wind, it flowers for much longer than other members of its sort growing in the open. Often the last flowers of the previous year are not removed until pruning in spring. Then all side shoots are again clipped back to two or three eyes.

In spring it is important to provide shade at the right time. The young shoots with the delicate, sensitive little leaves, grown so close under the glass, are soon damaged or even burnt by the often already intense rays of the sun.

Many fuchsia species with beautiful, elegant

flowers, if they are kept permanently in the pot, grow in a relatively steady way only in the initial stages and then quickly become woody. Many also flower only on two-year-old wood. Lovers of these wild forms can bring their favourites to greatest perfection as climbing plants growing freely. In the ground bed, where their vigorous roots can grow unfettered, *F. fulgens*, *F. fulgens rubra grandiflora*, *F. boliviana* and its varieties *luxurians* and *luxurians alba* demonstrate more than ever what vitality lies hidden in them.

In the relatively small greenhouses one will also be anxious, with today's heating costs, to use every little space to the optimum. Climbing fuchsias bring colour to those places which would rarely, if ever, be made full use of.

CHAPTER TEN

FUCHSIAS IN THE SMALL GREENHOUSE

Many people dream of one day acquiring a greenhouse. As already described in the preceding sections, it is certainly possible to cultivate fuchsias with great success without a greenhouse. Yet there is always the problem of overwintering in rooms and cellars that are often too warm. This problem at least no longer exists if the dream has finally been realised.

Before deciding to buy or to build oneself a greenhouse, which is not exactly cheap, one should be fully aware of how it is going to be used. Is it to serve only for the overwintering of fuchsias already in existence or do one's ambitions go beyond this? Are young plants to be brought on over the winter or is one already dreaming of standards and other ornamental forms of fuchsias?

For overwintering, a house which can be kept just frost-free (about 3–5°C) will do. A moderately warm greenhouse with an average temperature of 10–15°C on the other hand offers a great deal more opportunities. The comparatively low temperatures which fuchsia cultivation demands have not ultimately been conducive to any obvious fuchsia revival. With the increasing energy shortages, who can still justify running a warmhouse with high energy requirements? To say nothing of the strain on the pocket. Fuchsias are ideal plants in this respect, too. If the greenhouse is fitted with double glazing, or even triple glazing is available today, then this produces a further saving that is not to be underestimated. In a few years the higher purchase costs have been redeemed by the savings in energy.

The type of greenhouse or the size that is decided upon when buying naturally depends on one's needs and requirements. Today, everything from the small do-it-yourself model up to fully automatic de-luxe greenhouses is available. The diversity of types can hardly be covered properly in this book. One would therefore do well to get thoroughly acquainted with what is on offer at the shows or garden centres or in the catalogues of the manufacturers before buying.

When a certain small greenhouse has been decided on, the question arises of the best position for it. A place immediately beside the house is in many respects ideal. Long walks in all weathers are avoided and the connection to the heating, power and water supply mains is easier and cheaper to provide. Of all possible types of heating, the connection to the central heating in the house is particularly favourable in terms of cost. Thermostatic control of the heating produces a further saving.

So far as possible a greenhouse for fuchsias should be set up in a north–south direction so that the sides are facing east and west. The morning sun and the mild rays of the afternoon sun can be made full use of; the heat of the midday, however, is moderated by the shadow of the house. Even a tree a bit further away could cast light broken shadow at the hottest time on a hot summer's day if this were to be incorporated into one's considerations.

When cultivating fuchsias in the greenhouse, particular importance is attached to shading devices. Dry heat, which develops rapidly under glass on hot days, must be prevented by every means. The greatest problem lies here. Heating a greenhouse, in other words keeping it warm in winter, is a simple question of technology and cost. Creating in summer, in high outside temperatures, the cool and moist atmosphere that is absolutely essential for fuchsias if they are to thrive is, however, much more difficult. Shading provided on the outside, whether with blinds or with painted-on colours, is more effective than the same on the inside of the greenhouse. The latter is more likely to lead to an accumulation of heat, at any rate in smaller greenhouses. Greenhouses on a raised base are practical; the height thereby gained allows a few baskets with pendent fuchsias to be hung at the gable end without restricting freedom of movement in the greenhouse too much.

A greenhouse standing on open soil enables the plants to be grown beneath the bench as well. At the same time the evaporation from the ground beds contributes to greater air humidity.

The interior fittings such as benches, suspended shelves and so on are arranged according to one's respective wishes and requirements. There is a wide diversity of finished parts or accessories available.

An absolute must is several sufficiently large windows and ventilation vents. Two doors facing each other are ideal. Nothing hastens hot, stagnant air out of the greenhouse more quickly than a draught. If two doors are not provided for do not spare the expense of a ventilator, which must be installed in the gable wall opposite the door. It is amazing how quickly a few rays of sunshine, even in winter, push up the temperature in the greenhouse. In this connection we talk of the 'greenhouse effect'; the warmth that has penetrated remains trapped for a while in the inside of the greenhouse and is only very gradually emitted to the cooler outside air.

For this reason a thermometer, preferably of the minimum–maximum type, is one of the first pieces of equipment for a greenhouse. An elementary type of hygrometer, which indicates the relative air humidity, which is so important in fuchsia cultivation, can be obtained for a small outlay. What should be purchased on top of this in the way of labour-saving devices, from the electric air-humidifier to the fully automatic irrigation system, is decided solely by financial practicalities. Technology is certainly very useful and reassuring for people who have to attend to their business during the day and have no 'deputy gardener' in the family. In general, however, most of us will prefer to play the 'weather-maker' in the greenhouse ourselves and to look after the fuchsias with our own hands.

Finally the day has come; the greenhouse is fitted out ready and the plants can move in. All problems seem to be solved, and the care of the fuchsias becomes child's play. The plants visibly come to life, they are in the warm and damp and are getting enough light on all sides. Soon, however, we shall find out that even under glass there are problems. For the plants to thrive well depends as usual solely on our circumspection, conscientiousness and readiness to do the right thing at the right time. The conditions under which fuchsias flourish at their best are meanwhile known. On the greenhouse bench the plants are standing in pots, young plants often in very small pots which quickly dry out. In summer this means frequent watering. The work becomes easier if a layer of sand 2–3 cm deep is spread on the bench. The sand is kept constantly moist and the coolness from the evaporation produced does the plants good. Capil-

lary mats made of synthetic fibres can be bought in shops and these can store many times their own weight in water. If the pots are standing on the bed of sand they must be moved frequently so that the roots do not root themselves in the sand. With the synthetic mats this risk does not exist to the same degree. Both the bed of sand and the mats are laid on polythene so that the water can evaporate upwards and not run away through the bottom.

All seedlings or cuttings do not stand freely on the bench, anyhow, but are fed into moist peat in separate containers. Polystyrene boxes are particularly well suited for this purpose.

Because fuchsias resent dry heat, the hot days of summer sometimes cause problems for the greenhouse-owner. If the thermometer inside climbs above the 25°C mark, this means be on one's guard. Shading alone is no longer enough. Using the pressurised spray, not only the plants but also the glass, benches, pots and frames are veiled in mist. Water spilled on the ground in the gangway produces the desired coolness when it evaporates. Windows and doors are left wide open to speed up the cooling process. If it stays hot for days, the only thing left is to move the fuchsias under a tree in the garden.

As luck would have it, high temperatures ensure that in the evening the plants have dried up again. An important gardeners' rule states that plants should never enter the night with wet foliage. Spraying and watering in normal temperatures always takes place in the morning or at least in the first half of the day, if an attack by *Botrytis* or some other injurious fungus is not to be invited.

Once the fuchsias have produced buds and flowers —under glass the flowers are much bigger and the colours brighter and purer than in the open—then try not to catch the flowers directly when taking measures to raise the air humidity. Water spots and brown areas would really detract very much from the beauty of the flowers. If flowering plants are placed together and carefully shielded with a thin sheet of polythene, then they profit from the coolness without being sprayed on directly.

The second problem arises from the fact that not only the plants but unfortunately also various fungal and animal pests know how to appreciate the better living conditions under glass. Mostly they appear as a result of mistakes in cultivation (see Chapter 6). Under the favourable conditions in the greenhouse their rate of reproduction is so high that only vigilance and immediate control can guard against damage. In this respect prevention is better than cure.

The fuchsia-lover causes many problems for himself through his very enthusiasm. There are many types of fuchsia, some more beautiful than others, and meanwhile many are on sale. Through the years of work by the members of fuchsia societies the number available from gardeners has increased. Occasionally cuttings are received as a gift, cultivars are exchanged with friends or the very newest fuchsias are brought back home from trips to specialist nurseries. In short, the collection grows very quickly and the number of cultivated plants soon exceeds our means.

In the greenhouse the plants are now standing pot to pot much too close together. They become 'leggy' through lack of light, and because the air cannot circulate freely among the plants, *Botrytis* and rust gain ground. Fewer would in many cases mean more. If the plants are provided with the necessary living space, then they grow big and compact on strong shoots less prone to fungal attack.

Another temptation lies in the easy propagation of fuchsias. Who could bring himself to throw fine, healthy cuttings that keep on coming on to the compost heap? Beginners, though not only they, become addicted to a single activity which we can only call propagation mania. It is after all always a successful event to raise a new plant from a small shoot tip in a short time. If one wishes to give pleasure to fuchsia-lovers with these young plants, that is a commendable motive. It should never, however, lead to cramming and pressure on space in the greenhouse.

Fuchsia cultivation in the cold greenhouse

A coldhouse with its minimal heating costs can, with good planning, be used in a versatile way for growing fuchsias. It is kept just frost-free at 3–5°C and in the average winter requires no heating at all on many days. At night it is kept at these low levels with the help of some artificial heating. This heating has usually already been designed accordingly with the installation. The owner of a coldhouse sees this primarily as an overwintering place for his fuchsias and other non-hardy tub plants. From as early as February, when the days grow longer and the sun helps to produce higher temperatures in the greenhouse again, sowings can be made.

The fuchsias have completed their rest period and indicate this by putting forth new shoots. Cuttings which are taken early in the year from the first young shoots grow by early summer into plants with many shoots and capable of flowering, for the growing energy of all plants is, as we all know, particularly intense in the spring.

The low coldhouse temperatures would of course make rapid rooting of the fuchsia cuttings impossible. Here technology again comes to the rescue. Practical and functional propagators can be purchased. They are simply constructed and consist of a plastic box with a clear cover. They maintain the 'warm feet' that cuttings and sowings do not get in the relatively cool greenhouse by means of an electric heating cable laid in sand. A thermostat keeps the temperature constant at the set level. A propagator of this sort will find space on any greenhouse bench. Experienced home mechanics buy only the heating cable with thermostat and build their own propagator according to the respective dimensions of the bench. A polythene covering ensures that cuttings and seedlings are protected from unwelcome evaporation. This way one has a small warmhouse in the coldhouse. The extra power costs are minimal and are hardly of any consequence.

The temperate greenhouse

A day temperature of 12–16°C maintained in the small greenhouse offers every possibility to the fuchsia-lover. The night-time temperature can be lowered to 6–10°C without damaging the plants. Cuttings taken in the autumn grow to sturdy young plants without interruptions. They can be stopped often throughout the winter and thereby one arrives at a much greater number of flower shoots. Standards, pyramids and other large plants, including those fuchsias raised as climbing plants in the ground bed, can be trimmed into shape as early as autumn. The rest period, which even here is desirable, consists in watering more sparingly from time to time. Part of the foliage thus is preserved on the plant and the growth cycle is not broken altogether. New shoots break early in the year, with the result that one has available in May full-flowering plants for decorating the house and garden, whereas the plants overwintered indoors or in the coldhouse are not able to flower again until many weeks later.

Whether coldhouse or warmhouse, one should be

sure on one thing if heating energy is to be saved: with the coldhouse the thermostat can remain constant at 5°C, with the warmhouse 12–15°C. Anything over and above this is not necessary; it does not benefit the plants and is therefore wasted. At 5°C the plants really come to rest and do not put forth shoots again until the correct time. With the young plants, temperatures above 15°C in the warmhouse lead during the light-impoverished time of the year to over-long, weak young shoots which are always particularly susceptible to diseases.

Long day and short day

Fuchsias need different day lengths according to their origin and the cultivars resulting from constant cross-breeding in the physiological responses of organisms to changes in the lengths of day and night. This reaction varies from one cultivar to another.

With fuchsias, distinctions can be made between long-daylight plants, optional long-daylight plants and indifferent, neutral-to-daylight plants.

For long-day plants the critical day length is 12–14 hours. After at least five long days the formation of buds is triggered. In our latitudes in northern Europe this day length commences in late March. If the buds are induced, the development up to the open flower often takes eight weeks in single and semi-double cultivars and in fully double forms ten to twelve weeks. The group of long-day fuchsias includes such cultivars as, for example

'Cotton Candy'	'Marinka'
'Hollydale'	'Swingtime'
'Lord Byron'	'Tom Thumb'

Other fuchsias belong in the category of optional (qualitative) long-day plants. They flower the whole year through, thus also in the short days of winter with their poor light, although they experience a marked advancement in flowering in the long days. When brought in before the frost the flowers are sparser, the individual blooms also smaller and the colours no longer so intense.

Indifferent day-neutral fuchsia cultivars flower independently of day length and the existing light in summer and in winter, when they are offered the requisite temperatures of 12–15°C. Neutral forms are predominantly the *Fuchsia triphylla* hybrids and the species concerned in their origination, *F. triphylla*,

F. fulgens, *F. boliviana* var. *luxurians* and var. *luxurians alba*. Cultivars such as 'Gartenmeister Bonstedt', 'Traudchen Bonstedt', 'Mantilla', 'Elfriede Ott', 'Trumpeter' or 'Stella Ann' can flower uninterruptedly throughout the entire winter up to spring. If cuttings are required for propagation at this time, only a radical cutting-back will help and even then the first small pairs of leaves of the new shoots often appear already with complete flower buds. Other botanical species, too, such as *F. boliviana* var. *boliviana*, *F. splendens* and *F. cordifolia*, are neutral to day length and are therefore good winter flowerers in the greenhouse; likewise the cultivars which originate from *F. denticulata*, such as 'Dominyana' or 'Fanfare'. In every fuchsia collection some of these species and variants should therefore be represented. They extend the 'fuchsia year' by several months.

In short days, with less than 12 hours of daylight, fuchsias go through their vegetative growth phrase. All growing energy is spent on intensified shoot and leaf development, on the actual building-up of the plant. Of interest are tests which Adolf Otto carried out in Wolbeck, West Germany, in 1966. Thirteen fuchsia cultivars were planted out in a cold frame in June, and later, from 1 to 31 August, kept in the dark each day from 17.00 to 08.00 hours. With the exception of one cultivar ('Deutsche Perle'), the fuchsias stopped flowering in mid September and shooted vigorously. The artificially established short day had put the plants back into the vegetative phase again. Today, horticultural firms capitalise on these findings. They keep the mother plants in the dark in August and thereby have a richer yield of material for cuttings later.

Other investigations have revealed that cuttings which were taken from fuchsias in the vegetative phase definitely rooted more quickly.

All these factors are naturally very important in professional horticulture. The amateur will as a rule be able to find the few cuttings that he wishes to make in autumn without resorting to such measures.

Advancing flowering by exposure to light

Since scientists discovered the possibility of controlling plant culture through exposure to light or blacking out, much use has been made of this in horticultural practice. Particularly popular is the controlling of chrysanthemums, which can be purchased in flower throughout the entire year. Through additional lighting the short day turns into the long day, or conversely through blacking out the light the long day becomes a short day. The lighting industry has developed special fluorescent tubes, such as Gro-Lux, and lamps for this purpose which allow only those spectral colours which are essential for the plants' growth and flower development to come into effect. In the field of fuchsia cultivation there have been only a few studies in this interesting area.

In 1960 R. H. Sachs and C. F. Bretz of the University of California published the results of their extensive researchers with fuchsias under artificial light in the RHS journal (vol. 85, issue 11) and met with a great response in the fuchsia and garden press. They experimented with 20 fuchsia cultivars in different stages of development in order to find out whether and how fuchsias react to artificial light and what duration of illumination leads to early flowering. For all cultivars work was done with fuchsias in 10–12 cm pots which were raised in the short-length day and stopped twice. First light readings were taken in the open in the natural long day for comparison. The reading at midday on a clear, cloudless summer day was 80,000–100,000 lux, and in the shade it was still 10,000 lux. On a bright winter's day the readings in a cloud-free sky gave 5,000 lux. Based on these amazing light values work was done with lamps of high light intensity.

It was discovered that at an illumination below 5,000 lux bud development did not take place. For bud induction at least five but preferably more long days are required. In addition to the eight hours of daylight four hours of artificial light were provided at night. Of the 20 cultivars studies, 16 flowered in this 12-hour long day, among others 'Whitemost', 'Swingtime', 'Sleigh Bells', 'Flirtation', 'Amapola', 'Dark Eyes', 'Alice Kling', 'Bernadette', 'Dollar Princess', 'Jack Shahan', 'Pink Jade' and 'Lord Byron'. Bud development took place at temperatures between 10°C and 26°C. Further cultivation up to full flowering was made at 21–26°C.

For the amateur with a slightly more warmly run greenhouse it should be interesting to carry out further experiments with his or her fuchsias. Not all cultivars react equally well to control and it would be desirable if many more—similarly representative—tests were made, particularly with the cultivars that are by nature late-flowering. The professional gardener could, under artificial light, not only bring on the flowering of decidedly late-flowering forms and thereby also bring these 'problem children' on to the market in flower at the usual selling time for fuchsias, he could also bring forward entire propagation sets through illumination.

Practice of Illumination*
(from HANS GANSLMEIER*)*

About nine weeks before the intended date for flowering, the plants should already be in their final pots and possess shoots 3–5 cm long above the last stop. As the intensity of the natural daylight influences the development of the young bud, one should start with the illumination at the beginning of February at the earliest. The light intensity is 100–120 lux with incandescent lamps of 20–25 watts per m^2. Illumination period per night amounts to four hours in February, three hours in March, in each case from 22.00 hours. According to D. Vince-Prue (1977), the lengthening growth in fuchsias is greatly stimulated by incandescent lamps. It is better to use fluorescent tubes for illumination. These contain a smaller proportion of dark red light and therefore do not have a stimulating effect on the internodal lengthening. Although just a few long days produce an induction, light is to be given over a period of four weeks in order also to get a flower appearing on the succeeding shoots. It has proved useful to introduce five to ten short days after two weeks of illumination or not to illuminate at the weekends because under short-day conditions the development of vegetative side shoots in the leaf-axils is encouraged and the plant thereby becomes more bushy. A subsequent repeated illumination for a period of two weeks also produces further buds on the small, lateral shoots. During the period of illumination the temperature should not be lower than 15°C at night.

A day temperature of 18–20°C speeds up the further development of the bud. After 25 March the natural long day prevails and the illumination can be discontinued.

*Contributions on this theme have also been published by Professor Dr Karl Zimmer: *Deutscher Gartenbau* 7, 1978; 12, 1973; 12, 1964.

The plant cellar

Something that has been practised for some years in America with much success, namely converting a space in the house into a greenhouse, is seen only exceptionally in England and elsewhere. This is made possible today by Gro-Lux fluorescent tubes or lamps specially developed for illuminating plants. Now that coal cellars and other storage spaces stand empty, party cellars and hobby rooms have come into fashion. Why, then, not create a shelter for fuchsias in the cellar or in the loft? In plant show-cases and florists' windows, which receive little daylight, fluorescent tubes have long been installed with great success in order to improve the lighting.

The following description of how an empty, small cellar can be fitted out for fuchsia cultivation with the help of artificial light is based on an idea which was born years ago more out of necessity during a move of residence. What was initially thought of only as a temporary arrangement has in practice proven to be such a good answer that it can only be recommended that it be imitated.

Four fluorescent tubes suitable for illuminating plants (e.g. Gro-Lux), with reflectors for better light output, are fitted to a rectangular frame (1 × 1.6 m) with distances of 20 cm between them and connected up as per the instructions. The frame is suspended from the ceiling by means of reasonably strong chains. Chains are necessary so as to be able to vary the distance between lighting elements and plants. When the plants have grown a bit taller, the frame is also raised a few links. The plants are placed together on a bench under the light, and the distance between plants and fluorescent tubes should always be 25–30 cm.

In the 'temporary arrangement' mentioned above, all further conditions for a successful cultivation are also provided. A small window is kept open day and night and is shut only on frosty nights. The door is situated exactly opposite the window and has a 1-cm wide gap at the bottom which guarantees a constant exchange of air. Owing to the warm rays of the fluorescent tubes the temperature by day is almost always 13–15°C. It drops a few degrees at night of course but never so much that heating has to be provided. Low temperatures are particularly important when cultivating fuchsias under artificial light. If it is too warm the plants grow too quickly and develop weak shoots with long internodes. In rising temperatures buds and flowers are also dropped prematurely.

High doses of nitrogen should also be avoided for the same reasons. Preventive treatment against animal pests, but above all against *Botrytis*, guards against unpleasant surprises.

Even the hardy fuchsias had to spend the first winter after the move in pots and under artificial light. They are said to have grown strong enough by the end of May to be able to take their place in the new garden. Under the intense light of the tubes the leaves of *F. magellanica variegata* and *F. magellanica tricolor* achieved colours of undreamed-of beauty. Cultivars such as 'Autumnale' and 'President' had ruby-red lustrous leaves. 'Golden Marinka', 'Tropic Sunset' or 'Genii' were of a rare beauty. All species and cultivars retained this distinctive coloration in the hot summer of 1976, even when they were in the garden later, whereas in the subsequent wet and cold summers with little sun they displayed only a pale reflection of this loveliness.

Flowering fuchsias were still uncommon in this first winter in the cellar because I started off with quite young plants. From the end of February the cultivars 'Golden Dawn', 'Mrs Marshall', 'Citation', 'Violet Gem' and 'General Monk' flowered. At the end of March 'Fascination', 'Mrs W. Rundle', 'Brutus', 'Wood Violet', 'Flying Cloud' and 'South Gate' began to flower. When, at the beginning of March, the many overwintered standards started to put forth more shoots, two additional fluorescent tubes were fitted firmly to the ceiling. The stems were up to 1.5 m high and the distance of 30 cm from the light had to be maintained. Because of the constantly regular light and the warming rays, the standards vigorously sent out shoots from every eye, even from wood several years old. The result was much more profusely foliaged and thicker heads, which had never been achieved in preceding years without artificial light. In later years, when the bulk of the fuchsias were again housed in a greenhouse, controlled experiments were also conducted in the cellar with selected fuchsia cultivars to bring forward flowering under artificial light.

For representative tests with a large number of plants of a specified cultivar, the limited space of a cellar is of course not sufficient. For simple fuchsia cultivation under artificial light the duration of illumination, starting from eight hours in January, was also increased as the days became longer. In February there was uninterrupted light for ten hours, in March for 12 hours then up to May for 14 hours.

The programme in the experiments looked some-

A frame with fluorescent tubes for cultivation under artificial light.

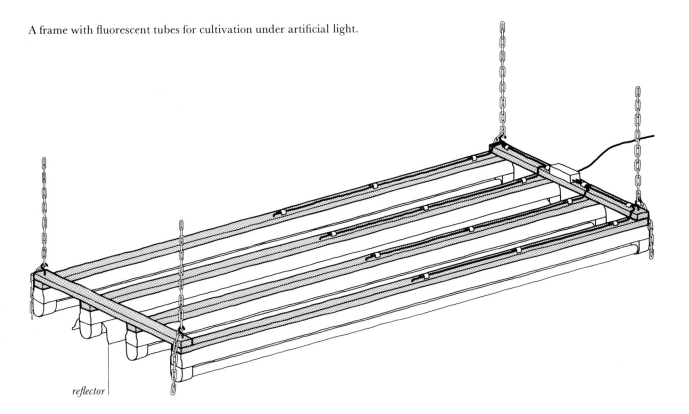

reflector

what different. A basic requirement for bringing flowering forward under artificial light is, with most cultivars, a sufficient physiological maturity. At the beginning of October, for bud induction, 14 hours of light were given for eight days and thereafter uninterrupted illumination for 12 hours daily. Using a preset timer, four hours of extra light were given once more from 22.00 hours. In December the first flowers appeared, and at Christmas 'Countess of Aberdeen', 'Estelle Marie', 'Bon Accord', 'Claire de Lune' (with particularly well-coloured foliage) and 'Amelie Aubin' were in full flower. The double cultivars 'Bernadette', 'Fascination', 'Kiwi', 'Stanley Cash', 'White King' and 'Papa Bleuss' flowered four weeks later, from the end of January. The colours of the white and blue forms were of a pure white and bright blue such as are never found under natural light conditions. Also perhaps of interest is the fact that the plants were illuminated continuously on some very cold nights, without damage. The overnight temperature must not drop below 13°C if the buds are to develop speedily to full flower. In conclusion it may be said that the cultivation of fuchsias in the greenhouse under natural light or alternatively indoors under artificial light have one thing in common: they prolong and increase one's joy in the plants in those very winter months when we often have more free time and can occupy ourselves attentively with looking after them.

Hardening of fuchsias

Most fuchsias which are raised under glass or artificial light are destined for the outdoors once the icy weather is over and the danger of overnight frosts is past, where they will decorate balconies, patios and the garden. So that the plants do not suffer any damage as a result of the change from the sheltered site to the more rugged one in the open air, they must undergo a transition phase for 10–14 days, i.e. be systematically hardened.

In the greenhouse the windows are left wide open at this time, even during the night. Fairly frequent spraying with clear cold water makes the leaves harder and more resistant. When the plants then finally come outdoors, they must without fail—this is exceptionally important—be hardened further. To this end, the plants are taken first to a shady, wind-sheltered place, preferably on the north side of the house, for one to two weeks. Plants which have not gone through such a phase of hardening and are straightaway exposed without a period of transition to the full light, which is much more intensve in the open than under glass, suffer damage to the leaves and are thereby also set back a long way generally in their development. The May sun, already strong, causes burning if it strikes the foliage of unprepared plants.

Unless wintry conditions persist unusually late, hardening can be started as early as around the end of April. Special care, however, is given at night. If the temperatures drop appreciably in the night, a light sheet of polythene should be placed over the plants to protect them.

CHAPTER ELEVEN

FUCHSIAS FOR SHOWS

In countries such as the USA, England or Holland fuchsia societies with large memberships have been active for many years now. Annual shows aimed at calling the attention of more and more people to the rewarding and lovely aspects of fuchsias are part of the regular programme. A show with particularly well-cultivated, profusely flowering fuchsias captivates many people, something which words and books with pictures and detailed descriptions are unable to do. On the other hand, for the members it is an obligation and at the same time a fascinating pursuit to raise particularly beautiful fuchsias of every conceivable growth style for the show and to enter into competition with one another. With this motivation, fuchsia-lovers realise great achievements. On top of this, medals and prizes encourage the competition.

Show specimens must satisfy higher standards and call for special cultivation. If special tasks are prescribed, and this is usually the case, one will have to try particularly hard to accomplish these.

CULTIVATION

There are three methods that are suitable for raising fuchsias for a show. Either cuttings are taken in the early year and one-year-old plants are raised from these; or older, overwintered plants are pruned back in late winter, placed in new soil and cultivated on. A third possibility for cultivating fuchsias, following the biennial method, has proved to be best for show plants and is superior to the first two.

Biennial fuchsias are plants which are not allowed to flower until the second year, in this case in the year of the show. They thus have two complete vegetative periods available for their development and accordingly grow to a magnificent condition with many flower shoots.

Cuttings are taken early in the year, about the end of May or beginning of June. At this time they are particularly healthy and vigorous. Large cuttings with at least three fully formed pairs of leaves are advantageous and these are rooted individually in 7-cm pots. At this time of the year rooting is possible without any additional soil warmth and takes only 14 to 21 days. Further cultivation through the summer is carried out as described in the chapter on propagation. Potting on is always done on time, without damaging the ball, and the plants are as much as possible raised in the open in a bright spot. Stopping each shoot throughout the summer after every second pair of leaves prevents flowering, which is not required until the next year. All growth is concentrated into the building-up of a large, robust plant with many shoots.

When the plants are brought in in October, they should stand in 12-cm pots (maximum). Throughout the winter, in the months of November, December and January, they will not of course grow very much, but should also not go through any pronounced rest phase. By frugal watering the pot is always kept just moist enough that the leaves do not drop. Cultivation, though, requires a minimum temperature of 5–8°C.

In late January–early February, when the days become longer and more light and sometimes even the first rays of sunshine stimulate new growth, the plant is repotted in fresh soil. Unlike those fuchsias which have undergone a complete winter rest, in those raised over two years many young, white fibrous roots will show. Repotting must therefore be done with appropriate care. Only so much of the old soil of the pot ball is removed that the plants will fit into the next smallest pot. They are thus potted back from the 12-cm pot to the 10-cm pot to begin with in order to encourage root growth strongly. From this point on the cultivation proceeds as in all other methods.

When the fuchsias are rooted in in the new pot they must be fed. It is preferable to use fertilisers with a high nitrogen content. In the meantime foliar feed is also given, but when doing this no fertilisers are used which could cause leaf spots.

Special attention must be paid to pest control. A show specimen is judged not only by the number of beautiful flowers it has but perhaps just as much on healthy, undamaged foliage and harmony of shape.

The routine pinching procedure is naturally very important. The more shoots, the more flowers the plants will boast on the day of the show. Whether pinching is done after every second pair of leaves or after every first fully developed pair depends on the cultivar. It is very important that pinching is stopped in time before the date of the show. With single cultivars there should be eight to ten weeks from the final pinching up to full flowering, in doubles 10–12 weeks. In this respect the work must be timed with the date of the show as the whole objective. From the moment when the first buds can be seen no further repotting should be done, either. From this point in time the plants are fed once a week with a fertiliser with a high potash content (N:P:K = 6:8:12).

Most growth types, including standards and baskets, can be raised to perfect show specimens by this biennial cultivation. All cultivars with short internodes and relatively small leaves are particularly suitable. Just a few of the wide variety available are

'Countess of Aberdeen'	'Mieke Meursing'
'Heidi Ann'	'Pink Darling'
'Lady Isobel Barnett'	'Plenty'
'Lena Dalton'	'Tom Thumb'

The sole disadvantage of biennial cultivation is that the plants become excessively large and therefore take up a lot of space. They must be given enough room, however, so that they can develop freely and without blemish in all directions. But what admiration these big plants will excite on the day of the show!

According to a list in the AFS bulletin, the time that a fuchsia requires from the last pinching up to full flowering is dependent on light and weather, but also on the characteristics of the individual cultivars. To this end the following is a summary of selected cultivars:

'Abbé Farges'	6 weeks
'Bon Accord'	9 weeks
'Dorothea Flower'	6 weeks
'La Campanella'	8 weeks
'Lakeside'	9 weeks
'Marinka'	8 weeks
'Mr Rundle'	7 weeks
'Mrs L. Swisher'	7 weeks
'Thalia'	10 weeks
'Tom Thumb'	8 weeks
'Upward Look'	9 weeks

If show plants are to be or have to be taken from overwintered stock several years old, it is important that in good time, but at least 24 weeks before the show date, the assigned plants are set up in a light and warm place again and brought to full lateral growth. If we reckon on about three to four weeks for the time from the first lateral growth, through to cutting and repotting, there should still be enough time up to the date of the show to be able to make three pinches. Here, too, we should aim for plants which have many shoots and flower profusely. With fuchsia cultivars with pendent growth particular care is to be given to supporting and tying. A harmonious shape which is uniformly foliaged from top to bottom should be the result. Canes are used unobtrusively and anything projecting outside the plant is cut away shortly before the date of the show. It goes without saying that pots and containers, unless brand new ones are used, must be washed clean. Thought must also be given to the size ratio of plant and container. A giant plant in a small pot does not look good and conversely a small plant should not stand isolated in a big container. The correct proportions lead to a harmonious overall impression at the outset.

TRANSPORTING THE PLANTS

It has proved successful to put the plants in the car not singly but always several together in a case so that they are able to support each other. The spaces between the pots are stuffed with crumpled damp newspaper. Wrapping the plants individually in paper has proved a failure; this way the plants are too easily damaged. Baskets are placed upright in a bucket which is half filled with damp sand to make it more stable. Exhibitions take place mostly in marquees or halls where the air is warm and dry. Before transporting their plants, circumspect fuchsia-lovers give them a particularly thorough watering once more. Immersing the pots in a larger receptacle is very effective.

With the actual stand arrangement care must be taken that the plants are presented to advantage. The best side should always be turned towards the observer. Each plant should also be checked one last time for withered flowers, seed pods or damaged leaves and any of these should be removed.

A concluding word on participating in shows in general. Shows should always be supported by as many participants as possible with the highest possible number of exhibits. They can be seen as the joint achievement of a horticultural society and effective only from a certain size upwards. As a rule plant-lovers are idealists. As no financial reward is to be expected, they see their mission as being to give pleasure to as many people as possible.

There will always be members who think nothing of a competition and attach no importance to awards. If these fuchsia-lovers for all that do take part—as it were *hors concours*—with their most beautiful plants, then this contributes a great deal to the general total picture and to the success of the exhibition.

CHAPTER TWELVE

HYBRIDISING

Seed extraction and sowing

Anyone who has been involved for some years with fuchsia cultivation will sooner or later want to harvest some of the abundantly produced seed pods and, out of sheer curiosity, to try sowing seeds.

Fuchsias, being so diverse, bear very different fruits. Many are perfectly spherical and tiny, barely 3 mm in diameter, while others are cylindrical and narrow, a good 2 cm and larger. *F. procumbens* from New Zealand bears berries the size of small plums. In a ripe state the colours of the fruits also vary; everything from the palest yellowish-green through dark green, dark red and violet shades to the deepest black can be found.

A ripe fruit is not hard and firm any more but soft and very succulent and gives a little when pressed with the finger. If they are carefully cut open with a razor-blade, it is easy to see that each berry has four chambers with a number of seeds in each chamber. Even the number of seeds in each fruit varies from a few up to over 100. Some will contain no seeds at all.

There are various methods of freeing the seeds from the succulent fruit flesh. In practice it has proved useful to cut the berry into four at the four dividing walls (usually quite visible from outside) of the individual chambers. Then the lot is placed on a piece of pale absorbent paper, e.g. a paper handkerchief or blotting paper, and the seeds are detached from the fruit flesh with a pointed instrument (a small knife blade); a wooden toothpick or a strong needle are also suitable.

Another method is to crush the berries in a cup, using a fork, and to fill the cup with water. The fertile seeds sink to the bottom of the cup and the flesh of the fruit is carefully poured off with the water. In both methods the flat, often sterile seeds can be finally separated from the roundish, fertile ones using a good magnifying glass. The seeds are then dried on an absorbent tissue for a few hours and if possible sown straightaway.

The actual technique of sowing is described in detail in the chapter on propagation. Anyone who does not have a greenhouse with a heated propagator at his disposal, and who would not want to risk sowings on the windowsill in the dark months of the year, can keep the dried seeds in a sealed container until the spring and only then sow them. As fuchsia seeds lose their full germinative power very rapidly, the sowing date should not be put off any longer than is necessary. Detailed studies of the duration of germinative capacity of fuchsia seeds are not available. From experience, seeds gathered in August and sown immediately germinate at a rate of 100 per cent at a soil temperature of 12–15°C. The germinative capacity decreases markedly with longer storage.

Another aspect is the period of germination of fuchsia seeds. It is possible that the first seeds germinate after a fortnight to three weeks, while one must wait many weeks more for the rest. In practice this means that the seedlings, once they have fully developed the first pair of real leaves, must be carefully taken out of the seed tray and pricked individually into small pots. When doing this, the fine roots should be handled very gently. The newly pricked-out young seedlings must be cultivated for a further period with soil heating. Not until the first small pot (5 cm) is well filled with roots can the plants be hardened and acclimatised to cooler temperatures. Fuchsias sown

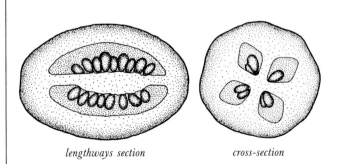

lengthways section   *cross-section*

Berry of *Fuchsia procumbens* cut open.

in August flower as early as the late summer of the following year.

Hybridising objectives

As already described, not too much patience is required to see the results of the first sowing. Whether it was worth the trouble, though, is another matter. Only in very rare cases do new fuchsia cultivars, representing an improvement on those already existing, result from such random berries of which at best the mother form is known. To add a few more dashing fuchsias to the 10,000-plus fuchsia cultivars so far known and some 6,000 registered (though not all are still in cultivation) may thus not be a desirable aim. Once interest has been aroused with the first attempt, carried out more out of the joy of experimenting, some thought should be given to where further improvements are desirable and attainable through controlled breeding.

If we take for example the *triphylla* hybrids, then we could try through controlled cross-breeding to achieve a greater resistance to low temperatures or else a better branching. An upright-growing and naturally well-branching fuchsia cultivar with the magnificent pure pink of 'Pink Galore' would be desirable. Many otherwise very good orange-coloured cultivars have the unfortunate characteristic of acquiring burn marks on the flowers in strong sun. Making the flowers more resistant would be a worthwhile breeding objective. Fuchsia cultivars which were reliably hardy everywhere in our climate and not just in a few regions favoured by nature would also certainly be gratefully welcomed.

There are more than enough fuchsias with white or cream-coloured sepals and red corolla. If a new cultivar brought forth a bright redcurrant-red which also did not change colour to blue on fading like e.g. 'Celia Smedley' by G. Roe, then that would be a sensational result. Whether it might be possible to cure many otherwise magnificent cultivars of this often unlovely fading remains to be seen. It would certainly be a breeding objective for an ambitious hybridist with the necessary know-how.

Some genetics

Besides an elementary knowledge of Mendelian genetics, a would-be hybridist should also possess wide knowledge of cultivars so that he or she does not make time-consuming, unnecessary detours on the long and often difficult road to new fuchsia varieties. For this reason, as parents two fuchsia cultivars are selected which are already quite close to the aim aspired to and which promise success. The cultivar which is to bear the fruit or seed berries is the female form and is named first when giving details of the parents. The pollen-parent, the male form, follows after it, e.g. 'Pink Galore' × 'Laurie'.

In practice it will soon be discovered that some cultivars are particularly good female types and others good male types. The good female parents are looked for among those cultivars which produce berries in abundance even when they have not been pollinated with a specific objective in mind. The cultivars which are self-cleaning, i.e. which shed faded flowers together with the seed vessel (berry) are not suitable for the purposes of breeding and are frequently sterile.

Famous female parents which have often been used for breeding are 'Alice Hoffman', 'La Campanella' and 'Rose of Castille'.

Good pollen parents, in other words male forms, are 'Citation', 'Flying Cloud' and 'Mrs W. Rundle'.

Such knowledge is of little use to the would-be hybridiser who has quite definite aims in mind. He has to select very particular parents for his breeding lines. Characteristics which are hereditary in a dominant way are, in fuchsias, the strong colours of red and blue, small flowers or the strong growth of a cultivar. Pastel tones are genetically recessive. If one crosses fuchsia hybrids, which at the same time are very complex in their hereditary factors, a concrete result is difficult to predict. As a hybridist one must muster a great deal of patience. Each new crossing leads to many surprises. Before science discovered that the heritage of all living organisms is stored in the chromosomes in the cell nucleus, many an endeavour to breed new fuchsia cultivars was determined by failures. New cultivars emerged more or less by chance.

A fuchsia species, i.e. the wild form, as a rule has two sets of chromosomes each with 11 chromosomes ($2 \times 11 = 22$) and is described as diploid (2n). *F. magellanica* and *F. lycioides* are exceptions; they naturally have a fourfold set ($4 \times 11 = 44$) and are accordingly tetraploid (4n). All cultivars with more than two chromosome sets are termed polyploid. In detail, diploid (2n), triploid (3n), tetraploid (4n), pentaploid (5n), hexaploid (6n), heptaploid (7n), octoploid (8n) and nonaploid (9n) fuchsias are known.

For the hybridist it is important to know that fuchsias with an odd number of chromosome sets (3n, 5n and so on) are generally unfruitful (sterile)—as also, incidentally, are many other plants. A pollination will lead either to no seeds or to seeds that are not viable. Hence it follows that viable seeds can be expected only when even-numbered polyploids (2n, 4n, etc.) are crossed with each other.

At the same time the cross-breeding of fuchsias with odd-numbered chromosome sets can lead to sterile descendants. If e.g. *F. splendens* (2n) is crossed with *F. magellanica* (4n), viable seeds are the result to begin with. From these, however, sterile, triploid fuchsias often develop which generally can no longer be used for further breeding work. According to Chaudhuri (who carried out extensive cytogenetic studies in the genus *Fuchsia* in 1956), though, odd-numbered polyploid fuchsias are not always sterile; rather, a generative propagation through so-called unreduced gametes can frequently be found.

This point is very important in the breeding of fuchsia hybrids, for it accounts for the emergence of pentaploid or heptaploid forms. A particular characteristic of odd-numbered polyploids is also that in the absence of seed appearance they are only vegetatively propagable.

The explanation for why plants with even-numbered chromosome sets are fertile but those with odd-numbered sets are infertile is simple: odd sets cannot be properly divided. After the fusion of female and male sexual cells—provided that fertilisation actually takes place—an irregular distribution of the chromosomes takes place among the filial cells, which then can generally no longer develop further in a normal way. With even-numbered sets the distribution occurs uniformly so that a normal development of the filial cells is possible.

Scientists of course in this case have the chance, through irradiation or colchicine treatment of the plants, to multiply the chromosome sets artificially. Theoretically, a hexaploid (6n) plant could be created from a triploid (3n) plant in this way which, as it now had an even-numbered set, would again be fertile. The modern techniques of tissue culture also offer solutions to the problem (embryo culture) in these cases.

In this respect the fuchsia-hybridist sometimes has it easier than the hybridist of other plants. What happens relatively frequently is that fuchsias which are triploid, pentaploid or heptaploid double their chromosome sets in a natural way. Many of the F_1 hybrids of *F. magellanica* × *F. fulgens* have done this repeatedly and there is a multitude of beautiful hybrids which can trace their line of ancestors back to these two wild forms. The two nearly white cultivars 'Rolla' (7n) and 'Countess of Aberdeen' (5n) also were and still are used for hybridising and have produced many good and well-known descendants.

Flower and pollination

Before taking the first steps on the road to practical hybridising, we should take a look at the structure of a fuchsia flower and the function of the individual parts of the flower. The pedicel is 20 mm to 8 cm long, either red or green according to cultivar, and carries the necessary nutrients to the flower. At the top of the pedicel is the seed vessel, which again can be red or green and contains the seed assets in its four chambers. Attached to this is the calyx; in the fuchsia this consists of the tube and four calycinal petals, the sepals. Projecting from the calyx, and partly attached to it, are the petals; these can be four in number in a single flower and five, six or seven in a semi-double, while flowers with many petals are termed double. The petals taken as a combined unit are called the corolla (flower head or crown). Projecting well outside the corolla is the style with the stigma, which is linked to the seed vessel through the length of the flower, and this is surrounded by eight filaments with the anthers. The fuchsia, through the open situation of its sexual organs, makes the process of pollination easy and uncomplicated. A few rules which have proved themselves in practice should, however, be noted. Plants which have been chosen as parents should be taken into cultivation as early in the year as possible. Because flowers are to appear quite early, pinching is not done and the plant is cultivated through without any delay up to the 12-cm pot limit. When this is filled with roots the flowers can soon be expected. Feeding should also be done sparingly. It is not growth that is being striven for but an early flowering, so that by the end of May at the latest flowering plants are at one's disposal.

The first flowers that appear on the parent plants are left untouched to begin with; they are to donate the pollen. The pollen needs a certain maturing period and must be in the correct, fully ripened

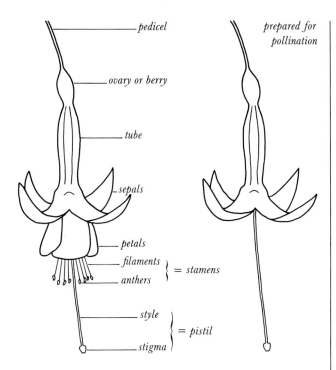

pedicel

ovary or berry

tube

sepals

prepared for pollination

petals

filaments ⎫
⎬ = stamens
anthers ⎭

style ⎫
⎬ = pistil
stigma ⎭

A fuchsia flower is composed of the seed vessel (ovary), from which the berries develop which later contain the seeds. The tube or hypanthium, which can be short and thick or long and narrow, forms, together with the four sepals, a single unit, the calyx, from which the four petals project which together form the flower head or corolla. Sepals and petals are often different in colour, e.g. red/white or red/blue, but can also be uniformly of one colour. The eight filaments, together with the anthers, form the stamen, and usually project far outside the corolla, together with an even longer style and stigma, which together form the pistil. A single fuchsia flower has four petals and a semi-double up to seven; all flowers which possess more petals are defined as double.

condition at the time when the further flowers of the two plants are developed to the point where they are just beginning to open. Whether the pollen is ready for release can be tested by running one's finger nail over an anther; if pollen grains are left on the nail the right time has been reached. Shortly before the flowers to be pollinated open naturally, a little assistance is given by using light pressure to spread the petals. To prevent the plant self-pollinating, the stamens and if necessary also the petals are cut away with a small, sharp pair of scissors (see illustration). Style and stigma are now isolated.

It will often be necessary to wait one or two days before pollinating, until the stigma becomes moist, tacky and thus receptive. To keep out any foreign pollination by wind or insects, a small piece of aluminium foil is wrapped around the stigma. In the warm hours of midday things have usually progressed far enough for one to be able to undertake pollination. The flower with its ripe pollen is cut away, the cover is removed from the stigma of the female parent. A light smearing on the moist stigma with the pollen, repeated once or twice to be on the safe side, until the stigma is completely covered with pollen, should suffice. Immediately after this the pollinated flower is enclosed in a small bag made of material permeous to air (e.g. muslin, nylon): a method which is well known, though it has the disadvantage that the danger of rotting inside the bag is very great.

In recent years a new method of protecting the pollinated flower has proven to be simpler and better with hybridisers. Up to now it was customary to place the whole flower into a small muslin bag or similar after the pollination. After the flower had released itself from the fruit the bag had to be taken off again because of the risk of rotting. Each time this carried the risk that flower or fruit broke off in the process. Today a product of the pharmaceutical industry is utilised, by means of which it is possible to handle the flower as gently as ever possible and reduce to a minimum the automatic strain on it. The product in question is those gelatine capsules in which the actual medicine is enclosed and which have nowadays largely replaced conventional capsules (Capsulae Operculatae). They are usually quite brightly coloured. For the foregoing purpose, however, they can also be obtained empty and wholly transparent. After pollination, half of one of these capsules is carefully pushed over the pistil and secured with a bit of cotton wool. Capsules with a volume of 1.0 or 0.5 cm^3 are the right size.

To prevent dates getting lost when the ripe fruit is shed, small pieces of plastic labels are fastened to the flower stalk with fine wire or thread; very narrow adhesive tape can also be used. To be on the safe side, the procedure is then immediately carried out again. If in the first pollinating operation A has been treated as the female parent and B as the male parent, then B is now used as the mother plant and A as the father plant. Finally, a label with the precise details and dates of the completed crossing, e.g. 'La Campanella' × 'White Spider' 01.06.1989, is given to each pollinated flower.

It is better not to rely on one's memory, and this should definitely not be done if several crossings are undertaken at the same time. For safety a supplementary notebook is set up and all the details of crossings are listed in this. Assuming that one was lucky and that the two parent cultivars chosen are well matched, it will soon be revealed whether the pollination was successful. What occasionally happens with fuchsias and other plants which have been the subject of intensive breeding over a lengthy period is that the sole effect of pollination is a stimulation of the seed vessel. It expands and develops, ripens, but contains nothing apart from its own dried-out seed-producers (ovaries). This need not necessarily mean that the plant is sterile. The reason may be an incompatibility, even with even-numbered chromosome sets. We can try to compensate for or overcome this difficulty by carrying out the crossing twice.

The withered flower will fall after some time and only the fertilised berry remains on the plant. The fruits are of course checked from time to time. Ripe seeds can be expected from about August. When cross-breeding with a fixed aim in mind, the excitement and anticipation are particularly great. How many seeds might be the result of our troubles? There could be many, but sometimes one is quite grateful if, with the help of a magnifying glass, three to five fully developed, fertile seeds can be found. If these are immediately sown, the first flowers of the fuchsias 'created' by oneself should, with a bit of luck and with good conditions for a speedy cultivation, be able to be marvelled at by July of the following year at the latest. Unfortunately, disappointment is also not uncommon.

The chances that something really new in growth, flower shape or flower colour will emerge in the fuchsias from the first cross-breeding attempt are minimal, only about one in 1,000. This means having to raise a large number of seedlings to increase the probability of success.

Anybody who has gained pleasure from hybridising but is disappointed by the first results should not give up yet. If the seedlings produced are intercrossed or are pollinated with their own pollen, the F_2 generation may perhaps first bring to light the latent hereditary characters and take the hybridist a step further on the road to the goal he has his sights on.

For the real fuchsia-lover it should be a matter of course to sort out weakly plants whose constitution leaves something to be desired and not to raise them at all at the outset. Although many hybridisers have developed brand new fuchsia cultivars in the last 140 years and more, this plant has so far not yet lost its vitality and its resistance to diseases. This speaks volumes for the sense of responsibility of the earlier hybridists.

Species, varieties and hybrids

For the beginner in hybridising, botanical knowledge is often lacking, so a short clarification of these terms follows.

Plants of a species, i.e. wild plants which have originated in the natural environment, are termed botanical species. A pure species produces with its own pollen, or pollinated by a plant of the same species, seedlings which are outwardly similar to the parents but are not completely identical in the genes. As in all living organisms that reproduce generatively (by seeds), differences exist. Even sibling seedlings often differ markedly from one another. A species is accordingly a collection of individuals. For this reason many species are subdivided into subspecies (ssp.) and varieties (var.), as e.g. *F. magellanica* var. *molinae*. Subspecies and varieties, however, have different ranks. A variety is subordinate to the subspecies. Within any species mutations can arise in a natural manner. Variants with multicoloured foliage, a lower growth habit or differently coloured flowers spring up. Mutations are changes in the genes caused by external influences such as climate, radiation, etc. Mutants, too, remain members of the species from which they have developed. It also makes no difference whether the varieties have originated in the species' natural habitat or in a garden, so long as they are not the result of hybridisation with another species. Examples are *F. boliviana* var. *luxurians alba* (syn. *F. corymbiflora alba*) or *F. magellanica* var. *macrostemma tricolor*. Even hybrids between varieties of the same species are always classified taxonomically under the species concerned.

Hybrids is the term given to the new fuchsias which have arisen as filial plants from a crossing of two species and thus are no longer genetically pure. By far the majority of today's fuchsias belong in this group. They come into being in cultivation, either through controlled cross-breeding by the hand of man or through pollination by insects or the wind.

The hybridist gives his hybrids a name, e.g. 'Annabel'. We can tell simply by the quotation marks that it is a cultivar that is being referred to. The term cultivar was introduced into botany so that at a glance a clear distinction can be made between the hybrids and the varieties.

A further group of often very beautiful fuchsia hybrids which originated in cultivation without the assistance of man, of insects and the like but in a natural way are the mutants, also known as 'sports'. One day, individual branches showing changes in the flower colour or in the foliage are seen on a plant. For instance, a red-and-blue flowering fuchsia has suddenly developed red-and-white flowers on one branch or a plant with uniformly green foliage suddenly bears branches with differently coloured, variegated leaves. 'Golden Marinka' or 'Green 'n' Gold' are examples of this. If propagation is done through cuttings taken from these mutated branches, a new cultivar has come into being. Such mutations frequently arise simultaneously in several areas or different fuchsia collections. There are many examples of this in the fuchsia literature. Today scientists are able to engineer such mutations artificially by doubling or splitting of chromosomes by means of radiation or colchicine.

The successful Dutch amateur hybridist Hermann J. de Graaff of Lisse has been kind enough to supply the following report. This account, with detailed data on the hybrid partners of his new fuchsias and advice given from practical experience, is thus very likely also to encourage one or two British fuchsia-lovers to hybridise new fuchsias:

As the son of one of the oldest local families of bulb-plant breeders, my particular interest in plant-breeding was only natural. To begin with I worked in the family business among other things on the new breeding of narcissi. At the same time I studied biology at the State University of Leiden, concentrating on genetics. I became a teacher. And after giving up our business I began—also to offset my work at the school—to get interested in fuchsias, which had hitherto in fact been a passion of my wife. In 1972 I began on cross-breeding. Initially without a plan, in order just to find out what was possible and how I could best proceed. The new cultivars 'Tour Eiffel' ('Alice Hoffman' ×), 'Joker' ('Lena ×), 'Firebird' ('Madame Goyaerts' ×), 'Petit Point' ('Alice Hoffman' ×), 'Medusa' ('Centerpiece' ×) and 'Belle de Lisse' ('Trailblazer' ×) stem from this early period, more or less as chance flukes.

The results, in which I purposely include the plants rejected by the VKC (Dutch Fuchsia Society's Committee of Inspection), showed that cross-breeding with red and lilac parent plants too often produced red and lilac descendants again. Hardly much that is new is likely to be expected from this colour combination. Crossing with cultivars of other colours, however, resulted in really attractive novelties. In particular the comparatively new 'La Campanella' produced very good results. Unfortunately, it is no longer possible to clarify the origin of this cultivar, but presumably its hereditary factors contain a large number of recessive characters which create many rare colour tones in its descendants. The frequently encountered propensity for pendent growth is also very attractive. From 'La Campanella' I obtained the pendent fuchsias 'François Villon', 'La Bergère', 'Le Berger', 'Troika', my first success in 1976, and 'Nutshell'. Upright-growing cultivars were 'First Kiss', 'Mia van der Zee' and 'Contramine', the last with prominent flowers.

Good orange is still quite rare in fuchsias. Because of this fact and my special liking for botanical fuchsias, I got around to working with 'Speciosa' (a hybrid from *F. splendens* and *F. fulgens*). 'Machu Picchu', 'Je Maintiendrais', rejected by the VKC but marketed by the English firm of Wills, as well as 'Oranje Boven' are the preliminary result. Owing to my inexperience in the early days and because my cats have caused something of a muddle here, I am no longer able to name with certainty the female parents of 'Baroque Pearl', 'Flim Flam' and 'Westergeest'.

Attempts to breed small-flowered cultivars produced 'Flamingo' ('Flash' ×) and 'Twiggy' (*F. magellanica* × *F. lycioides*). 'Dark Spider', a lax plant with flowers of 'Spider' type with very dark corolla, has 'Brutus' as its female parent.

Only in recent years has it become possible for me, by using a new method when pollinating, to specify exactly the male parents as well. 'Loeky' ('Joy Patmore' × 'Impudence') is the first in a new breeding line. The flower shape, erect sepals and horizontally spread corolla, is so far found only in a few colour variations. Here, then, there is still further good work that can well be done.

Naturally I am also keen to breed a yellow fuchsia. Can the yellow in the calyx of *F. procumbens* be combined with the yellow in the corolla of *F. splendens*? The first crossing attempts showed that it is difficult to get from these wild species a plant with which something can be started off. The yellow of *F. splendens* is not fast in the sun, no more than the white is in fuchsias. The flowering period is often not favourable. The plants do not flower so profusely as most cultivars, and the growth also leaves something to be desired. A result cannot be achieved so quickly. This is made worse, too, because of the annoying habit of fuchsias of often developing sterile seeds. Nevertheless, the only way of arriving at genuine new forms takes us through wild forms. In the latter there is still much unused gene material ready for the modern hybridiser.

In the Netherlands there has for some time been within the fuchsia society a group under my leadership known as the 'Hybridisation Group'. It is the aim of this group to arrive, through working together, at results such as are otherwise obtainable only under the much better conditions which professional hybridists e.g. in the USA now enjoy. Success with breeding depends in large part on the amount of the material with which one is able to work.

The wanted list includes, among others, double orange-coloured flowers or combinations of orange and white. By using a computer, the theoretical work to this end is already done. Now we must only wait to see whether results appear in practice.

Our group also wishes to try to learn more about the genetic background of the characteristics of our fuchsias. Only in this way can we reach the stage where cross-breeding of fuchsias is no longer simply a game of chance but we can proceed with specific objectives in mind.

A few hints for beginners:

Give the names of the parent plants only when you are absolutely certain.

Sow as early in the year as possible, so that the seedlings flower in the same summer and it can be decided which plants you wish to retain. Then you will not need to do all the work of bringing useless plants through the winter.

You should work with as many seeds as possible. On average only one in 100 seedlings is worth keeping.

The seedlings should grow under normal conditions, so that weak plants are selected against in a natural way.

Straight after the first flowering, everything that does not really represent anything special should be thrown away. There are already enough mediocre cultivars.

From hybrids which do not show the expected characteristics after the first generation (F_1) you should breed a second generation (F_2) by fertilising the flowers with their own pollen. This way recessive characteristics can also come forward.

Chromosome numbers of some fuchsias

How far we can rely on the following chromosome table by Mr Chaudhuri of Manchester University (1956), which was published in the BFS yearbook for 1974, ought first to be clarified by new zytological tests. According to J. O. Wright, the species set out as *F. cordifolia* is believed to have been in reality a hybrid of *F. splendens* and *F. lycioides* an élite form of *F. magellanica*.

Fuchsia species

F. cordifolia	22
F. denticulata	22
F. fulgens	22
F. lycioides	44
F. magellanica var. *molinae*	44
F microphylla	22
F. procumbens	22
F. splendens	22
F. magellanica 'Pumila'	44
F. magellanica 'Longipedunculata'	44
F. magellanica	44
F. coccinea	44

Diploid

'Dominyana'	(Dominy 1852)	22
'Fanfare'	(Reiter 1941)	22
'Speciosa'		
'Thalia'	(Bonstedt 1906)	22

Triploid

'Caledonia'	(Lemoine 1899)	33
'Koralle'	(Bonstedt 1905)	33
'Gartenmeister Bonstedt'	(Bonstedt 1905)	33

Tetraploid

'Carnea'	(Smith 1861)	44
'Checkerboard'	(Walker and Jones 1948)	44
'E. A. Babbs'	(Wood 1949)	44
'Andenken an H. Henkel'	(Rehnelt 1897)	44
'Loveliness'	(Lye 1869)	44
'Marinka'	(Rozain-Boucharlat 1902)	44
'Mrs W. P. Wood'	(Wood 1949)	44
'Tangerine'	(Tiret 1949)	44
'Tom Thumb'	(Baudinat 1850)	44
'Venus Victrix'	(Gulliver 1840)	44
'Thompsonii'	(Thompson 1840)	44
'Riccartonii'	(Young 1833)	44

Pentaploid

'Amy Lye'	(Lye 1885)	55
'Annie Earle'	(Lye 1887)	55
'Countess of Aberdeen'	(Dobbie Forbes)	55
'Duchess of Albany'	(Rundle 1891)	55
'Globosa'	(c. 1833)	55
'Gustave Doré'	(Lemoine 1880)	55
'Letty Lye'	(Lye 1877)	55
'Masterpiece'	(Henderson 1891)	55
'Mrs Marshall'	(Jones)	55
'Mrs W. Rundle'	(Rundle 1883)	55
'Pee Wee Rose'	(Niederholzer 1939)	55
'Prince of Orange'	(Banks 1872)	55
'Sunray'	(Milne 1872)	55

Hexaploid

'Alice Hoffmann'	(Kiese 1901)	66
'Balkonkönigin'	(Neubronner 1895)	66
'Beauty'	(Banks 1866)	66
'C. J. Howlett'	(Howlett 1911)	66
'Coachman'	(Bright)	66
'Display'	(Smith 1881)	66
'Dolores'	(Niederholzer 1944)	66
'Dorothy'	(Wood 1946)	66
'Elegans'	(Bull 1866)	66
'Epsii'	(Epps 1840)	66
'Fascination' syn. 'Emile de Wildeman'	(Lemoine 1905)	66
'Henri Poincaré'	(Lemoine 1905)	66
'Hidcote Beauty'	(Webb 1949)	66
'Immaculate'	(Wood 1943)	66
'Jubilee'	(Lye 1897)	66
'Lady Boothby'	(Raffill 1939)	66
'Lord Lonsdale'		66
'Morning Mist'	(Berkeley Nursery 1951)	66
'Ophelia'		66
'Starlite'	(Bull 1868)	66
'Ting-a-Ling'	(Schnabel-Paskesen 1959)	66

Heptaploid

'Ballet Girl'	(Veitch 1894)	77
'Bon Accord'	(Crousse 1861)	77
'Charming'	(Lye 1895)	77
'Clipper'	(Lye 1897)	77
'General Gallieni'	(Lemoine 1899)	77
'Golden Treasure'	(Carter 1860)	77
'Mme Cornelissen'	(Cornelissen 1860)	77
'Mme Danjoux'	(Salter 1843)	77
'Muriel'		77
'President Roosevelt'	(Garson 1942)	77
'Rolla'	(Lemoine 1913)	77
'Rose of Castille improved'	(Banks 1869)	77
'Royal Purple'	(Lemoine 1896)	77
'Serena'	(Whiteman 1944)	77
'Snow Cap'	(Henderson 1880)	77
'Telegraphe'	(Lemoine 1886)	77
'Whitemost'	(Niederholzer 1942)	77

Octoploid

'Conspicua'	(Smith 1863)	88
'Hamburger Markt'		88
'Dollar Princess'	(Lemoine 1912)	88
'Jules Daloges'	(Lemoine 1907)	88
'Mrs Popple'	(Elliot 1895)	88
'White Phenomenal'	(Lemoine 1869)	88
'San Leandro'	(Brand 1949)	88
'Pacific Grove'	(Niederholzer 1947)	88
'Purple Heart'	(Walker and Jones 1950)	88

CHAPTER THIRTEEN

CULTIVARS

Thousands of fuchsia cultivars have been developed in the course of the last 150 years. Leo. B. Boullemier of Britain in his world-wide acknowledged *Check List of Species, Hybrids and Cultivars of the Genus Fuchsia* records and details between 8,000 and 10,000 fuchsias. So it was a great problem to decide on a selection for this book. In the following, therefore, only those cultivars are described which are more widely available. The numbers given after the cultivar names are the AFS Register numbers.

Fuchsia triphylla *and its hybrids*

Today's widespread and popular *triphylla* hybrids, with their mostly dark foliage which often has a metallic irradiance, have, in terms of cultivation history, been taken notice of by hybridists and used for cross-breeding only very recently. They flower profusely and for a long period in brilliant orange, garnet-red or ruby-red colours. The flowers appear in thick clusters at the end of the shoots.

Fuchsia triphylla is the fuchsia discovered *c.* 1695 by Plumier in the foothills of Santo Domingo, a small, bushy shrub 40–60 cm tall with brilliant coral-red, terminal flower clusters. For almost 30 years nothing more was heard of this fuchsia species until Philip Miller raised the first plants from seed in the apothecary garden at Chelsea. Unfortunately, these plants were soon lost again. Then the seeds collected by the American Thomas Hogg in 1873 in Santo Domingo produced plants in the botanic gardens of New York which also found their way to England. These were distributed by the renowned English market-garden of Henderson & Son of St John's Wood as *F. racemosa*, although a plant sent to Kew in 1882 was unequivocally identified there as *F. triphylla*. At all events it

seems very unlikely that a company of international repute such as Henderson should have known nothing of the existence of a plant which must have been in cultivation in England for almost three full decades.

In this connection it is also significant that the first colour illustration of the species *F. triphylla* did not appear until 1892 in *The Garden* and caused something of a stir. If we take a look at these dates, it is hardly possible that the first 'Thalia' which was raised by Turner in 1855 would have been a *triphylla* hybrid, as many authors state. It appears more likely that two different fuchsia cultivars have been confused with each other, especially since the breeders of that time often knew nothing at all of one another or of what other gardeners were breeding. Duplications were therefore frequent, 'Hebe' being a typical example of this. The cultivar of this name which is still in cultivation originates from Stokes 1848. At about the same time the breeders Standish, Harrison, Bell and Mayle gave their new cultivars the same name. It is small wonder, then, if mix-ups have occurred and still are occurring, for now and then one of the early breeds does still turn up again.

In *Gardener's Chronicle* of 1875, a cultivar named as 'Thalia' is described as a fuchsia with white tube (a seedling of 'Venus Victrix'), which was probably a Turner introduction but seems no longer to be available. Even if Turner (1855) cannot have been the breeder of the first *triphylla* hybrid, however, it is no surprise, given the passion for fuchsias at that time, that other breeders soon began to work intensively with the new species *F. triphylla*. Subsequently, *F. boliviana* Roezl (1873) and *F. corymbiflora* Ruiz and Pavon (1802) as well as *F. fulgens* De Candolle (1828, Mexico) were also used for crossing with *F. triphylla*.

The *triphylla* hybrids and types are descendants of the species *F. triphylla*. Other long-tube hybrids are *triphylla* types. The types and hybrids are:

'Andenken an Heinrich Henkel' (Rehnelt 1897, G) *triphylla* type
(*F. corymbiflora* × 'Magnifica')
Brought on to the market by the Henkel company of Darmstadt, West Germany, in 1901; it was also named after the company owner Heinrich Henkel. Foliage dark green, underside reddish; flowers long, vivid carmine-red, in clusters. Good autumn and winter flowerer in the greenhouse. Rehnelt himself wrote in the magazine *Gartenwelt* (Garden World) of 6.4.1901: 'Without exaggerating it can be said that the wealth of blossom of young plants may be difficult to surpass. In this it is the least like the *triphylla* hybrids, but, as well as other good qualities, it has the advantage over these of lasting foliage. The plants do not become bare and unsightly in the winter.' It is thus not an actual *triphylla* hybrid but is classified in this group by all authors.

'August Siebert' (Bonstedt 1914, G) *triphylla* hybrid
Has the longest-tubed flower, which is dark cherry-red and hangs down in big, many-flowered clusters. It has dark foliage.

'Benita' (Rogers 1912, GB) *triphylla* type
('Gartenmeister Bonstedt' × *F. splendens*)
Flowers with long, thin tube, uniformly scarlet-red; foliage bronze-green. Growth lax and dwarfish.

'Bernard Rawlins' (Thorne 1959, GB) *triphylla* type
Having flowers with almost white, long tube and orange corolla, falls outside the range of the colour scale normal in the *triphylla* types. The growth is upright and not very strong, this cultivar was very rarely ever seen and is certainly not in cultivation today, being replaced as a white *triphylla* by Gouldings 'Our Ted'.

'Billy Green' (breeder unknown; introduced by Rawlins 1966, GB) *triphylla* type
It is a strong-growing, upright cultivar with olive-green foliage and long, elegant, salmon pink flowers in clusters. A standard can be raised in only one year.

'Bornemanns Beste' (Bonstedt 1906) *triphylla* hybrid
It is particularly strong-growing, and when freely planted out grows quickly into big, healthy shrubs. All *triphylla* hybrids bred by Carl Bonstedt were brought on to the market by his friend Georg Bornemann, gardener in Blankenburg.

'Clio' (Bonstedt 1907, G) *triphylla* hybrid
The very long, dainty-tubed flowers in large clusters are deep pink; green foliage is exquisite. The plant is medium-tall and bushy.

'Coralle' (Bonstedt 1905, G) triphylla hybrid
Dark green foliage and uniformly coral-red flowers. Is probably the most widespread *triphylla* hybrid today with 'Thalia', very often misnamed 'Koralle'.

'Elfriede Ott' (Nutzinger 1965, A) *triphylla* type
('Coralle' × *F. splendens*)
The rather small leaves are of a dull olive-green; growth lax. The flowers with long tube are salmon pink and the slightly darker corolla single, though having the appearance of a semi-double or double flower. Everything together produces a harmony of great beauty. The cultivar is neutral to day length and given the appropriate basic requirements is a good winter flowerer.

The breeder Karl Nutzinger, of the institute nursery of Admont in Steiermark, Austria, has made further contributions to the expansion of the assortment of *triphylla* types. All cultivars raised by him are particularly well suited as garden or border plants.

'Erika Köth' (Nutzinger 1965, A) *triphylla* type
('Coralle' × *F. boliviana*)
Strong-growing balcony and border cultivar with small orange-coloured tubular flowers. Makes a charming small standard in a relatively short time.

'Eros' (Lemoine 1878, F) *triphylla* hybrid
(*F. triphylla* ×)
Creamy-yellow orange flowers. It was described in the magazine *The Garden* as 'a new race of fuchsia' (vol. 71, p. 453).

'Eros' (Bonstedt 1907, G) *triphylla* hybrid
Pink tubular flower will light tips. Whereas in the other Bonstedt cultivars the clusters as well as the individual flowers hang down elegantly, in this one they grow upwards. This cultivar is low-growing and grows rigidly upright.

'Fürst Otto zu Werningerode' (Gireoud in Sagan 1898, G) triphylla hybrid
(*F. triphylla* × 'Surprise')
The long tubular flowers are brilliant pink, paler at the end, the petals carmine-red; dark foliage.

'Gartenmeister Bonstedt' (Bonstedt 1905, G) *triphylla* hybrid
Foliage dark bronze-red; of vigorous growth. The long-tubed flowers are uniformly brick-red and differ from the flowers of the cultivar 'Thalia' only in becoming thicker in the lower part of the tube.

'Elfriede Ott'

'Mary'

'Georg Bornemann' (Bonstedt 1915, G) *triphylla* hybrid

This cultivar is given particular prominence by Bonstedt: 'The main advantage of this cultivar for us, however, lies in the fact that it makes it possible now to raise all cluster-flowering fuchsias also to the form of standards as graftings grow on to it easily. This was hitherto not possible because they do not develop properly on base plants such as "Riccartonii" and others. It thereby opens up a possibility for use of this elegant class which will be particularly welcome in regular gardens.' If we look at the growing vigour of 'Bornemanns Beste', we might suppose that Bonstedt's 'Georg Bornemann' has been renamed, as has happened with many old cultivars.

'Göttingen' (Bonstedt 1904, G) *triphylla* hybrid

Foliage dark purple, underside reddish; tube and sepals salmon-orange, corolla vermilion.

'Grasmere' (Travis 1964, GB) No. 1151 *triphylla* type (*F. cordifolia* × *F. lycioides*)

Although the flowers of this handsome cultivar are of *triphylla* type, it does not, however, belong directly in this group, as a look at the parent species will reveal. As this cultivar bears flowers in clusters in common with the *triphylla* hybrids, however, it is placed with them for simplicity's sake, for it does not fit in well with the fuchsias bearing axillary flowers. This naturally lax fuchsia with large leaves and long, thin tube and with uniformly coral-red flowers is of strong, self-branching growth. Particularly beautiful as edge planting in larger containers.

'Grossherzogin Adelheid' (Rehnelt 1903, G) *triphylla* hybrid
(*F. corymbiflora* × *F. triphylla*)

This cultivar was brought on to the market in Trier, West Germany, by Lambert and received a certificate of merit from the association of market-gardeners. Leaves dark green, shot with bronze, reddish on underside; flowers long, coral-red with orange-red petals.

The many shapes and colours demonstrate the intensive breeding work done with fuchsias. 1 = 'Purple Heart', 2 = 'Tennessee Waltz', 3 = 'Marinka', 4 = 'Carmel Blue', 5 = 'Fan Dancer', 6 = 'Franz Noszian', 7 = 'Jamboree', 8 = 'Dilly-Dilly', 9 = 'Swingtime', 10 = 'Dirk van Delen', 11 = 'Pink Ballet Girl', 12 = 'Chang', 13 = 'Starlite', 14 = 'Red Spider', 15 = 'Falling Stars', 16 = 'Winston Churchill', 17 = 'Leonora', 18 = 'Constance', 19 = 'South Gate', 20 = 'Kwintet', 21 = 'Curtain Call', 22 = 'Royal Velvet', 23 = 'Flying Cloud', 24 = 'Wings of Song'.

'Harry Dunnett' (Baker-Dunnett 1974, GB) No. 1198 *triphylla* type
The long, banana-shaped tube is red, the sepals old-pink and the tiny corolla shrimp-pink; foliage mid-green, velvety with amber-coloured veining. Growth upright.

'Irmgard Bonstedt' (Bonstedt 1914, G) *triphylla* hybrid
Low-growing and very profusely flowering. Colour of the flowers as in 'Georg Bornemann'.

'Leverkusen' (Hartnauer 1928, G) *triphylla* type
In 1923 a seedling of 'Andenken an Heinrich Henkel' developed in the factory nursery of the Bayer company. It has normal fuchsia foliage which appears reddish only in new growth, and flowers of the *triphylla* type but with an obviously shorter tube. The flower is uniformly salmon-carmine with drooping sepals. 'Leverkusen' is a good bed plant of compact, more broad than tall growth. It reacts to wide fluctuations in temperature by dropping flowers and buds.

'Lilo Vogt' (Nutzinger 1976, A) *triphylla* type
('Coralle' × *F. boliviana*)
A lax fuchsia with very long, elegant, old-pink tubular flowers. Unfortunately the sepals open only in favourable conditions. Perhaps it needs more warmth than our summers generally offer.

'Mantilla' (Reiter 1948, USA) No. 1 *triphylla* type
The brilliant carmine-red flower is exquisite with its very slender tube, pointed projecting sepals and neat corolla. Filaments and pistil are only a little paler in tone. The olive-green, reddish-flushed and reddish-veined, finely denticulate foliage forms a good background. The flowers grow to 9–10 cm in length. Particularly attractive as a wall basket in a sheltered position. 'Mantilla' was the first fuchsia registered with the AFS.

'Mary' (Bonstedt 1894, G) *triphylla* hybrid
(*F. triphylla* × *F. corymbiflora*)
A cultivar with dark foliage, red-veined and slightly pilose, and long, bright ruby-red flowers. It originated in Bonstedt's Rostock period. Unfortunately the cultivar is rather delicate and not particularly sun-tolerant. For this reason, in later cultivations Bonstedt used *F. fulgens* as the partner in cross-breeding.

'Otto Fürst' (Bonstedt 1904, G) *triphylla* hybrid
Long flowers with pink tube and somewhat paler petals. The foliage is more bluish-green.

'Otto Nordenskold' (Rehnelt 1903, G) *triphylla* type
Long, very thin, coral-red tube and short, cinnabar-red petals. The foliage is dark green with reddish underside.

'Perle' (Bonstedt 1907, G) *triphylla* hybrid
Delicate pearl-pink, dainty tubular flowers, almost white at the tip, in clusters; strikingly pale foliage. Growth low and strongly branched.

'Präsident W. Morio' (Nutzinger 1976, A) *triphylla* type
('Coralle' × *F. fulgens rubra grandiflora*)
Named after the president of the German dahlia, fuchsia and gladioli society. The rather small flowers are a mixture of pink and orange. This plant of lax growth is particularly well suited for the planting of boxes and tubs.

'Puck' (Bonstedt 1914, G) *triphylla* hybrid
A dainty and low-growing cultivar whose flowers are more separated and upright, with sepals white inside, so that they resemble little stars.

'Rocket' (Reiter 1942, USA) *triphylla* type
('Gartenmeister Bonstedt' × 'Mrs Victor Reiter')
It has similar flowers to 'Leverkusen' and reddish-green foliage. Of bushy, upright growth.

'Rubin' (Vieweg 1893, G) *triphylla* hybrid
(*F. boliviana* × *F. triphylla*)
In foliage and in the colour of the flowers this cultivar is extremely similar to the cultivar 'Mary'. Over several issues of the 1901 volume of *Möllers Deutsche Gärtner-Zeitung* a dispute went on between the breeders Bonstedt and Vieweg: each claimed to be the originator. Not until around the turn of the century did the director of the botanic garden at Göttingen, Carl Bonstedt, and Friedrich Rehnelt of the botanic garden at Giessen achieve a real breakthrough with new cultivars of the cluster-flowering fuchsias.

'Schönbrunner Jubiläum' (Nutzinger 1976, A) *triphylla* type
('Coralle' × *F. fulgens* var. *fulgens rubra grandiflora*)
The long and large flowers are of a very bright red and outstanding substance; the start of flowering is unfortunately somewhat late. To counter the rather stiff growth it is necessary to pinch even the young plants frequently and thereby encourage a more bushy growth.

'Stella Ann' (Baker-Dunnett 1974, GB) No. 1199 *triphylla* type

Extremely free-flowering cultivar with poppy-red, very long tube and coral-red sepals with green tip. The small corolla is deep orange. The foliage is olive-green, veined red with reddish underside. The upright and bushy growth makes this cultivar a good bedding plant.

'Superba' (Veitch & Son 1895, GB) *triphylla* hybrid
(*F. triphylla* × *F. boliviana*)
'Superba' is synonymous with 'Mary' (see p. 000), sometimes called 'Mary Superba'.

'Thalia' (Bonstedt 1905, G) *triphylla* hybrid
The foliage is sage-green with metallic lustre and leaves tapering to a point. The long flowers have an evenly straight, narrow tube of glowing orange-red with sepals of the same colour. Very robust and strong-growing. Good as a bedding-out plant in full sun. Probably the most popular of all *triphyllas*.

'Tickled Pink' (Reedstrom 1957, USA) No. 308 *triphylla* type
Long tube dark pink; the very pointed sepals are dark pink outside, white inside. This produces a very good contrast with the pink-coloured corolla.

'Timlin Brened' (Baker-Dunnett 1974, GB) No. 1200 *triphylla* type
This subtle beauty with long, flamingo-pink tube, shell-pink sepals with green tip, and coral-red corolla is somewhat fastidious and reacts to any change in cultivation or temperature by dropping its buds. One must be careful and more sparing when watering.

'Tourtonne' (van Süchtelen 1968, NL) *triphylla* type
('Leverkusen' × 'Waternymph')
A particularly warmth-loving cultivar with long tube, the flower is uniformly rose-coloured; foliage bronze-green. Of upright growth.

'Traudchen Bonstedt' (Bonstedt 1905, G) *triphylla* hybrid
(*F. triphylla* ×)
The flowers with long pale pink tube and similarly coloured sepals have only a slightly darker corolla. The foliage is dark green, slightly pilose, with a bronze glint, underside reddish. Flowers in particularly dense clusters, in great abundance and almost without a break.

'Triphylla Hybrida' (Lemoine 1895, F) *triphylla* hybrid
(*F. triphylla* × *F. boliviana*)
Very long, scarlet-red tube, the short petals are

vermilion-red, flowers up to 10 cm long; the green foliage is shot with reddish on the underside.

'Trumpeter' (Reiter 1946, USA) *triphylla* type
Very long and strong tube. The flower is wholly salmon-pink, the foliage brownish-green and the growth, in contrast to all the Bonstedt cultivars, markedly lax. Very beautiful and very distinctive.

'Whiteknights Ruby' (J. O. Wright 1976, GB) No. 1357 *triphylla* hybrid
(BFS Silver Certificate of Merit, Reading Show 1977)
Mr Wright of the University of Reading has applied completely new methods to breeding with this *F. triphylla* × *F. procumbens* hybrid. The result is very beautiful. The long tube is cardinal-red, at the base more purple, and the small sepals are likewise purple and held almost horizontally. The corolla together with the stamens is uniformly light purple. Growth upright, with dark, velvety, red-veined foliage which is reddish on the underside like the leaf stalks.

'Winterblüher' (Bonstedt 1914, G) *triphylla* hybrid
Stands out through its strikingly large, succulent leaves and rigid, upright growth. Because it begins to flower late, the blossom persists through the winter.

The sun tolerance of the fuchsia *triphylla* hybrids is, along with their richness of colour, their most prominent quality. Frequent pinching of the young plants increases the profusion of flower, for each branch that develops ends in a cluster of flowers.

With adequate water provision and regular feeding they flower without break up to late autumn. In larger tubs or in ornamental beds their beauty is enhanced still more by underplanting with flat-growing, grey-foliaged plants such as *Helichrysum* or *Senecio*. In beds, an edge planting with colourfully foliaged fuchsias such as 'Sunray', 'Golden Glow' or 'Golden Treasure' is also very attractive.

For overwintering, these warmth-loving fuchsias require somewhat higher temperatures than the other fuchsias, about 8–10°C.

Anybody who has a greenhouse or winter garden at his disposal can cultivate the *triphylla* hybrids right through and can also take pleasure in the plants as they flower unremittingly throughout the winter.

F. fulgens var. *rubra grandiflora*

Fuchsias with colourful or multicoloured foliage

Fuchsia cultivars which possess leaves of various colour combinations, diverging from the green foliage of most cultivars, are called 'variegated fuchsias'. They are raised for the beauty of their decorative leaves. Although some cultivars also bear very fine-looking flowers, the majority do not flower until late in the season and produce small red and blue flowers.

The origin of the variegated fuchsias varies. Some are breeds, in other words hybrids, but most have arisen through mutations from normal green-foliaged cultivars. The best-known example is 'Golden Marinka', a sport of 'Marinka' with golden-margined foliage which has retained the flower shape and colour and all other characteristics of the original cultivar. Although, in spontaneous mutations such as this, often only a part of the plant changes, the change is absolutely constant (fixed) if the mutated branches are taken for propagation by cuttings. Now and then, however, retrogressive forms with the original green foliage occur. These green shoots, which are stronger in growth than the colourfully foliaged ones, must soon be cut away so that they do not overgrow or even supplant the variegated new development.

Colourfully foliaged fuchsias are as varied in their growth characteristics as the rest of the fuchsia cultivars. Plants can be found for every use wished for. They can be trained as hanging baskets, planted with pendent cultivars, as standards, bonsais or other ornamental forms. A bit more patience is needed, however, for the brightly foliaged cultivars are as a rule slower in their development. A few departures from the cultivation of the other fuchsias must be noted if optimal success is to be obtained with this group.

Light, a lot of light, is the first basic requirement for cultivation. Many varieties even tolerate positions in full sunlight. Only in a bright situation do the plants develop their full colour. Many cultivars produce only normal green leaves in shady positions. With sufficient soil moisture they are also suitable for hot positions which for fuchsias are otherwise not very beneficial.

'Mantilla'

Watering demands some consideration and intuition. The soil should almost dry out before watering again. In this group of fuchsias overwatering very easily leads to leaf drop, and if the worst comes to the worst even to loss of the plant. This danger is greatest in the young stage. Watering over the foliage, often helpful in green-foliaged fuchsias, or spraying leads to brown, unsightly spots on the leaves in variegated cultivars. For this reason work should also not be done with mineral foliar feeds. On the other hand we use nitrogen-rich fertilisers during the entire season in order to stimulate the desired leaf growth. The compost, too, must be especially permeable; with one part of loam-based soil. Pure peat composts can be made moist again only with difficulty once they have dried out.

More than 50 cultivars with multicoloured leaves are known and new ones are increasingly being added to this number. Many are always on offer at specialist nurseries, forming part so to speak of the standard assortment. Others can be found only in amateur collections, but it is worth looking for them.

FUCHSIA CULTIVARS WITH MULTICOLOURED FOLIAGE

'Autumnale' (Meteor, c. 1880)
(syn. 'Burning Bush' or 'Rubens')
FLOWERS: red and blue, late, single.
FOLIAGE: in warm autumn colours, brown, copper, yellow and little green.
GROWTH: broadly spreading.

'Blue and Gold' (Reedstrom 1956, USA) No. 254
FLOWERS: pink, mauve and blue, double.
FOLIAGE: golden-yellow.
GROWTH: upright.

'Cloth of Gold' (Stafford 1863, GB)
FLOWERS: red and purple, single, late.
FOLIAGE: golden-yellow, rosy-bronze when older.
GROWTH: upright and bushy.
Various cultivars are in circulation under this name.

'Coquet Gold' (Ryle 1976, GB) No. 1398
(Sport of 'Belsay Beauty')
FLOWERS: white, violet and purple, single.
FOLIAGE: pale green with lemon-yellow margin, many leaves entirely yellow.
GROWTH: upright and bushy.

'Day by Day' (Wagtails 1971, GB)
(Sport of 'Emile Zola')
FLOWERS: scarlet and purple, single.
FOLIAGE: green, cream and cherry-red.
GROWTH: upright and bushy.

F. magellanica* var. *macrostemma tricolor
(syn. *gracilis tricolor*)
FLOWERS: red and purple, single.
FOLIAGE: grey-green flushed with red.
GROWTH: upright, hardy.

F. magellanica* var. *macrostemma variegata
(syn. *gracilis variegata*)
FLOWERS: red and purple, long and narrow, single.
FOLIAGE: green, spotted and margined white, sometimes with red blush.
GROWTH: upright, bushy, hardy.

'Genii' (Reiter 1951, USA)
(correct name 'Jeane')
FLOWERS: red and mid-blue, early and free-flowering, single.
FOLIAGE: yellow with red midrib and red stalks.
GROWTH: upright, positively hardy.

'Gilda' (Handley 1971, GB) No. 986
FLOWERS: coral-pink, each petal with a red edge, double.
FOLIAGE: pale green with golden margin.
GROWTH: upright.

'Gold Brocade' (Tabraham 1976, GB)
FLOWERS: red and mauve, fading to pink, single.
FOLIAGE: gold-green, veined deep red.
GROWTH: strong, upright and bushy.

'Genii'

'Goldcrest' (Thorne 1968, GB)
FLOWERS: pink and lavender, single.
FOLIAGE: gold-green.
GROWTH: lax and bushy.

'Golden Gate' (Niederholzer 1940, USA)
FLOWERS: red and purple, single.
FOLIAGE: yellow-green.
GROWTH: compact and bushy.

'Golden Glory' (Gorman 1970, USA) No. 930
FLOWERS: orange, uniform, single.
FOLIAGE: golden-yellow with red base.
GROWTH: loose and bushy.

'Golden Lena' (Nottingham 1978, GB)
(Sport of 'Lena')
FLOWERS: pink and magenta, semi-double.
FOLIAGE: green, margined and mottled gold.
GROWTH: lax and bushy, hardy.

'Golden Marinka' (Weber 1955, USA) No. 401
(Sport of 'Marinka')
FLOWERS: red, single.
FOLIAGE: green with golden margin and red veins.
GROWTH: upright, with red branches.

'Golden Treasure' (Carter 1860, GB)
FLOWERS: scarlet and purple, late, single.
FOLIAGE: green with gold.
GROWTH: upright and bushy.

'Golden Violet' (Prentice 1966, USA) No. 665
FLOWERS: white and violet, double.
FOLIAGE: yellowish with pale green and red stalks.
GROWTH: lax.

'Goldilocks' (Haag 1950, USA)
FLOWERS: red and white, semi-double.
FOLIAGE: golden-yellow.
GROWTH: small and bushy.

'Gold Leaf' (Gadsby 1974, GB) No. 1222
FLOWERS: old-pink and white, single.
FOLIAGE: golden-yellow.
GROWTH: lax, bushy.

'Graf Witte' (Lemoine 1899, F)
FLOWERS: red and purple, single.
FOLIAGE: yellowish-green with red midrib and red veining.
GROWTH: upright, strong-growing and bushy.

'Green 'n' Gold' (Rasmussen 1954, USA)
(Sport of 'Glendale')

FLOWERS: uniformly coral-red, single.
FOLIAGE: small, green with golden margins.
GROWTH: upright and bushy.
A red-and-blue flowering cultivar is also distributed under the same name.

'Herbe de Jaques' (Schneider 1978, USA) No. 1439
(Sport of 'Corallina')
FLOWERS: red and purple as in 'Corallina'.
FOLIAGE: green, golden and red.
GROWTH: lax.
Almost identical to 'Tom West'.

'Humboldt Holiday' (Hasset 1980, USA) No. 1533
('Mary Ellen' × 'Cosmopolitan')
FLOWERS: white/violet and pink, large multicoloured blossom, double.
FOLIAGE: golden-green with red leaf veins.
GROWTH: pendent and many-branched.

'Judy' (Weaver 1977, USA) No. 1431
(Sport of 'Amapola')
FLOWERS: dark pink, single.
FOLIAGE: green, white and yellow.
GROWTH: lax.

'Little Rascal' (So Yun 1974, USA) No. 1182
FLOWERS: red and purple, small, single.
FOLIAGE: dark green and light green mixed, the young foliage and the branches are red.
GROWTH: lax.

'Mexicali Rose' (Castro 1962, USA) No. 515
FLOWERS: red and magenta with orange-coloured spots, double.
FOLIAGE: golden-yellow.
GROWTH: upright.

'Mindrum Gold' (Ryle 1975, GB) No. 1251
FLOWERS: pink and violet, double.
FOLIAGE: golden-green.
GROWTH: compact, low.

'Morning Glow' (Gadsby 1975, GB) No. 1302
FLOWERS: pink and pale blue, semi-double.
FOLIAGE: golden-yellow, later light green.
GROWTH: upright and bushy.

'Morning Light' (Waltz 1960, USA) No. 441
FLOWERS: tube and base of sepals red, sepals white and corolla lavender, double.
FOLIAGE: golden-yellow, red midrib.
GROWTH: lax.

'Mumtaz' (Hazard and Hazard, USA, date unknown)
FLOWERS: red and white, long, double.
FOLIAGE: yellowish-green with pink centre.
GROWTH: upright.

'Pink Lemonade' (Foster 1974, USA) No. 1172
FLOWERS: red and white, single.
FOLIAGE: lemon-yellow with pink-magenta veining.
GROWTH: upright and bushy.

'Pixie' (Russell 1960, GB)
(Sport of 'Graf Witte')
FLOWERS: small, cherry-red and mauve, single.
FOLIAGE: yellowish-green, red-veined.
GROWTH: vigorous, upright.

'President' (Standish 1841, GB)
FLOWERS: red and purple, single.
FOLIAGE: green with very strong red suffusion.
GROWTH: loose, bushy.

'Rosecroft Beauty' (Eden 1969, GB)
(Sport of 'Snowcap')
FLOWERS: red and white, semi-double.
FOLIAGE: light green with narrow cream-coloured margin and cherry-red spots.
GROWTH: upright and bushy.
Has the habit of reverting.

'Sabine' (Tolley 1971, GB) No. 1158
FLOWERS: pale to dark pink, single.
FOLIAGE: yellowish-green.
GROWTH: lax.

'Samson' (Peterson 1957, USA) No. 287
FLOWERS: with long pink tube and long sepals, corolla purple and large-bloomed, double.
FOLIAGE: pale green with pale yellow.
GROWTH: lax.

'Santa Clara' (Pennisi 1969, USA) No. 833
FLOWERS: red, white and purple, double.
FOLIAGE: green and gold.
GROWTH: lax.

'Sharpitor' (National Trust c. 1974, GB)
FLOWERS: small and dainty, whitish-pink, single, similar to 'Mrs W. P. Wood' or *F. magellanica* var. *molinae*.
FOLIAGE: pale green with cream-coloured margin.
GROWTH: upright and bushy.
In the 1975–8 Wisley Trials was awarded a certificate for particular hardiness.

'Silver Jubilee' (Hobbs 1976, GB) No. 1381
FLOWERS: red and white, double.
FOLIAGE: green and yellow with red branches.
GROWTH: upright and bushy.

'Stanford' (Hazard and Hazard, USA)
FLOWERS: red and white, single.
FOLIAGE: dark red.
GROWTH: upright and bushy.

'Strawberry Delight' (Gadsby 1970, GB) No. 873
FLOWERS: red and white, red-tinged, double.
FOLIAGE: yellowish-green with bronze, older foliage green.
GROWTH: lax.

'Sundance' (Handley 1974, GB) No. 1194
FLOWERS: pink and burgundy, single, large-flowered.
FOLIAGE: pale yellow-green.
GROWTH: lax.

'Sunray' (Milne 1872, GB)
FLOWERS: red and purple, single.
FOLIAGE: very colourful, several shades of green, white through cream to yellowish tones, the whole tinged with reddish cast.
GROWTH: upright.

'Ted's Rainbow' (Zerlang 1977, USA) No. 1404
FLOWERS: pink and purple, single.
FOLIAGE: dark green, light green and yellow: red leaf veins.
GROWTH: upright and bushy.

'The Small Woman' (Wagtails 1969, GB)
(Sport of 'Lovable')
FLOWERS: pink and lavender, large and double.
FOLIAGE: green, speckled gold.
GROWTH: lax.

'Tom West' (Meillez 1853, F)
FLOWERS: red and purple, late, single.
FOLIAGE: pale green with cream.
GROWTH: lax upright.

'Tour Eiffel' (de Graaff 1976, NL)
FLOWERS: salmon-pink, single.
FOLIAGE: green and bronze, red-veined with red branches and stalks.
GROWTH: lax.

'Tropic Sunset' (Antonelli 1965, USA) No. 635
('Autumnale' ✕)
FLOWERS: carmine and dark purple, double.
FOLIAGE: small, reddish-brown with light green mar-

gin, red stalks.

GROWTH: lax and many-branched.

'Wave of Life' (Henderson 1869, GB)
FLOWERS: scarlet and purple, single.
FOLIAGE: golden-yellow with pink stalks and branches.
GROWTH: lax.

'White Gold' (York 1953, USA) No. 190
FLOWERS: pure white with pink veins, single.
FOLIAGE: golden-yellow with red veins and red stalks, older foliage green.
GROWTH: lax and bushy.

'Whiteknights Glister' (J. O. Wright 1980, GB) No. 1594
(Sport of *F. magellanica* var. *molinae* × *F. fulgens*)
FLOWERS: reddish-white and purple.
FOLIAGE: green with cream-coloured margin.
GROWTH: upright, slow-growing.

'White Pixie' (Merrist Wood 1968, GB)
(Sport of 'Pixie')
FLOWERS: carmine and white with pink veining, single.
FOLIAGE: yellowish-green, red-veined.
GROWTH: upright and bushy.

Registration of new cultivars

The registration service of the American Fuchsia Society (AFS) was set up in 1948, with the aim of bringing some order to the nomenclature of fuchsias and preventing two or more new cultivars being given the same name by chance in the future. In the past, in the long cultural history of fuchsias, the latter situation had occurred with regrettable frequency.

This meritorious work was soon acknowledged by the International Society for Horticultural Science (ISHS) and in 1967 the AFS was appointed as the International Registration Authority for Fuchsias.

The AFS has welcomed this and encourages the hybridists to have their new fuchsia hybrids registered. The registered cultivars are published annually in the March bulletin of the American Fuchsia Society. Given the wide circulation of this publication, this is the best way of informing fuchsia-fanciers throughout the world of the new introductions. There is no fee for registration. The incumbent registrar compares the intended names with all those so far registered, reserved or otherwise catalogued in any way and either gives his approval to the choice of name or, if the name is already in existence, recommends that another name be found.

Applications for registration should be submitted in time and as early as possible before the annual deadline (15 November), irrespective of whether an application for name reservation is under consideration or not. It is advisable to request the blank forms from the registrar early in the year and to return them as complete as possible. Comprehensive and detailed descriptions of the new cultivars are essential in order that they may be distinguished from fuchsias already in existence.

A numbered 'Certificate of Registration' is delivered to the hybridiser for each registered cultivar.

Reservation and registration applications and the correspondence relating to these matters are to be sent to the following address:

Dee Logan,
Recording Secretary/International Registrar
8710 South Sherida Avenue
Reedley
California
93654
USA

Recent fuchsia cultivars

The following list contains only fuchsia cultivars which were registered and introduced in 1986.

'Aberconwy' (Howarth, GB) No. 2023
'Adrian Young' (Young, GB) No. 1983
'American Nikki' (Walker, USA) No. 1945
'Anacapa' (Schneider, USA) No. 2012
'Anni Adriaens' (Vrindts, B) No. 2026
'Atlantic Star' (Redfern, GB) No. 1981
'Audrey Dahms' (Dahms, Collard, GB) No. 1957
'Baby Two Step' (Schneider, USA) No. 2013
'Becky Torrie' (Laburnum, GB) No. 1985
'Belinda Allen' (Gadsby, Allen, Saxondale, GB) No. 1974
'Bella Madina' (Weeks, GB) No. 1963
'Berba' (Bats-Wesseling, NL) No. 1928
'Berbanella' (Bats-Wesseling, NL) No. 1929
'Berba's Trio' (Bats-Wesseling) No. 1930
'Bits' (Wilkins, Higginbottom, Richardson, Austr.) No. 1950

'Blue McKenzie' (Laburnum, GB) No. 1986
'Bob Armbruster' (Walker, USA) No. 1952
'Bosworth Field' (Laburnum, GB) No. 1987
'Bradgate Park' (Laburnum, GB) No. 1988
'Bud Stubbs' (Garrett, USA) No. 2019
'Buena Maria' (Garrett, USA) No. 2021
'Burnside' (Downs, GB) No. 1951
'Candy Kisses' (Laburnum, GB) No. 1989
'Carmelflora' (Stubbs, USA) No. 1941
'Channel Island' (Schneider, USA) No. 2014
'Christine Windsor' (Windsor, GB) No. 1966
'Cissbury Gem' (Hobbs, GB) No. 1968
'City of Adelaide' (Richardson, Austr.) No. 1949
'Clarence's Redhead' (Schneider, USA) No. 2015
'Clarendon Park' (Pidcock, Laburnum, GB) No. 1990
'Claudine Sanford' (Sanford, USA)
'Clock Tower' (Pidcock, Laburnum, GB) No. 1991
'Cricket' (Storvick, USA) No. 2025
'Cropston Magna' (Laburnum, GB) No. 1991
'Cupcake' (Stubbs, USA) No. 1815
'Cynthia' (Pidcock, Laburnum, GB) No. 1993
'Deborah Young' (Young, GB) No. 1984
'Dee Starr' (Richardson, Austr.) No. 1947
'Elf's Own' (Woolley, GB) No. 1961
'Emily Salisbury' (Reynolds, GB) No. 1980
'Erica Julie' (Tite, GB) No. 1956
'Eric's Hardy SD' (Weeks, GB) No. 1964
'Ethel Weeks SD' (Weeks, GB) No. 1965
'Evelyn Gentry' (Rawlins, Thames, GB) No. 1973
'Expo '86' (Wood, USA) No. 2022
'Fancy Sockeye' (Brough, GB) No. 1975
'Florrie Bambridge' (Windsor, GB) No. 1967
'Fondant Cream' (Laburnum, GB) No. 1994
'Goose Green' (Laburnum, GB) No. 1995
'Helen Veach' (Schneider, USA) No. 2016
'Hubert Lambert' (Vrindts, B) No. 2027
'Jack Caunt' (Caunt, GB) No. 1958
'Jam Roll' (Brough, GB) No. 1976
'Jan' (Hill, GB) No. 1962
'Jasper' (Howwarth, GB) No. 2024
'Jean Pidcock' (Pidcock, Laburnum, GB) No. 1996
'Jean Temple' (Wood, USA) No. 2010
'King Richard III' (Laburnum, GB) No. 1997
'La Costa' (Garrett, USA) No. 2020
'Lady Diana' (Stevens, Austr.) No. 2017
'Lady Jane Grey' (Laburnum, GB) No. 1998

'La Houtainoise' (Vrindts, B) No. 2028
'La Legia' (Vrindts, B) No. 2029
'Lesley Anne' (Richardson, Austr.) No. 1948
'L'Esperance' (Vrindts, B) No. 2030
'Lindsay Ann' (Brightwell, NZ) No. 1940
'Madame Elise Machiels' (Vrindts, B) No. 2031
'Marco Boy' (Bats-Wesseling, NL) No. 1931
'Mardale' (Laburnum, GB) No. 1999
'Martin Hayward' (Rowell, GB) No. 1969
'Midnight Blue' (Laburnum, GB) No. 2000
'Minx' (Brough, GB) No. 1977
'More Applause' (Plows, USA) No. 2009
'North Cascades' (Wood, USA) No. 2011
'President Francois Charlier' (Vrindts, B) No. 2032
'Princesse De Liege (Vrindts, B) No. 2033
'Proud Beauty' (Laburnum, GB) No. 2001
'Radings Gerda' (Reiman, NL) No. 1932
'Radings Inge' (Reiman, NL) No. 1933
'Radings Karin' (Reiman, NL) No. 1934
'Radings Marjorie' (Reiman, NL) No. 1935
'Radings Michelle' (Reiman, NL) No. 1936
'Radio Leicester' (Pidcock, Laburnum, GB) No. 2002
'Rainbow Warrior' (Laburnum, GB) No. 2003
'Rebecca Williamson' (Redfern, GB) No. 1982
'Robert Bruce' (Stubbs, USA) No. 1942
'Ronald L. Lockerbie' (Richardson, Austr.) No. 1946
'Rose-N-Blue' (Walker, USA) No. 1953
'Ruth West' (Drapkin, USA) No. 1955
'San Pasqual' (Stubbs, USA) No. 1944
'Sarah Hadfield' (Rowell, GB) No. 1970
'Sipke Arjen' (Reiman, NL) No. 1937
'Sister Bass' (Laburnum, GB) No. 2004
'Smoky-N-Lovely' (Walker, USA) No. 1954
'Stan Wilkins' (Laburnum, GB) No. 2005
'Stephanie' (Vrindts, B) No. 2034
'Sue Rose' (Caunt, GB) No. 1959
'Summer Wine' (Laburnum, GB) No. 2006
'Terry Green' (Caunt, GB) No. 1960
'Tethys' (Vrindts, B) No. 2035
'Timothy Brian' (Schweitzer, USA) No. 2018
'Tizzy' (Walker, USA) No. 1943
'Uppingham Lass' (Johnson, GB) No. 2007
'Ville De Liege' (Vrindts, B) No. 2036
'Walz Kleinduimpje' (Waldenmaier, NL) No. 1938
'Walz Knipperbol' (Waldenmaier, NL) No. 1939

A TO Z OF CULTIVARS

'Abbé Farges' (Lemoine 1901, F)
TUBE: light red.
SEPALS: light red.
COROLLA: lilac-pink, single to semi-double.
STAMENS: light red.
PISTIL: light red.
FOLIAGE: mid-green, small.
GROWTH: upright and bushy.
An extremely profusely flowering cultivar which reacts very well to pinching. It is equally decorative as a pot plant, as a table standard and as a good show plant with its beautiful structure. Beware, the wood is very brittle.

'Achievement' (Melville 1886, GB)
TUBE: carmine-red.
SEPALS: carmine-red.
COROLLA: plum-blue, red base, single.
STAMENS: red.
PISTIL: red.
FOLIAGE: light green, particularly the young leaves.
GROWTH: upright, well branched.
A plant that has stood the test of time. Big, well-shaped flowers on a problemless plant which will not disappoint even a beginner.

'Aika' (Bögemann 1982, G) No. 2199
(*F. magdalenae* × 'Ting-a-Ling')
(Certificate of Merit of the VKC at Aalsmer)
TUBE: light pink, darker streaks.
SEPALS: pink at first, then lighter, green tips.
COROLLA: deep pink, base pink, single.
STAMENS: light pink, enclosed.
PISTIL: light pink.
FOLIAGE: mid-green, glossy.
GROWTH: lax-upright.
This new German breed is distinguished by great vitality and enormously profuse flowering. The exquisitely shaped flower is something quite new. Versatile use as hanging basket, bush or standard.

'Aintree' (Need 1964, GB)
TUBE: ivory.
SEPALS: pink.
COROLLA: intense rose-red, single.
STAMENS: ivory.
PISTIL: white.
FOLIAGE: dark green and glossy.
GROWTH: upright and bushy.
Charming pot and bedding-out plant which also tolerates sun.

'Alaska' (Schnabel 1963, USA) No. 585
TUBE: white.
SEPALS: white, broad, with green tips.
COROLLA: white, double.
STAMENS: light pink.
PISTIL: white.
FOLIAGE: dark green.
GROWTH: upright and bushy.
Strong-growing with good branching. For such a large-flowered fuchsia it bears an astonishing number of flowers. As the flowers are accordingly heavy, good support is necessary. All in all white cultivars, the flowers are at their most beautiful under glass or in a covered, shady position outdoors. Problem-free in cultivation, 'Alaska' is one of the best white double fuchsias.

There is another American cultivar with the name 'Alaska' (Roth 1956) which is also white and double but has smaller flowers. This cultivar is supposed to have blue tips to the white sepals.

'Aldham' (Dunnett 1978, GB) No. 1514
TUBE: white.
SEPALS: white with slightly pink underside, upright.
COROLLA: snow-white, medium-sized, double.
STAMENS: reddish.
PISTIL: reddish.
FOLIAGE: dark green with red veins, finely denticulate.
GROWTH: lax-upright.

Thickly double, beautifully shaped flowers which appear in great masses. Superb as hanging basket. Whether the growing strength is sufficient for a standard must be put to the test.

'Alice Hoffmann' (Kiese 1901, G)
TUBE: light red.
SEPALS: light red and glossy.
COROLLA: white, red-veined, semi-double.
STAMENS: light red.
PISTIL: light red.
FOLIAGE: bronze-green, small.
GROWTH: upright and bushy.
This low-growing cultivar is particularly well suited for bed planting. It is a profuse flowerer and very robust, the flowers being borne very visibly above the foliage. In sheltered positions or in regions with a mild climate it is hardy.

'Alice Kling' (Wilson 1959, USA) No. 413
TUBE: uniformly dark red.
SEPALS: uniformly dark red.
COROLLA: uniformly dark red, medium-sized, single.
STAMENS: red.
PISTIL: red.
FOLIAGE: mid-green.
GROWTH: strong-growing with long internodes.
Many-branched, strong-growing climbing fuchsia which quickly reaches a good height and flowers unremittingly throughout the entire summer. Resistant to heat.

'Alison Ewart' (Roe 1976, GB)
('Eleanor Leytham' × 'Pink Darling')
TUBE: pink, short and thick.
SEPALS: pink, small with green tips.
COROLLA: pink/mauve, single.
STAMENS: pink.
PISTIL: light pink.
FOLIAGE: dark green with red veins.
GROWTH: upright and bushy.
This cultivar grows compact and bushy, i.e. it is naturally self-branching. The relatively small flowers appear early and in great abundance. In England it is very popular as a show plant. It is seen frequently as a bush as well as a table standard.

'Alison Ryle' (Dr M. Ryle 1968, GB) No. 1112
('Tennessee Waltz' × 'Lena Dalton')
TUBE: fuchsia-pink.
SEPALS: fuchsia-pink with light tips.

COROLLA: deep lavender-blue, pink veins, semi-double.
STAMENS: red.
PISTIL: pink.
FOLIAGE: dark green.
GROWTH: upright, well branched.
Good bedding-out cultivar which tolerates full sun.

'Alsternixe' (Nutzinger 1971, A)
TUBE: red.
SEPALS: red.
COROLLA: blue, single.
STAMENS: red.
PISTIL: red.
FOLIAGE: dark green.
GROWTH: upright and strong.
This cultivar is especially suited for bed planting in larger areas. The dainty flowers of brilliant colour clothe the plant in great numbers. Whether this derivative of *F. magellanica gracilis* is hardy would be worth testing.

'Ambassador' (Jones & Machado 1962, GB)
TUBE: white with pink flush.
SEPALS: white, underside pink.
COROLLA: violet and purple, fading to lilac and pink, single.
STAMENS: pink.
PISTIL: pink.
FOLIAGE: mid-green, red midrib.
GROWTH: upright and strong-growing.
The single flower is very big and well shaped, the buds long and elegant. Good as a bush as well as a standard.

'Amelie Aubin' (Eggebrecht 1884, G)
TUBE: white.
SEPALS: white with green tips.
COROLLA: carmine, white at the base, single.
STAMENS: pale pink.
PISTIL: white.
FOLIAGE: light green.
GROWTH: lax; with supports can also be raised as a bush.
It has long internodes and branches only after frequent stopping. Good as profusely flowering hanging basket plant or as edge planting in large containers. On a standard, which can grow to many years of age, the bright, well-shaped flowers stand out particularly well.

'Angel's Dream'

'Bonnie Lass'

'Bow Bells'

'Berba's Trio'

'Annabel'

'America' (Niederholzer 1941, USA)
TUBE: white, thin and very long.
SEPALS: white with pink tinge, underside cherry-red with white border.
COROLLA: crimson, base veined whitish-pink, single.
STAMENS: pale pink.
PISTIL: pale pink.
FOLIAGE: light green.
GROWTH: lax cascade.
A slow-growing cultivar of great beauty, but not at all easy to care for. Needs a cool, shady position in summer. During the winter rest the temperature must not drop below 10°C.

'Amy Lye' (Lye 1885, GB)
TUBE: greenish-white.
SEPALS: cream, green tips.
COROLLA: orange to coral-red, single.
STAMENS: pink.
PISTIL: white.
FOLIAGE: dark green, red midrib, new growth bronze.
GROWTH: spreading, with supports and pinching can also be trained as a bush.
Good, old cultivar on which the much-cited Lye's hallmark may be placed without any reservation. Characteristic of 'Amy Lye' and a good distinguishing mark is the obvious wrinkles in the petals. Strong-growing, problem-free and suitable for all growth forms. The bright colours against the dark foliage are a feast for the eyes.

'Andromeda' (De Groot 1968, NL)
(*F. regia* var. *typica* × 'Upward Look')

TUBE: light red.
SEPALS: light red, green tips.
COROLLA: lilac-pink, lighter at the base, red-veined, single.
STAMENS: cherry-red.
PISTIL: cherry-red.
FOLIAGE: dark green, small.
GROWTH: upright.
From each leaf-axil of this bushy plant come four to six of the dainty sideways-upward pointing, well-shaped flowers. Grows naturally bushy and makes a very good small standard. Also good as a bedding-out plant.

'Angela Leslie' (Tiret 1959, USA) No. 382
TUBE: pink.
SEPALS: pink, underside darker.
COROLLA: pale pink with darker pink veins, double.
STAMENS: pink, sometimes with petaloids.
PISTIL: pink.
FOLIAGE: mid-green.
GROWTH: upright, bushy and well branched.
For a pastel-coloured fuchsia with such big flowers it is amazingly strong-growing. It likes shady and cool conditions. Owing to the heavy flowers it must be supported.

'Angeline' (Dunnett 1979, GB) No. 1515
TUBE: white, long and thin.
SEPALS: white with pink tinge, green tips.
COROLLA: campanula and violet, with pink spots, very full double.
STAMENS: pinkish-white.

PISTIL: white.

FOLIAGE: mid-green, narrow.

GROWTH: trailer, short internodes, well branched.

Profusely flowering hanging-basket cultivar. The thickly double corolla on the long, elegant tube is exquisite and characteristic.

'Angel's Dream' (Stubbs 1973, USA) No. 1079 ('Pink Galore' × 'White King')

TUBE: white.

SEPALS: white with pink tinge.

COROLLA: white, pink base, double.

STAMENS: pink.

PISTIL: pink.

FOLIAGE: dark green with red veins and stalks.

GROWTH: trailer, well branched.

This fuchsia is a hanging-basket plant as we would like one to be. Long-drooping branches studded with large spectacular flowers. Part of the petals are fused with the elegantly upright sepals. This causes a two-tiered effect which makes the flower look bigger. The little 'mouse-tooth' marks on the petals can also be found in many other Stubbs cultivars.

'Angel's Flight' (Martin 1957, USA) No. 320

TUBE: white with pink wash.

SEPALS: pink, underside darker at the base.

COROLLA: white, veined red, double.

STAMENS: pink.

PISTIL: white.

FOLIAGE: mid-green.

GROWTH: lax-upright or trailer; with support also as a bush.

A particularly charming cultivar among the almost white ones. The sepals are centred elegantly and gracefully around the tube. It is easy to cultivate in a cool, shady, sheltered position.

'Annabel' (Dr M. Ryle 1977, GB) No. 1476 ('Ingram Maid' × 'Nancy Lou')

TUBE: white with pink streaks, long.

SEPALS: white with pink tinge, upright.

COROLLA: white with quite faint pink veins, double.

STAMENS: light pink.

PISTIL: light pink.

FOLIAGE: light green, yellowish at the tip.

GROWTH: upright.

This is an outstanding almost white fuchsia which was awarded the BFS silver Certificate of Merit in Manchester, 1977. The rather free growth neverthe-less supports the heavy, long, beautifully shaped flowers well.

'Auntie Jinks' (Wilson Jack 1970, GB)

TUBE: pinkish-red, long.

SEPALS: white with red border, upright, often rolled or curled.

COROLLA: dark cherry-red, lighter at the base, single.

STAMENS: pink.

PISTIL: pink.

FOLIAGE: dark green, small and pointed, finely den-ticulate.

GROWTH: trailer, very elastic, densely branched.

This 'Checkerboard' seedling produces a fabulous abundance of flowers and can be cultivated as a hanging basket splendidly and without problems.

'Aunt Juliana' (Hanson 1950, USA) No. 1320

TUBE: carmine-red.

SEPALS: carmine-red.

COROLLA: clear lavender-blue, veined red, double.

STAMENS: red.

PISTIL: red.

FOLIAGE: mid-green.

GROWTH: trailer.

This sport of 'Uncle Jules' is a rather superior hanging-basket plant with large, wonderfully shaped flowers. With good cultivation and in a protected position, perhaps on the house wall, it is of singular beauty.

'Aviator' (Diener 1939, USA)

TUBE: red.

SEPALS: red, long and narrow, elegantly turned.

COROLLA: ivory-white, slightly red-veined, long, single.

STAMENS: red.

PISTIL: red.

FOLIAGE: light green, conspicuously red-veined.

GROWTH: upright and vigorous.

A very attractive older cultivar which definitely de-serves a wider popularity.

'Baby Chang' (Hazard & Hazard 1950, USA)

TUBE: orange-red, long.

SEPALS: orange-red, upright, green tips, underside yellowish-green.

COROLLA: orange, single.

STAMENS: orange, enclosed.

PISTIL: yellowish.

FOLIAGE: small, mid-green.

GROWTH: natural trailer, very elastic.

Enchanting miniature flowers with the pagoda shape of 'Chang'. Frequent pinching results in extremely profuse flowering. It is also a good winter flowerer in the greenhouse.

'Balkonkönigin' (Neubronner 1896, G)
TUBE: light pink.
SEPALS: pale pink, green tips.
COROLLA: dark pink, single.
STAMENS: light pink.
PISTIL: white.
FOLIAGE: mid-green with red veins.
GROWTH: trailing cascade.
This well-proven fuchsia falls right over the edge of the pot just like a waterfall. To fill a hanging basket sufficiently seven plants are needed. The wealth of blossom on well cared-for plants is fabulous. However, it is no secret that not everybody grows this successfully—great care is required.

'Ballerina' (Götz 1967, G)
TUBE: red.
SEPALS: red.
COROLLA: white, single.
STAMENS: red.
PISTIL: pink.
FOLIAGE: dark green.
GROWTH: upright and bushy.
Balcony and bedding-out fuchsia that flowers early and very profusely.

'Barbara' (Tolley 1971, GB) No. 1155
TUBE: light pink.
SEPALS: pink, underside darker.
COROLLA: pink, single.
STAMENS: dark pink.
PISTIL: pink.
FOLIAGE: mid-green.
GROWTH: upright and bushy.
This seedling of the well-tested cultivar 'Display' is extremely free-flowering and tolerates the sun well. Growth form produces an upright plant, suitable for training only as a standard.

'Beacon Rosa' (Bürgi-Ott 1972, CH)
TUBE: rose-red.
SEPALS: rose-red.
COROLLA: pink, slightly veined, single.
STAMENS: pink.
PISTIL: pink.
FOLIAGE: dark green.
GROWTH: upright and well branched.
More pleasing in colour than the old 'Beacon'. Also

very suitable as a bedding-out plant. Good resistance to rain.

'Beauty of Bath' (Colville 1965, GB)
TUBE: whitish-pink.
SEPALS: whitish-pink, underside darker, edged red, green tips.
COROLLA: creamy-white, long, double.
STAMENS: pale pink.
PISTIL: whitish-pink.
FOLIAGE: mid-green, glossy.
GROWTH: upright and bushy if stopped early.
Robust and profusely flowering, almost white cultivar. The flowers are long and well shaped. Distinguished from 'Angel's Flight', with which it is frequently confused, by the stiffly upright growth with strong branches but also by the non-rolled, red-edged sepals.

'Beauty of Exeter' (Letheren 1890, GB)
TUBE: salmon-pink, long.
SEPALS: salmon-pink.
COROLLA: slightly darker salmon-pink, semi-double.
STAMENS: pink.
PISTIL: whitish-pink.
FOLIAGE: yellow and green.
GROWTH: lax-upright, robust.
Only regular, early stopping brings this beautiful-flowered plant to an attractive shape. Particularly good as a standard.

'Beauty of Swanley' (Lye 1875, GB)
TUBE: waxy white with pink tinge.
SEPALS: waxy white, upright, green tips.
COROLLA: baby-pink, single.
STAMENS: white.
PISTIL: white.
FOLIAGE: mid-green.
GROWTH: broadly upright, with supple branches and short internodes.
The subtle charm of the flowers needs to be observed at close range. The delicate beauty is, for all that, content with little care and produces a fullness to the flowers which look as if they are made of porcelain. Good as a bush or standard.

'Bellbottoms' (Castro 1972, USA) No. 1029
TUBE: light salmon-pink, long.
SEPALS: light salmon-orange, underside darker, green tips, long and narrow.
COROLLA: smoky-orange, lighter at bottom, single.

'Bicentennial'

'Blush of Dawn'

STAMENS: salmon-pink.
PISTIL: salmon-pink.
FOLIAGE: light green.
GROWTH: upright.
One of the prettiest flowers in this colour arrangement. Radiant, elegant and large-flowered. Flowers at different periods; in the greenhouse even in winter.

'Belle de Lisse' (de Graaff 1977, NL)
'Trail Blazer' ×)
TUBE: whitish-pink.
SEPALS: whitish-pink, green tips.
COROLLA: pale lilac-pink, double, the outer petals are shorter than the inner ones.
STAMENS: pink.
PISTIL: pink.
FOLIAGE: light green, large.
GROWTH: lax-upright; will trail.
Free-flowering new form from Holland, of beautiful shape and colour, which will make its way.

'Berba' (Bats 1979, NL) No. 1928
('Mevrouw Goyaerts' ×)
TUBE: white, very long, up to 5 cm.
SEPALS: pink, underside deep pink, green tips, upright.
COROLLA: deep rose-red with darker edges, salmon-pink spots at the base, semi-double.
STAMENS: red.
PISTIL: light pink.
FOLIAGE: mid-green, medium-sized.
GROWTH: stiff trailer, good self-brancher.

Very suitable for wall baskets, distinguished by its very large flowers and very long tube with pale red-purple and orange petaloids. Received Certificate of Honour from Dutch Committee of Inspection, Aalsmeer.

'Berba's Trio' (Bats 1983, NL) No. 1930
('Le Campanella' × 'Bridesmaid')
TUBE: white to rose-red.
SEPALS: rose-red, underside crepe-like, green tips.
COROLLA: a) white with purple-blue patches, b) white with red veining at the base, c) purple-blue with red veins, single.
STAMENS: rose-red.
PISTIL: pale pink.
FOLIAGE: small, mid-green with red stalks.
GROWTH: lax; will produce stiff trailer.
Anybody who loves colour will be lost in wonder at this cultivar. Quite new, different combinations of the three basic colours can be seen in individual flowers. Only the rose-red calyx with the upright sepals is common to all. To propagate true types cuttings must be taken from shoots with multicoloured flowers.

'Berkeley' (Reiter 1955, USA) No. 233
TUBE: light pink.
SEPALS: light pink, broad, upright.
COROLLA: brilliant Tyrian-red, double.
STAMENS: light pink.
PISTIL: whitish-pink.
FOLIAGE: mid-green.
GROWTH: lax.

'Blue Veil'

'Brentwood'

'Carnival'

Large roundish flowers which appear in masses. After the first climax of flowering the plant takes a short rest, only then to flower inexhaustibly through until the frosts. Very well suited for the planting of balcony boxes or for the edge of larger containers.

'Berliner Kind' (Eggebrecht 1882, G)
('Schneewittchen' × 'Goliath')
TUBE: scarlet-red, short.
SEPALS: scarlet-red, waxy, green tips.
COROLLA: milky-white, slightly veined, fully double, of perfect shape.
STAMENS: pink.
PISTIL: white.
FOLIAGE: dark green, red midrib, red stalks.
GROWTH: lax-upright.
With all cultivars that have been in cultivation over such a long time and are still widespread today first-rate quality can be taken as a matter of course. Such is also the case here. The roundish flowers are of outstanding substance and so remain beautiful for days on end. They literally overwhelm the plant, which does not grow very tall (about 30 cm) but branches well.

'Bianca' (Pennisi 1967, USA) No. 715
TUBE: white and short.
SEPALS: white.
COROLLA: white, large, double.
STAMENS: white.
PISTIL: white.
FOLIAGE: mid-green.
GROWTH: trailer.
The branches, even when supported, are almost too weak to bear the heavy flowers. Not to be confused with 'La Bianca' of Tiret.

'Bicentennial' (Paskensen 1976, USA) No. 1344
TUBE: white, long and thin.
SEPALS: light orange, salmon underside.
COROLLA: magenta petals with orange stripes surrounded by orange petaloids, double.
STAMENS: pink.
PISTIL: whitish-pink.
FOLIAGE: mid-green.
GROWTH: lax-upright semi-trailer.
This cultivar was brought out to mark the 200th-year celebrations of the USA. The medium-sized flowers are well shaped and of great illuminating power, especially in a sunny position. The plant is naturally self-branching and is particularly suitable for hanging baskets.

'Bishop's Bells' (Gadsby 1970, GB) No. 869
TUBE: rose-red.
SEPALS: rose-red, green tips, extremely long and broad.
COROLLA: violet and purple, pink-veined, semi-double.
STAMENS: pink.
PISTIL: pink.
FOLIAGE: mid-green.
GROWTH: upright.
A 'Caroline' seedling with beautiful flowers; must be stopped early and repeatedly if a bushy plant is aspired to.

'Blue Pearl' (Martin 1955, USA) No. 325
TUBE: short, compact, white with green.
SEPALS: pinkish-white, broad, creped surface.
COROLLA: blue and violet, pink base, double.
STAMENS: rose-red.
PISTIL: whitish-pink.
FOLIAGE: dark green, red stalk, finely denticulate.
GROWTH: lax-upright, vigorous.
A still popular, older cultivar. The large, roundish-flat flowers appear in batches. Each petal is finely tooth-edged. Good feeding shortens the break between periods of flowering.

'Blue Pinwheel' (Stubbs 1970, USA) No. 902
TUBE: light red, long and thin.
SEPALS: light red, narrow and rolled.
COROLLA: lavender-blue, pink at the base, single.
STAMENS: pink.
PISTIL: pink, very long.
FOLIAGE: mid-green.
GROWTH: trailing cascade.
The name is well chosen. With a little imagination the elegant sepals form the shape of a fan blower. Strong-growing, free-flowering hanging-basket plant which also looks attractive as a miniature standard.

'Blue Ribbon' (Fuchsia-La 1967, USA) No. 695
TUBE: pale pink.
SEPALS: pale pink, joined with the corolla.
COROLLA: white, angular, double.
STAMENS: pale pink.
PISTIL: pale pink.
FOLIAGE: mid-green.
GROWTH: lax-upright.
It is often stated with surprise: 'But the flower is not blue at all!' Blue Ribbons are bestowed as a distinction at the fuchsia shows in America when a cultivar has particular qualities.

'Blue Veil' (Pacey 1980, GB)
TUBE: pure white.
SEPALS: pure white, broad.
COROLLA: lobelia-blue, double.
STAMENS: red.
PISTIL: red.
FOLIAGE: mid-green.
GROWTH: strong trailer.
A cultivar with a lovely colour combination, and fully double, well-shaped flowers which do not turn reddish even when faded.

'Blush of Dawn' (Martin 1962, USA) No. 516
TUBE: greenish-white.
SEPALS: white with green tips, pale pink underside.
COROLLA: quite pale lilac-pink, double.
STAMENS: light cherry-red.
PISTIL: white.
FOLIAGE: mid-green.
GROWTH: lax-upright.
This delicately coloured, large-flowered cultivar exhibits its full beauty only in the greenhouse. The pastel colours become slightly spotted by the rain. Also very attractive as a wall basket under a porch.

'Bobby Shaftoe' (Ryle 1970, GB) No. 1113
TUBE: white.
SEPALS: white, green tips.
COROLLA: white with some pink at the base, semi-double.
STAMENS: cherry-red.
PISTIL: white.
FOLIAGE: dark green, small.
GROWTH: upright.
Very attractive, well-branched growth with short internodes. Well-formed flowers in enormous profusion.

'Boerhave' (van Wieringen 1970, NL)
TUBE: deep red and very long.
SEPALS: deep red, narrow, tapering to a point.
COROLLA: rosy and purple, single.
STAMENS: cherry-red.
PISTIL: dark pink, very long.
FOLIAGE: mid-green, veined red.
GROWTH: stiff trailer.
A good, strong-growing hanging-basket cultivar with extraordinarily long, slender flowers.

'Bon Accord' (Crousse 1861, F)
TUBE: white.
SEPALS: white.
COROLLA: pale pink and purple, single.
STAMENS: pale pink.
PISTIL: white.
FOLIAGE: mid-green and small.
GROWTH: rigid, upright.
This is the best-known cultivar of a small group of fuchsias with upward-pointing flowers. In America, but also elsewhere, it is offered by many gardeners under the name 'Erecta Novelty'. Both cultivars are perfectly identical. To complete the confusion: Dr Essig, in his checklist of 1934, describes 'Erecta Novelty' as red, white and slightly pink, the corolla with pink edge and upright flowers. Perhaps 'Erecta Novelty' was originally an independent cultivar after all? Whatever the case may be, what is cultivated today under the name of 'Bon Accord' is a versatile, very decorative fuchsia with that 'something special'.

'Bon Bon (Kennett 1963, USA) No. 592
TUBE: green and white, very long.
SEPALS: quite light pink, underside somewhat darker.
COROLLA: almost white, slightly tinged pink, double.
STAMENS: light pink.
PISTIL: white.
FOLIAGE: mid-green.
GROWTH: lax bush on trailer.
An enchanting fuchsia not all that easy to cultivate. The long branches with the distinctively shaped flowers look good in a hanging basket. It should be stopped several times as a young plant. Unfortunately, it only seldom survives a winter rest, so some young plants from the autumn propagation should always be kept available.

'Bonnie Lass' (Waltz 1962, USA) No. 522
TUBE: snow-white, long and thin.
SEPALS: snow-white on outside, pale pink beneath, steeply upright, long and narrow.
COROLLA: bright blue-violet, fading attractively to reddish, single to semi-double.
STAMENS: cherry-red.
PISTIL: white.
FOLIAGE: dark green.
GROWTH: upright.
This cultivar is profusely flowering with long, elegant flowers of bright colours. Prefers a cool, shady spot. For the rest, attentiveness to care is advisable as already stated for other white and blue fuchsias.

'Capri'

'Daisy Bell'

'Caroline'

'Bouffant' (Tiret 1949, USA) No. 32
TUBE: red and long.
SEPALS: red.
COROLLA: white, slightly veined red, single.
STAMENS: red.
PISTIL: red.
FOLIAGE: mid-green with red veining.
GROWTH: trailing.
A strong-growing, profusely flowering cultivar with good effect from a distance. It branches relatively well and the long shoots show up best in larger containers. Problem-free to cultivate and every cutting roots.

'Bountiful' (Munkner 1963, USA) No. 564
TUBE: white and long.
SEPALS: pinkish-white, underside somewhat darker, long with green tips.
COROLLA: milky-white, slightly veined pink, double.
STAMENS: pink.
PISTIL: pale pink.
FOLIAGE: mid-green.
GROWTH: upright and bushy.
The name is very well chosen and aptly describes the abundant wealth of flower and the excellent growth of this fuchsia. As a bush it requires supports to be able to carry the weight of the many heavy flowers, and of course a good feeding. An espalier of 'Bountiful' in the greenhouse or in a very well sheltered spot is imposing.

'Countess of Aberdeen'

'Bow Bells' (Handley 1972, GB) No. 1051
TUBE: greenish-white.
SEPALS: white, green tips.
COROLLA: magenta, darker at the edges, white at the
base, single to semi-double.
STAMENS: light pink.
PISTIL: white.
FOLIAGE: light green.
GROWTH: lax-upright; if supported also upright.
An early-flowering cultivar with large flowers of good
substance.

'Brentwood' (Evans & Reeces 1936, USA)
('Rolla' × 'Duchess of Albany')
TUBE: white, waxy.
SEPALS: white, green tips.
COROLLA: cream, pale green edges, semi-double.
STAMENS: white.
PISTIL: white.
FOLIAGE: dark green, small.
GROWTH: upright, well branched.
The charming, medium-sized flowers appear in
batches. Even under ideal conditions the plant is
delicate and requires best, attentive care. The culti-
var probably had its true value as a breeding plant in
the years from 1930 to 1950.

'Bridal Veil' (Waltz 1963, USA) No. 586
TUBE: white.
SEPALS: white, green tips, creped on the underside.

'Citation'

'Caspar Hauser'

COROLLA: cream-white, fully double.
STAMENS: pale pink.
PISTIL: white.
FOLIAGE: dark green and small.
GROWTH: lax-upright or trailer.
A fairly robust, white cultivar which like all white fuchsias needs a shady, sheltered position. Not particularly sensitive to heat.

'Brutus' (Lemoine 1897, F)
TUBE: cherry-red.
SEPALS: cherry-red.
COROLLA: dark purple, pink base, single.
STAMENS: red.
PISTIL: red.
FOLIAGE: mid-green, red veins.
GROWTH: upright and bushy, strong-growing.
Like many Lemoine breeds 'Brutus' has also proved itself well over many decades. The plant is very versatile, especially for the raising of large plants.

'Buddha' (Fuchsia-La 1968, USA) No. 799
TUBE: white, long and thick.
SEPALS: white with pink tinge, underside pink, green tips, broad.
COROLLA: beautiful wine-red with some pink spots, double.
STAMENS: pink.
PISTIL: white to pink.
FOLIAGE: dark green.
GROWTH: lax-upright.
A powerful grower which also flowers comparatively diligently. The branches are brittle and break easily. They must always be supported well so that the heavy, beautifully shaped flowers are not damaged.

'Caledonia' (Lemoine 1889, F)
TUBE: cherry-red, very long and thin.
SEPALS: cherry-red, not reflexed.
COROLLA: crimson and red, single.
STAMENS: cherry-red.
PISTIL: cherry-red.
FOLIAGE: mid-green.
GROWTH: upright and bushy, with elastic, thin stalks.
A particularly attractive fuchsia with elegant, dainty flowers. Under good conditions it is even relatively hardy.

'Callaly Pink' (Ryle 1974, GB) No. 1334
TUBE: white, streaked pink.
SEPALS: white, underside pink, upright, green tips.

COROLLA: shrimp-pink, single.
STAMENS: pink.
PISTIL: whitish-pink.
FOLIAGE: mid-green, red midrib.
GROWTH: upright and bushy.
Medium-sized pink flowers of excellent substance. The plant is strong-growing and can be raised well as a bush or else as a standard. Very decorative and floriferous.

'Cameron Ryle' (Ryle 1971, GB) No. 1024
('Lena Dalton' × 'Citation')
TUBE: white.
SEPALS: white with green tips, underside rosy.
COROLLA: purple-blue, reddish when faded, semi-double.
STAMENS: pink.
PISTIL: white.
FOLIAGE: mid-green.
GROWTH: upright and bushy.
A particularly profusely flowering cultivar with medium-sized, handsome flowers in the white and blue combination so much desired.

'Candlelight' (Waltz 1959, USA) No. 391
TUBE: white.
SEPALS: white, underside pale pink.
COROLLA: violet and purple, fading to red, double.
STAMENS: pink.
PISTIL: white.
FOLIAGE: dark green.
GROWTH: upright.
As in many white and blue fuchsias, we also get the impression with this one that the plant is carrying two kinds of flowers. With such thickly foliaged fuchsias and succulent branches it is advisable to keep a good watch for *Botrytis* attack.

'Capri' (Schnabel-Paskesen 1960, USA) No. 418
TUBE: short and thick, greenish-white.
SEPALS: radiant white, with green tips, underside creped.
COROLLA: bluish-violet, fully double, with many petals.
STAMENS: pale pink.
PISTIL: white.
FOLIAGE: dark green, with red midrib.
GROWTH: lax-upright or trailer.
Only in the greenhouse in fact do the gigantic flowers reach their true beauty. If the name should give the impression of a blue as in the grotto of Capri, then the

reality unfortunately falls far short of the imagination.

'Cardinal Farges' (Rawlins 1958, GB)
(Sport of 'Abbé Farges')
TUBE: light red.
SEPALS: light red.
COROLLA: white with red veins, single to semi-double.
STAMENS: light red.
PISTIL: light red.
FOLIAGE: mid-green, small.
GROWTH: upright and bushy.
With the mutation only the flower colour has changed. All other characteristics, the well-branched growth, the early and enduring profuse flowering and good resistance to rain, are as in the original cultivar, unfortunately including the brittleness of the wood. A good show and garden plant.

'Carlisle Bells' (Mitchinson 1983, GB) No. 1744
TUBE: pale pink, streaked red.
SEPALS: white, long, underside pink.
COROLLA: blue, lighter at the base, single.
STAMENS: whitish-pink with red anthers.
PISTIL: whitish-pink, very long.
FOLIAGE: mid-green with red veins and stalks.
GROWTH: upright, well branched.
A plant with many outstanding features. If a cool, bright but not sunny place is found for it, the bright colours remain clean and pure for a long time and hardly change colour even when fading. Add to this, the enchanting wide-open bell shape of the flower, as we know it from 'Citation'. Plants stopped twice build themselves up to well-shaped, very harmoniously structured bushes. Also very well suited for standards.

'Carmel Blue' (Hodges 1956, USA) No. 247
TUBE: white, long.
SEPALS: white, green tips.
COROLLA: blue, fading to purple, single.
STAMENS: pink.
PISTIL: white.
FOLIAGE: mid-green.
GROWTH: upright and bushy.
The lovely blue of the elegant, long flowers unfortunately fades to a reddish-purple with age. The sun colours the initially snow-white tube and sepals pink. If the plant is kept in a cool and shady situation, this particularly beautiful colour combination can be enjoyed for longer. Look out for attack by red spider. Also known in the trade under the name of 'Bavaria'.

'Carnival' (Tiret 1956, USA) No. 250
TUBE: white and long.
SEPALS: snow-white and glossy, pale green on outside, curled back to the tube.
COROLLA: spiraea-red, very radiant, double.
STAMENS: white.
PISTIL: white.
FOLIAGE: grass-green.
GROWTH: lax bush or trailer.
These flowers compel attention and stand out best on a standard or raised on the espalier. A hanging basket with this cultivar will always make an impression as well.

'Caroline' (Miller 1967, GB)
TUBE: creamy-pink.
SEPALS: light pink, underside darker, green tips.
COROLLA: light lavender, pink at the base, single.
STAMENS: pink.
PISTIL: whitish-pink.
FOLIAGE: mid-green.
GROWTH: upright.
A lovely fuchsia which one would be delighted to possess. The fact that 'Citation' is the female parent cannot be missed in the shape of the flower; this classic shape is not all that common. Take special care with the watering-can and do not pot on to larger pots too quickly. Anybody who takes note of these two points will have success with it. A preventive treatment against *Botrytis*, especially in the spring, is also advisable.

'Cascade' (Lagen 1937, USA)
('Rolla' × 'Amy Lye')
TUBE: white with pink tinge.
SEPALS: white with pink tinge.
COROLLA: dark carmine-red, single.
STAMENS: pink.
PISTIL: pink.
FOLIAGE: light green, margins finely denticulate.
GROWTH: as a cascade.
'Cascade' is a perfect example of this growth type. The very flexible branches hang over the edge of the pot like a waterfall. Good basket plant which is also vigorous enough for larger structures.

'Caspar Hauser' (Springer 1983, G)
('Major Heaphy' ×)
TUBE: scarlet-red, glossy.
SEPALS: scarlet-red, glossy, underside creped.
COROLLA: mahogany-red (RHS 187C), each petal

edged black, double.
STAMENS: red.
PISTIL: red.
FOLIAGE: light green, red stalks, denticulate.
GROWTH: upright and bushy.
Anybody seeing 'Caspar Hauser' for the first time is fascinated by its matchless, quite distinctive colour combination. The flower with the handsomely rolled corolla and the exquisite, silky gloss on the petals is of good substance and therefore long-lasting.

The plant is strong-growing and branches well. No problems with overwintering. It is thus worthwhile bringing on large perennial plants which then flower in extreme profusion.

'Cecile' (Whitfield 1981, USA) No. 1609
TUBE: pink, short and thick.
SEPALS: pinkish-red, green tips, upright.
COROLLA: lavender-blue, pink base, double.
STAMENS: pink.
PISTIL: light pink.
FOLIAGE: mid-green, heart-shaped.
GROWTH: trailer.
This cultivar possesses all the marks of a good basket plant. Medium-sized, fully double flowers, each petal neatly folded and crimped. With good cultivation five plants should be sufficient to fill a 30-cm hanging basket.

'Celia Smedley' (Roe 1970, GB)
('Joy Patmore' × 'Glitters')
TUBE: greenish-white.
SEPALS: pinkish-white, underside darker and creped, with green tips.
COROLLA: pure redcurrant-red, not turning blue, white at the base, single.
STAMENS: pink.
PISTIL: white.
FOLIAGE: mid-green, denticulate.
GROWTH: rigidly upright, very strong-growing.
One of the best English cultivars, equally good as a pot plant or as a bedding plant, in sun or shadow. The rather rigid growth must be countered by frequent stopping. Makes a very attractive standard in one season.

'Centrepiece' (Fuchsia Forest 1964, USA) No. 604
TUBE: rose-red.
SEPALS: rose-red and broad.
COROLLA: pink petaloids surround the lavender-blue petals, semi-double.

STAMENS: pink.
PISTIL: white.
FOLIAGE: mid-green.
GROWTH: lax-upright.
Produces large flowers in profusion and for a long time. Particularly attractive as a hanging basket planted with at least five plants.

'Chang' (Hazard & Hazard 1946, USA)
TUBE: orange-red.
SEPALS: orange-red, underside lighter, green tips.
COROLLA: brilliant orange, single.
STAMENS: pale pink.
PISTIL: white.
FOLIAGE: large, light green.
GROWTH: upright, broadly spreading.
This seedling of *F. cordifolia* fascinates because of its not very big but radiant flowers of the most showy orange. Every bloom resembles a small pagoda. The growth is self-willed and even frequent stopping cannot change this much. Planted out as a standard, in a sunny spot in the garden, it is an unsurpassed eye-catcher.

'Charlotte' (Handley 1976, GB) No. 1366
TUBE: rosy-pink.
SEPALS: rosy-pink, steeply upright.
COROLLA: salmon-pink, single.
STAMENS: pale pink.
PISTIL: pale pink.
FOLIAGE: dark green, dentate, veined red, red stalks.
GROWTH: upright, bushy and well branched.
The beautifully shaped corolla consists of four almost round, slightly crimped and folded petals. Although this cultivar is not particularly strong-growing, it ought to yield a charming table standard.

'Charming' (Lye 1895, GB)
('Arabella Improved' × 'James Lye')
TUBE: carmine.
SEPALS: cherry-red, held high.
COROLLA: rosy-purple, lighter at the base, single.
STAMENS: red.
PISTIL: red.
FOLIAGE: light green, yellowish at tips of shoots.
GROWTH: upright and bushy.
An old cultivar, easy to grow, which in 1929 received a merit medal from the RHS.

'Checkerboard' (Walker & Jones 1948, USA)
TUBE: red and long.

SEPALS: basally red, merging to radiant white.
COROLLA: rather darker red, single.
STAMENS: white.
PISTIL: white.
FOLIAGE: dark green, denticulate.
GROWTH: upright.
The contrasting colour change of red and white is aptly described by the name 'Checkerboard'. A very robust fuchsia for every use. The profusion of flowers leaves nothing to be desired: this cultivar should have a place of honour in every collection. Standards of this cultivar grow very old.

'Cheers' (Annabella Stubbs 1979, USA) No. 1499
TUBE: coral-pink.
SEPALS: coral-pink, with pale pink streaks, underside darker, broad and tapering.
COROLLA: orange and red, strongly double with over 40 petals.
STAMENS: pink.
PISTIL: pink.
FOLIAGE: dark green, coarsely dentate.
GROWTH: lax-upright; will trail with weights.
With a few supports this new cultivar can be trained to a fine-looking bush with lovely flowers. Without supports it sufficiently fills a large hanging basket. A somewhat sheltered position is advisable.

'Cheviot Princess' (Ryle 1977, GB) No. 1433
('Pink Cloud' × 'Lena Dalton' seedling × 'Athela')
TUBE: white, short with characteristic thickening.
SEPALS: white, long, horizontal.
COROLLA: spiraea-red, lustrous, single, bell-shaped.
STAMENS: rosy.
PISTIL: white.
FOLIAGE: dark green, glossy.
GROWTH: bushy and well branched, upright, strong-growing.
Received a BFS silver Certificate of Merit in Manchester in 1977. A cultivar of a strong luminosity which is well suited for use in beds or balcony boxes.

'Chillerton Beauty' (Bass 1847, GB)
TUBE: light pink.
SEPALS: pale pink, underside darker, green tips.
COROLLA: purple, with pink veining, single.
STAMENS: whitish-pink.
PISTIL: pink.
FOLIAGE: mid-green.
GROWTH: upright and bushy.
This cultivar is almost 150 years old and is still cultivated. That alone speaks for the quality of this fuchsia. It is versatile in use and makes a good standard in a short time.

'Circe' (Kennett 1965, USA) No. 639
TUBE: pale pink.
SEPALS: pale pink.
COROLLA: consists of four large light blue petals surrounded by pink petaloids, semi-double.
STAMENS: pink.
PISTIL: whitish-pink.
FOLIAGE: mid-green, red stalks.
GROWTH: upright.
The pastel flowers open wide and are without exception of outstanding substance. The growth is also strong enough for larger training forms, e.g. standard.

'Citation' (Hodges 1953, USA) No. 153
TUBE: light red.
SEPALS: light red, narrow and steeply upright.
COROLLA: white, pink veins, single, large and bell-shaped.
STAMENS: light red.
PISTIL: light red.
FOLIAGE: mid-green, older leaves are veined red.
GROWTH: upright and bushy.
If this 'prima donna' among the fuchsias has its special needs fulfilled, is fed always at the right time and regularly, is placed in half shade and protected against *Botrytis*, it develops its large, generously shaped, beautiful flowers unremittingly. Hardly anyone can resist the classic beauty and charm of this out-of-the-ordinary flower shape.

'City of Pacifica' (Reedström 1962, USA) No. 546
TUBE: white.
SEPALS: white, very long and narrow.
COROLLA: light blue, fading to pink, double.
STAMENS: light pink.
PISTIL: light pink.
FOLIAGE: mid-green.
GROWTH: upright, long internodes.
The charm of the relatively large flowers lies in their pastel colours and their elegantly curved sepals. Unfortunately the plant is rather sparse-flowering. Requires without fail a shady position.

'Clair de Lune' (Rozain-Boucharlat, date unknown, F)
TUBE: pale orange-salmon, waxen.

SEPALS: pale orange, green tips, splayed.
COROLLA: yellowish-orange, single.
STAMENS: orange.
PISTIL: orange.
FOLIAGE: large, bronze-green.
GROWTH: lax-upright.
Strong-growing, prolific-flowering plant with long, elegant flowers of good substance. Very good also as a medium-tall standard, in which the head should consist of at least five tiers.

'Cloverdale Jewel' (Gadsby 1974, GB) No. 1218
('Cloverdale' × 'Lady Isobel Barnett')
TUBE: pink.
SEPALS: pink, upright.
COROLLA: wisteria-blue, pink-veined, semi-double.
STAMENS: pink.
PISTIL: whitish-pink.
FOLIAGE: mid-green.
GROWTH: upright and bushy.
This dainty plant with its medium-sized flowers blossoms profusely even in a small pot. Also very attractive as a miniature standard.

'Cloverdale Pearl' (Gadsby 1974, GB) No. 1219
(unknown seedling × 'Grace Darling')
TUBE: pinkish-white.
SEPALS: pink, darker at the edges, green tips.
COROLLA: pearl-white, slightly veined, single.
STAMENS: pink.
PISTIL: whitish-pink.
FOLIAGE: dark green, red midrib.
GROWTH: upright.
Very good cultivar with flowers of pearl-like quality, also easy to care for and branches well. In Britain exhibitors use this cultivar as a 'banker' (i.e. one that is 'sure' to gain an award).

'Coachman' (Bright, GB)
TUBE: light salmon-coloured.
SEPALS: light salmon-coloured, green tips.
COROLLA: orange-red, single.
STAMENS: pink.
PISTIL: light pink.
FOLIAGE: light green, large.
GROWTH: lax-upright and bushy.
This long-tried cultivar flowers profusely and early, but makes brief pauses in flowering. It likes a sunny position and needs to be fed well. The strong growth should be used for training large plants, which can become very old.

'Constance' (Berkeley Hort. Nursery 1935, USA)
TUBE: pink.
SEPALS: coral-pink, underside darker, green tips, creped.
COROLLA: plum-blue, pink ground, double.
STAMENS: coral-pink.
PISTIL: pink.
FOLIAGE: dark green, small and pointed, on reddish branches.
GROWTH: upright and bushy; in warm position lax-upright.
Striking, unusual, round flower shape on relatively long tube. Even the sepals surround the corolla in a perfect curve. This seedling of 'Pink Pearl' resembles the female parent apart from the darker corolla. Very many flowers, especially on older plants; problem-free in cultivation.

'Constellation' (Schnabel 1957, USA) No. 289
TUBE: white.
SEPALS: white, with green tips.
COROLLA: creamy-white, double.
STAMENS: white.
PISTIL: white.
FOLIAGE: dark green.
GROWTH: upright.
This is one of the best white fuchsias and, if it is repeatedly stopped as a young plant, quickly grows to a plant with many shoots. Keep in a cool and shady position.

'Contramine' (de Graaff 1978, NL)
('La Campanella' ×)
TUBE: white to light pink.
SEPALS: white to pink tinge, steeply upright.
COROLLA: violet, pink at the base, single.
STAMENS: pink.
PISTIL: white.
FOLIAGE: mid-green, red midrib.
GROWTH: upright, lax.
Dainty, bell-shaped flowers which project sideways and appear in prolific profusion even on quite young plants. This cultivar is not particularly strong-growing.

'Coquet Bell' (Ryle 1973, GB) No. 1114
('Lena Dalton' × 'Citation')
TUBE: rosy-pink.
SEPALS: pink, with green tips.
COROLLA: lavender, red-veined, pink at the base, single to semi-double.

STAMENS: dark pink.
PISTIL: whitish-pink.
FOLIAGE: mid-green.
GROWTH: upright.
A very compact-growing, abundantly flowering fuchsia which tolerates sun. It should also look good as a standard.

'Corsair' (Kennett 1965, USA) No. 640
TUBE: greenish-white.
SEPALS: white, green tips.
COROLLA: blue, later purple, white base and white streaks on the outer petals.
STAMENS: pale pink.
PISTIL: white.
FOLIAGE: dark green, red midrib.
GROWTH: upright.
Anyone would be delighted to possess fuchsias such as this, with such attractive flowers. They are, however, by no means so easy to cultivate. It is precisely the white and blue fuchsias that are almost all difficult and make particular demands. Even 'Venus Victrix', the original female parent of this fuchsia category, is fastidious. White and blue fuchsias can be divided in a rather simplified way into two groups. One has small, supple foliage on thin branches such as 'Carmel Blue' or 'Preston Guild'; the other group has strong, succulent shoots and large, sappy foliage such as 'Corsair'. Both demand painstaking cultivation in very porous soil and particular care with watering. They also unfold their full beauty only in the humid but well-ventilated greenhouse. Those with supple foliage are easily attacked by whitefly or red spider and the succulent types by *Botrytis*. A regular preventive spraying programme is therefore a must if one would like to get effective results with white and blue fuchsias.

'Countess of Aberdeen' (Dobbie-Forbes 1888, GB)
TUBE: creamy-white.
SEPALS: pale pink.
COROLLA: creamy-white with slight pink tinge, single.
STAMENS: pale pink.
PISTIL: white.
FOLIAGE: mid-green, small.
GROWTH: upright, bushy.
This very popular and charming old cultivar has a very bushy growth with short internodes and is therefore prone to *Botrytis*. Does not particularly like too much stopping and cuttings often need a long time to root. It is best propagated in the spring from quite

soft shoot tips. If it can stand in a sheltered, shady spot, the flowers remain pure white and the entire magic of the delicate flowers, which appear in enormous masses, can develop to the full. At shows, it is presented to advantage as a table standard.

'Crinoline' (Reiter 1950, USA)
TUBE: green and white.
SEPALS: white, green tips.
COROLLA: light, rosy lavender, double.
STAMENS: light pink.
PISTIL: white.
FOLIAGE: mid-green.
GROWTH: upright.
The plant is of compact, unusually tidy growth and flowers in enormous profusion and for a long time.

'Curtain Call' (Munkner 1961, USA) No. 479
TUBE: pink to carmine-red.
SEPALS: pink to carmine-red.
COROLLA: Bengal-pink to carmine-red, double, each petal has delicate tooth-marks at the lower edge.
STAMENS: pink.
PISTIL: whitish-pink.
FOLIAGE: dark green, large and glossy.
GROWTH: lax-upright; will trail with weights.
The flowers are large and well shaped. Four of them always appear in each leaf-axil (usually there are only two). This cultivar is easy to confuse with 'Cara Mia', which, however, is not so fully double and does not have the dentate petals either.

'Cyndy Robin' (Stubbs 1982, USA) No. 1662
('Applause' × 'Snowfire')
TUBE: flesh-coloured, short.
SEPALS: light pink to pink, broad, long.
COROLLA: pink to coral-red, double.
STAMENS: pink.
PISTIL: whitish-pink.
FOLIAGE: mid-green, sharply dentate.
GROWTH: trailer.
Like many Stubbs introductions this one, too, is a good, strong-growing hanging-basket plant. It produces batches of very large flowers which open wide as they develop. The position should be shady but as bright as possible so that the flowers acquire their full colours.

'Cyril Holmes' (R. Holmes 1976, GB) No. 1336
('Percy Holmes' × 'Hidcote Beauty')
TUBE: white, waxen.

SEPALS: white, underside reddish, green tips.

COROLLA: salmon-pink, single.

STAMENS: short, hardly protruding beyond the corolla.

PISTIL: white, very long.

FOLIAGE: light green, heart-shaped.

GROWTH: upright and bushy.

The attractive pale foliage forms a perfect background for the exquisitely shaped pastel flowers. The four sepals in the single corolla are undulate and almost angular. Strong-growing and versatile in use, including for larger, ornamental forms.

'Daisy Bell' (introduced by Mieseke, USA, breeder unknown) No. 1420

TUBE: white with orange tinge.

SEPALS: light orange with green tips.

COROLLA: salmon-pink, green tips, single.

STAMENS: pale pink.

PISTIL: cream.

FOLIAGE: light green with copper-red centre.

GROWTH: trailer.

Strong-growing, effective trailing cultivar which looks particularly good in wall baskets. Exceptionally profusely flowering. Like all variegated fuchsias it is susceptible to overwatering. Pretty and unusual.

'Dancing Flame' (Stubbs 1981, USA) No. 1621 ('Novella' × 'Applause')

TUBE: light orange, streaked darker, short.

SEPALS: orange, the underside somewhat darker.

COROLLA: orange and carmine, darker centre, double.

STAMENS: pink.

PISTIL: pink.

FOLIAGE: mid-green, serrated leaf margin.

GROWTH: lax-upright.

Most cultivars from California love warm conditions and are particularly colourful in hot periods of weather. In 'Dancing Flame' the first flowers on young plants lack substance, but this situation returns to normal with increasing physiological maturity. Three plants are enough to fill a 30-cm hanging basket.

'Danny Boy' (Tiret 1961, USA) No. 483

TUBE: white to light pink.

SEPALS: light pink, underside dark pink, creped, upright.

COROLLA: dark red, outer petals mixed orange, large-flowered, double.

STAMENS: pink.

PISTIL: whitish-pink.

FOLIAGE: dark green.

GROWTH: upright, strong-growing.

In proportion to the size of the flowers this cultivar is very floriferous and the plant structure is strong enough to bear this rich display.

'Daphne Arlene' (Putley 1948, GB) (Synonymous with 'Shuna')

TUBE: waxen-white.

SEPALS: waxen-white, broad and short.

COROLLA: coral-pink, single.

STAMENS: white.

PISTIL: white.

FOLIAGE: truncated, dark green, small.

GROWTH: upright.

A sport of 'Countess of Aberdeen' with small, roundish flowers of stronger colours. As the plant grows only very slowly, it is particularly suitable for pot cultivation and flowers prolifically even in small pots.

'Dark Eyes' (Erickson 1958, USA) No. 351

TUBE: carmine.

SEPALS: carmine.

COROLLA: clear violet and blue, pink ground, double, particularly beautiful camelia-type flowers.

STAMENS: pink.

PISTIL: pink.

FOLIAGE: mid-green, glossy, red leaf veins.

GROWTH: spreading, lax-upright.

Of the red and blue fuchsias this is one of the most beautiful of all. It branches well but must be adequately supported because of the abundant heavy flowers.

'Dark Secret' (Hodges 1957, USA) No. 300

TUBE: greenish-white.

SEPALS: waxen-white outside, underside pale pink, green tips, creped, broad.

COROLLA: dark violet, outer petals with pink patches, double.

STAMENS: white.

PISTIL: white.

FOLIAGE: dark green.

GROWTH: upright, bushy.

Like all large-flowered white and blue fuchsias this one, too, needs to be looked after with some care, especially when watering. The magnificent flowers, however, are ample compensation for all the effort.

'David Lockyer' (Mrs E. Holmes 1968, GB)

TUBE: white.

SEPALS: white.

COROLLA: dark red and light red with white streaks, double.

STAMENS: light pink.

PISTIL: white.

FOLIAGE: dark green.

GROWTH: upright.

Characteristic of this cultivar is the second corolla which grows out of the thick centre of the first and causes the flower to appear very long.

'Dee Copley' (Copley Gardens 1964, USA) No. 617

TUBE: pink to light red, long and thin.

SEPALS: light red, broad, upright, creped.

COROLLA: very beautiful royal blue, red stripes in the folds of the petals, double.

STAMENS: pinkish-red.

PISTIL: pinkish-red.

FOLIAGE: dark green.

GROWTH: upright and elastic.

Very colourful and lovely cultivar. The medium-sized flowers cover the plant almost completely at times.

'Derby Imp' (Gadsby 1974, GB) No. 1220

TUBE: light red.

SEPALS: light red.

COROLLA: blue, fading to purple, single.

STAMENS: light red.

PISTIL: light red.

FOLIAGE: mid-green.

GROWTH: lax-upright; with support also as bush.

Only a dainty little flower but very prettily shaped. Several plants together in a hanging basket are freely covered with flowers; may need weights.

'Derby Star' (Gadsby 1975, GB)

('Cliffs Hardy' × 'Shy Look')

TUBE: pinkish-white.

SEPALS: pinkish-white, horizontal.

COROLLA: wisteria-blue, white base, slightly veined, single.

STAMENS: pink, almost enclosed.

PISTIL: pink, very long.

FOLIAGE: dark green.

GROWTH: horizontal, broadly spreading, well branched.

The growth of this cultivar is rigid and each new branch again pushes out horizontally. Even with every possible device it is still impossible to obtain a properly shaped bush. The very pretty, delicate

flowers are also held sidewards and upwards on long, strong stalks.

'Deutsche Kaiserin' (Weinrich 1870, G)

TUBE: carmine-red.

SEPALS: carmine-red.

COROLLA: carmine-red, single to semi-double.

STAMENS: carmine-red.

PISTIL: carmine-red.

FOLIAGE: dark green, suffused red.

GROWTH: trailer.

Also an irrepressible, older balcony fuchsia which one can still come across now and then. Profusely flowering with elongated, rather sombre flowers.

'Diana Wills' (Gadsby 1968, GB) No. 976

TUBE: white, waxen.

SEPALS: white, green tips, held obliquely downwards.

COROLLA: spiraea-red, outer petals with white and pink streams, double.

STAMENS: pink.

PISTIL: white.

FOLIAGE: mid-green, red veining.

GROWTH: upright and bushy, medium-tall.

Is particularly happy in half shade and then produces a mass of its charming, very colourful flowers.

Later breeds from Cliff Gadsby have perhaps become more popular. It is, however, worth while looking for this cultivar.

'Dilly Dilly' (Tiret 1963, USA) No. 577

TUBE: white.

SEPALS: light pink, underside pink, green tips.

COROLLA: light blue to lavender, pink base, double.

STAMENS: pink.

PISTIL: light pink.

FOLIAGE: mid-green, large, serrulate margin.

GROWTH: lax-upright; will trail with weights.

For a plant with relatively large flowers in such delicate pastel colours its cultivation is simple and problem-free. It is particularly suitable as a hanging-basket plant, but can also be raised as a decorative pot plant using a few stakes.

'Dirk van Delen' (Steevens 1971, NL)

TUBE: light pink.

SEPALS: pink with green tips.

COROLLA: pink, single.

STAMENS: light pink.

PISTIL: light pink.

FOLIAGE: dark green.

GROWTH: upright and bushy.

This strong-growing, enormously prolific pot and bedding cultivar also makes a standard with a beautiful head in a short time.

'Display' (Smith 1881, GB)
TUBE: rose-red.
SEPALS: rose-red.
COROLLA: pink, single.
STAMENS: pink.
PISTIL: pink.
FOLIAGE: mid-green.
GROWTH: bushy and well branched.

The almost unicoloured flowers of the coolie's hat type are pretty and unusual. The plant possesses a robust root system and for that reason has long proved itself as a bedding plant. With only two stoppings a many-branched, profusely flowering bush can be obtained which hardly needs to be supported. The growing power is sufficient for all larger forms of training such as standard, pillar or pyramid.

'Dollar Princess' (Lemoine 1912, F)
TUBE: cerise.
SEPALS: cerise, upright.
COROLLA: dark purple, double.
STAMENS: red.
PISTIL: red.
FOLIAGE: dark green.
GROWTH: lax-upright and bushy.

A versatile cultivar with rather small but perfectly shaped flowers in large masses. Charming as a small stem.

'Dominyana' (Dominy 1852, GB)
(Originally quoted as *F. spectabilis* × *F. serratifolia* but now considered to be *F. macrostigma* × *F. denticulata*)
TUBE: long, scarlet-red.
SEPALS: short, scarlet-red.
COROLLA: short, scarlet-red, single.
STAMENS: red.
PISTIL: red.
FOLIAGE: bronze-red to dark red, large.
GROWTH: rigidly upright, tall, must be stopped frequently and early.

The trumpet-shaped, long flowers develop very slowly and last for a long time, being of outstanding substance. Young plants and badly fed ones flower sparsely. If older specimens which have flowered in winter in the greenhouse are planted out at the end of May in a warm, sheltered spot in the garden, they flower there for a second time in particular profusion.

'Dorothea Flower' (Thornley 1969, GB) No. 1009
('Hawkshead' × 'Venus Victrix')
TUBE: white, long.
SEPALS: white on outside, underside pale pink.
COROLLA: bluish-violet with pink base, single.
STAMENS: pink.
PISTIL: whitish-pink, very long.
FOLIAGE: mid-green, red midrib.
GROWTH: upright and bushy, slow-growing.

The entire plant makes a graceful and elegant impression. It stands out to particular advantage in a wall basket at eye level. Its susceptibility to *Botrytis*, especially in winter, should be borne in mind and guarded against accordingly.

'Dr Topinard' (Lemoine 1890, F)
TUBE: light red.
SEPALS: light red.
COROLLA: white, red veins, single.
STAMENS: pink.
PISTIL: whitish-pink.
FOLIAGE: dark green.
GROWTH: upright, bushy.

There are still many cultivars from the very productive French breeder Lemoine in circulation. This clearly speaks for their quality. The medium-sized flowers with widely exposed, plate-shaped corolla which appear in masses and without a break are particularly fine-looking.

'Duchess of Albany' (Rundle 1891, GB)
TUBE: creamy-white, waxen.
SEPALS: creamy-white.
COROLLA: cherry-pink, single.
STAMENS: pink.
PISTIL: white.
FOLIAGE: light green, slightly pilose.
GROWTH: upright, strong-growing.

The medium-sized, elegant flowers in their bright colours are very attractive and have a particularly harmonious effect on a well-raised standard.

'Dutch Mill' (Petersen 1962, USA)
TUBE: light red.
SEPALS: light red.
COROLLA: light blue and violet, lighter at the bottom, pink veins, single.

STAMENS: pink.
PISTIL: pink.
FOLIAGE: mid-green, red-veined.
GROWTH: upright.
Very strong, somewhat disorderly growth with natural, prolific branching. Well suited to planting out in beds, at the least it should be cultivated in larger pots. Profuse flowerer with exquisite flower shape through which the name is aptly chosen, for the sepals give the impression of windmill sails.

'Earl of Beaconsfield' (Laing 1878, GB)
(*F. fulgens* × 'Perfection')
TUBE: salmon-pink, very long, of wax-like substance.
SEPALS: salmon-pink with green tips.
COROLLA: salmon-orange, short, single.
STAMENS: pink, short.
PISTIL: salmon-pink.
FOLIAGE: relatively large, light green.
GROWTH: lax-upright.
Anyone who does not yet have this beautiful cultivar with its long, elegant flowers in his or her collection should look out for it. It is really worth its becoming more widespread. Early stopping is important. With a few stakes to support the initially loose growth, a very attractive bush can be formed.

'East Anglian' (Thorne 1960, GB)
TUBE: flesh-pink.
SEPALS: pink with red streaks.
COROLLA: pink with orange, single.
STAMENS: pink.
PISTIL: white.
FOLIAGE: mid-green, red when older.
GROWTH: stiffly upright.
The large flowers are of waxen substance and remain attractive for a long time. This cultivar could also yield a fine standard. On its introduction it immediately received several awards. Although the plant seems robust, it still loves a sheltered position.

'Easter Bonnet' (Waltz 1955, USA) No. 225
TUBE: pink.
SEPALS: pink, white and green tips.
COROLLA: deep pink, darker at the base, double.
STAMENS: pink.
PISTIL: white.
FOLIAGE: olive-green.
GROWTH: lax-upright.
A good, versatile, double, pink cultivar, which has received an award in America.

'Eleanor Clark' (Clark Dave & Fuchsiavale 1980, GB) No. 1539
TUBE: phlox-pink, streaked darker.
SEPALS: phlox-pink, held high.
COROLLA: shrimp-pink, darker-veined, single.
STAMENS: pink.
PISTIL: pink.
FOLIAGE: light green, small, dentate.
GROWTH: upright and bushy.
This sport of the well-tested cultivar 'Symphony' has more subdued colours which remain at their best in the shade. Versatile in use, but particularly good as an ornamental bush.

'Eleanor Leytham' (Roe 1973, GB)
('Countess of Aberdeen' × 'Pink Darling')
TUBE: white.
SEPALS: white with slight pink flush.
COROLLA: baby-pink, single.
STAMENS: white.
PISTIL: white.
FOLIAGE: small, light green, creped.
GROWTH: stiffly upright.
The dainty flowers on a correspondingly dainty plant have a quite special charm.

'Elisabeth' (Nutzinger 1966, A)
('El Camino' × 'W. Churchill')
TUBE: light red.
SEPALS: light red, shiny.
COROLLA: light blue, rosette-shaped, small-flowered, double.
STAMENS: pink.
PISTIL: pink.
FOLIAGE: small, dark green.
GROWTH: upright.
Very good pot and bedding cultivar of neat growth and profusely flowering. Each flower looks like a pretty small rosette.

'Elise Mitchell' (Ryle 1980, GB) No. 1576
TUBE: pink.
SEPALS: pink, white towards the tip, green tips.
COROLLA: quite light lavender, pink on some petals, double.
STAMENS: pink.
PISTIL: white.
FOLIAGE: mid-green, denticulate, small.
GROWTH: upright, well branched.
The enchanting, gentle colours develop best in shade. With a bit of protection from the weather it is very good as a pot or balcony plant.

'Elizabeth' (Whiteman 1941(?), GB)
TUBE: opal-pink, very long.
SEPALS: opal-pink, green tips.
COROLLA: rose-red, single.
STAMENS: light pink.
PISTIL: light pink.
FOLIAGE: mid-green and large.
GROWTH: upright and vigorous.
The long, elegant flowers are so beautiful that one willingly puts up with the difficulty of raising a good plant from this cultivar. It is best shown off in a wall basket.

'Emile de Wildeman' (Lemoine 1905, F)
(syn. 'Fascination')
TUBE: red.
SEPALS: carmine-red, waxen.
COROLLA: pink, veined cerise, double.
STAMENS: cerise.
PISTIL: cerise.
FOLIAGE: mid-green with red veins.
GROWTH: upright and bushy.
A well-proven cultivar but it does prefer a sheltered position under cover. In the greenhouse it begins to flower early in the year as one of the first fuchsias. Even on the windowsill in a not-too-warm room it holds out well.

'Enchanted' (Tiret 1951, USA)
('Titanic' × 'Yuletide')
TUBE: rose-red.
SEPALS: rose-red.
COROLLA: very beautiful mid-blue, speckled red, large double flower.
STAMENS: pink.
PISTIL: light pink.
FOLIAGE: mid-green.
GROWTH: lax-upright.
This sibling seedling of 'Swingtime' is a particularly beautiful cultivar for balcony boxes and tubs and flowers in great profusion.

'Ernestine' (Stubbs 1981, USA) No. 1616
(('Trade Winds' × 'Dee Dee') × 'Fan Tan')
TUBE: flesh-coloured.
SEPALS: orange-pink.
COROLLA: orange and scarlet, double.
STAMENS: pink.
PISTIL: light pink.
FOLIAGE: mid-green, large, serrated leaf margin.
GROWTH: upright.

'Ernestine', like all Stubbs breeds, is vigorous and strong-growing. As the large flowers pull the branches down, it must be unobtrusively supported and tied in good time. The firm foliage is shunned by pests. This cultivar has good resistance to heat.

'Estelle Marie' (Newton 1973, USA) No. 1082
TUBE: green and white.
SEPALS: white with green tips.
COROLLA: blue with white base, fades to purple, single.
STAMENS: whitish-pink.
PISTIL: white.
FOLIAGE: small, dark green.
GROWTH: upright.
Although the parentage is not known for certain, we can assume that 'Bon Accord' is one of the parents. Habits, leaf shape and not least the upright-held flowers allude to this. The pure blue in the corolla and the markedly larger flower are—if you like—an improvement on 'Bon Accord'.

'Evensong' (Colville 1967, GB)
TUBE: pink.
SEPALS: white with green tips, pink at the base, upright.
COROLLA: white, single.
STAMENS: whitish-pink.
PISTIL: white.
FOLIAGE: light green.
GROWTH: upright.
In the greenhouse, raised in the pot as a bush or in a roofed-over patio position, the classic, almost white flowers come into effect well. Easy-to-grow white fuchsias such as this are rare.

'Falling Stars' (Reiter senior 1941, USA)
('Morning Mist' × 'Cascade')
TUBE: scarlet-red.
SEPALS: scarlet-red, underside orange-red.
COROLLA: very dark, almost brown, velvety red, single.
STAMENS: pink.
PISTIL: light pink.
FOLIAGE: light green, suffused bronze.
GROWTH: lax-upright.
From the point of view of flower colour an extraordinary fuchsia. Raised as a standard the flowers are particularly striking at eye level. To achieve a thick head, the shoots with their relatively long internodes must be frequently pinched. One of the few fuchsias which not only tolerates full sun but actually needs it.

'Fan Dancer' (Castro 1962, USA) No. 513
TUBE: carmine-red.
SEPALS: carmine-red.
COROLLA: lavender with pink and red spots, pink-veined, double.
STAMENS: pink.
PISTIL: red.
FOLIAGE: mid-green.
GROWTH: lax bush or trailer.
The special thing about this colourful cultivar is the almost square flower shape and a peculiarly shaped seed-vessel. Unfortunately it is difficult to raise to a reasonably good shape. It is easier with two-year-old plants on the framework of old wood.

'Fanfare' (Reiter senior 1941, USA)
(*F. denticulata* × *F. leptopoda*)
TUBE: red, streaked carmine, very long.
SEPALS: red with green tips.
COROLLA: orange, single, tiny.
STAMENS: pink.
PISTIL: pink.
FOLIAGE: dark green, large and glossy.
GROWTH: upright with pendulous lateral branches.
If 'Fanfare' is not stopped it quickly grows a metre tall and on the pendulous side shoots produces the very beautiful, elegant, often 8-cm long flowers in clusters. Even with frequent stopping it makes only an upright bush. It is valuable on account of its late flowering, which in the greenhouse persists over the winter.

'Ferdinand Mahnke' (Mahnke 1910, G)
TUBE: red.
SEPALS: red.
COROLLA: white with red veining, single.
STAMENS: red.
PISTIL: pink.
FOLIAGE: dark green, small.
GROWTH: upright and bushy.
A long-tested, profusely flowering bedding cultivar which can still be met with frequently.

'Fiery Spider' (Munkner 1960, USA) No. 452
TUBE: reddish, long.
SEPALS: orange, tips green, long and narrow.
COROLLA: red with orange, single.
STAMENS: pink.
PISTIL: whitish-pink.
FOLIAGE: light green.
GROWTH: trailer.

This elegant flower is really beautiful, consisting of nothing but Gothic arches (these unusual flowers, with the tips still joined while the flower is half open, give the effect of bowed arches). Three to five plants in a hanging basket are sufficient.

'Fiona' (Clark W. 1958, GB)
(Jones Cup and Award of Merit of the BFS 1958)
TUBE: white.
SEPALS: white with green tips.
COROLLA: beautiful blue, fading to reddish-purple, single.
STAMENS: pink.
PISTIL: white.
FOLIAGE: mid-green.
GROWTH: lax-upright.
This cultivar is very strong-growing and because of its long, overhanging shoots it needs a lot of space. The long, elegant sepals open only gradually and over one to two days form a lovely lantern which frames the bright blue corolla and causes it to shine through. It reaches its full beauty, though, only in a position under cover sheltered from rain.

'Fire Mountain' (Stubbs 1980, USA) No. 1536
('Novella' × ('Applause' × 'Bicentennial'))
TUBE: flesh-coloured.
SEPALS: pale orange and pink.
COROLLA: orange and carmine, marked with orange, double.
STAMENS: flesh-coloured.
PISTIL: cream.
FOLIAGE: mid-green, red veins, serrulate.
GROWTH: lax-upright semi-trailer.
In the shade the plant has good resistance to heat. For the flowers to acquire their proper colours requires a bright position. In young plants the corolla may turn out less full—i.e. single rather than double flowers.

'First Lady' (Stubbs 1973, USA) No. 1080
('Pink Galore' × 'White King')
TUBE: pink.
SEPALS: pink, with darker streaks, becoming lighter towards the tips.
COROLLA: deep pink, double, with dentate petals.
STAMENS: dark pink.
PISTIL: pink.
FOLIAGE: dark green with red veins.
GROWTH: lax-upright semi-trailer.
Better for the greenhouse or for very sheltered places, where it must be kept in a cool and shady position. Care required with repotting, watering and feeding.

'Fiery Spider'

'Fiona'

Enchanting, large, round flowers, always individually separated.

'Flashlight' (Gadsby 1971, GB) No. 977
TUBE: light pink.
SEPALS: light pink, green tips.
COROLLA: pale lilac-pink, single.
STAMENS: light pink.
PISTIL: white.
FOLIAGE: light green.
GROWTH: medium upright.
This seedling of 'Flash' × *F. magellanica* var. *molinae* forms a neat bush, studded with miniature flowers. It ought to derive a certain hardiness from its parents. All tests in this respect, however, have come to nothing. On a table standard the delicately coloured flowers make a beautiful show.

'Flirtation Waltz' (Waltz 1962, USA) No. 523
TUBE: white.
SEPALS: white, underside pink, green tips.
COROLLA: pale pink, double.
STAMENS: pink.
PISTIL: white.

FOLIAGE: light green.
GROWTH: upright.
An exceptionally good fuchsia. The upright growth is self-supporting and branches quite naturally. Raised up on a stake it forms without much trouble a pillar that flowers all over, or if planted out—though in the

'Elizabeth'

shade—is a very decorative bedding plant. The hybridiser Waltz has developed a number of outstanding fuchsias.

'Florentina' (Tiret 1960, USA) No. 432
TUBE: snow-white, long.
SEPALS: snow-white, fused with the corolla.
COROLLA: burgundy-red, double.
STAMENS: pink.
PISTIL: whitish-pink.
FOLIAGE: mid-green, red-veined, red stalks.
GROWTH: lax-upright to semi-trailer.
The large flowers have an unusual, very attractive colour combination which strikes the eye. The plant is problem-free and with good cultivation flowers very profusely.

'Flowerdream' (Rijff 1983, NL)
('Merry Mary' × 'Bora Bora')
TUBE: white with violet stripes.
SEPALS: white, underside pink.
COROLLA: white with carmine-red areas, double.
STAMENS: pink.
PISTIL: white.
FOLIAGE: mid-green, matt, red stalks.
GROWTH: trailer.
A good sun-tolerant, profusely flowering new cultivar. The brighter the position, the better colours the flowers develop.

'Flyaway' (Crockett 1965, GB) No. 820
TUBE: greenish-white.
SEPALS: white, underside pink, steeply upright.
COROLLA: violet and purple, pink at the base, double.
STAMENS: pink.
PISTIL: whitish-pink.
FOLIAGE: mid-green, large.
GROWTH: upright.
Large-flowered, floriferous cultivar. Succulent branches on the thickly foliaged bush demand our watchfulness for *Botrytis*. Otherwise a good, robust fuchsia in sun or shade.

'Flying Cloud' (Reiter 1949, USA)
TUBE: white, long, about 13 mm.
SEPALS: white.
COROLLA: white, slightly veined pink at the base, double.
STAMENS: pale pink.
PISTIL: white.
FOLIAGE: dark green.

'Flowerdream'

'First Lady'

'Frauke'

GROWTH: rather flatly spreading; as a bush must therefore be supported.

'Flying Cloud' was one of the first white, double fuchsias from America and has lost none of its popularity. Like all white fuchsias, it must be cultivated in shade. In the sun the flowers become pink. Very good as a standard.

'Foolke' (Bögemann 1984, G)
(*F. excorticata* × 'Ting-a-Ling' seedling × *F. perscandens* × *F. magellanica* var. *molinae* seedling)
TUBE: long, shiny like wax, dark lilac (RHS 64[a]).
SEPALS: narrow, acute horizontal, dark lilac.
COROLLA: aubergine (RHS 187[a]) fading to deep wine-red (RHS 187[b]), single.
STAMENS: violet with blue pollen.
PISTIL: violet, stigma cream.
FOLIAGE: mid-green, small, tapering.
GROWTH: rigidly upright with long internodes.
Unthought-of possibilities lie hidden in the almost inexhaustible, complex gene potential of the genus *Fuchsia* and its cultivars. 'Foolke' is a fine example of this. If a hybridiser ventures to incorporate new species in cross-breeding, as Lutz Bögemann has here with the two 'New Zealanders' from the section *Skinnera*, then such sensational, completely new colour combinations are the outcome. Even the bright blue pollen of the species has turned up again. The gracefully designed flowers are of outstanding substance and remain fresh for a long time. Perhaps Lutz Bögemann will succeed—in a further generation—in presenting these magnificent flowers on a well-branched compact plant.

'Forget-Me-Not' (Banks 1866, GB)
TUBE: light pink.
SEPALS: light pink.
COROLLA: light blue, older flowers mauve, single.
STAMENS: pink.
PISTIL: pink.
FOLIAGE: mid-green, glossy.
GROWTH: upright.
The small-flowered fuchsias with their abundant wealth of blossom are particularly charming. This old cultivar is versatile in use. Stopping must be begun early, though, so that the plant becomes bushy.

'François Villon' (de Graaff 1978, NL)
TUBE: creamy-white, long.
SEPALS: creamy-white, underside pink, horizontal.

COROLLA: dark brick-red, single.
STAMENS: pink.
PISTIL: pink, very long.
FOLIAGE: mid-green.
GROWTH: trailer.
An exceptionally floriferous cultivar with medium-sized, narrow, elegant flowers. The growth, which immediately at the rim of the pot drops downwards like a cascade, is well suited for filling hanging baskets or baskets.

'Franz Noszian' (Nutzinger 1976, A)
('Coralle' × (*F. boliviana* × *F. splendens*))
TUBE: rose-red, short and compact.
SEPALS: rose-red.
COROLLA: light pink with darker veins, semi-double.
STAMENS: rose-red.
PISTIL: rose-red.
FOLIAGE: mid-green, small leaves.
GROWTH: upright and bushy.
As in many Nutzinger breeds, here, too, we find an enormous wealth of flowers on a robust, problem-free plant.

'Frau Hilde Rademacher' (Rademacher 1925, G)
TUBE: scarlet-red.
SEPALS: scarlet-red.
COROLLA: brilliant lilac and blue with pink spots, double.
STAMENS: cerise.
PISTIL: cerise.
FOLIAGE: mid-green with red veins.
GROWTH: lax-upright.
The blue of the corolla is particularly picturesque. As a plant very robust and also suitable for the garden. In a well-sheltered place it has been hardy for several years. Branches well and flowers very profusely.

'Frau Ida Noak' (Lemoine 1911, F)
TUBE: red.
SEPALS: red.
COROLLA: violet, double.
STAMENS: red.
PISTIL: pink.
FOLIAGE: dark green.
GROWTH: upright and bushy.
An incredibly early and profusely flowering old cultivar. Unfortunately, under this name one is almost always offered 'Display', especially in Holland. The two cultivars are, however, so different in flower shape and colour that it is well worth while looking out for the real 'Frau Ida Noak'.

'Frauke' (Bögemann 1981, G)
('Speciosa' × 'Ting-a-Ling')
TUBE: long, thin, apricot and salmon-pink.
SEPALS: narrow, pointed, at start like the tube, then cream with green tips.
COROLLA: salmon-orange, single.
STAMENS: salmon-pink, almost enclosed.
PISTIL: cream, long.
FOLIAGE: grey-green, finely pilose.
GROWTH: upright, slightly lax.
This new cultivar from the Ostfriesland region of West Germany shows good resistance to weather and heat, thus an excellent plant for sunny garden beds. It flowers without interruption, predominantly at the tips of the shoots.

'Frosted Flame' (Handley 1975, GB) No. 1273
TUBE: white and waxen.
SEPALS: white outside, pale pink inside, long and narrow, green tips.
COROLLA: brilliant fiery-red with darker edge, paler lines at bottom, single.
STAMENS: whitish-pink.
PISTIL: pink.
FOLIAGE: grass-green.
GROWTH: trailer.
Of the numerous new good cultivars with which the late English hybridist Enid Handley of Derby enriched the fuchsia world over the last ten years and more, this is one of the best. The magnificence and number of the bright and beautiful flowers is so great that one is hardly aware of any foliage among them.

'Gay Fandango' (Nelson 1951, USA)
TUBE: dark pink.
SEPALS: dark pink, underside bright light red.
COROLLA: purple and pink with orange, pink at the base, double.
STAMENS: cherry-red.
PISTIL: pink.
FOLIAGE: mid-green, in whorls of three or four.
GROWTH: lax-upright.
Strong-growing and versatile, including as a standard. Older plants in particular flower in great profusion. The denticulate leaves arranged in whorls and the exceptionally good branching create a promising situation for the raising of large plants.

'Gay Senorita' (Schmidt 1939, USA)
('Heron' × 'Pride of Exeter')

TUBE: red.
SEPALS: red.
COROLLA: lilac and pink, single.
STAMENS: red.
PISTIL: pink.
FOLIAGE: dark green.
GROWTH: upright.
The early flowering and the beautiful, campanulate, large flowers are plus points for this very popular and widespread cultivar. Particularly attractive in balcony boxes or tubs.

'General Monk' (not known)
TUBE: cherry-red.
SEPALS: cherry-red.
COROLLA: beautiful almost pure blue, white at bottom, pink-veined, double.
STAMENS: cherry-red.
PISTIL: cherry-red.
FOLIAGE: mid-green, small.
GROWTH: upright, well branched; hardy in most districts.
Does not grow very tall, so good as pot plant or for edge planting in the garden.

'Genni' (Fuchsia-La Nursery 1968, USA) No. 801
TUBE: light cerise.
SEPALS: light cerise, very long and rolled up, green tips.
COROLLA: white, red-veined, semi-double.
STAMENS: light pink.
PISTIL: whitish-pink.
FOLIAGE: mid-green, large, red-veined, red stalks.
GROWTH: lax bush or trailer.
Fast-growing basket plant. The elegantly rolled, very narrow, long sepals are particularly attractive and characteristic of this cultivar.

'Georgana' (Tiret 1955, USA)
TUBE: pink.
SEPALS: pink, underside darker, green tips.
COROLLA: dark lavender with pink areas and pink-veined, double.
STAMENS: dark pink.
PISTIL: pink.
FOLIAGE: mid-green and large.
GROWTH: upright.
Very large flowers which are numerous and almost too heavy for the plant's structure. Support necessary. Good feeding clearly stimulates flower development.

'Fire Mountain'

'Groenekan's Glorie'

'Gesäuseperle' (Nutzinger 1946, A)
TUBE: white.
SEPALS: white.
COROLLA: rose-red, single.
STAMENS: pink and white.
PISTIL: white.
FOLIAGE: mid-green.
GROWTH: lax-upright, strong-growing.
This cultivar emerged from the first attempt by the Austrian hybridist Nutzinger to obtain new fuchsias. A strong-growing, robust plant which produces large flowers unremittingly and is well suited for balcony boxes or large tubs. It is confusingly similar to the old cultivar 'Amelie Aubin'.

'Glendale' (Evans and Reeves 1936, USA)
TUBE: coral-pink.
SEPALS: coral-pink.
COROLLA: coral-pink, single.
STAMENS: coral-pink.
PISTIL: coral-pink.
FOLIAGE: mid-green.
GROWTH: upright, strong and bushy.
This self-coloured cross between *F. lycioides* and 'Fireflush' flowers very profusely and early in clusters at the end of the shoot. Good for using as bedding plant or for larger tubs.

'Glitters' (Erickson 1963, USA) No. 579
TUBE: waxy-white.
SEPALS: waxy-white, underside salmon-coloured.
COROLLA: orange-red, single.
STAMENS: pink.

PISTIL: pink.
FOLIAGE: mid-green.
GROWTH: upright, strong.
Medium-sized flowers are produced in incredible amounts on strong, very tall-growing plants. Cultivation presents no problems. Particularly good bedding cultivar for positions in full sun.

'Golden Dawn' (Haag 1951, USA)
TUBE: salmon-pink.
SEPALS: salmon-pink.
COROLLA: reddish-orange, single.
STAMENS: pink.
PISTIL: pink.
FOLIAGE: light green.
GROWTH: medium upright.
Must be stopped early and often to balance out the rather rigid growth. Profusely flowering cultivar which can also be used well in fully sunny position.

'Goldsworth Beauty' (Slococks 1952, GB)
TUBE: light cherry-red.
SEPALS: light cherry-red, pale tips.
COROLLA: very dark purple-blue, single.
STAMENS: cherry-red.
PISTIL: pink and white.
FOLIAGE: dark green.
GROWTH: upright and bushy.
At first glance there is nothing exceptional about this cultivar. The flowers are of classic shape and in typical fuchsia colours. The quality of the plant and the harmonious structure, however, are clearly different from those of other similar fuchsias. The plant

grows to an attractive pyramid shape even without our assistance.

'Golondrina' (Niederholzer 1941, USA)
TUBE: rose madder, long.
SEPALS: rose madder, long and narrow.
COROLLA: magenta with darker edges and pink veins, single.
STAMENS: rose madder.
PISTIL: rose madder, very long.
FOLIAGE: mid-green with red veins.
GROWTH: spreading upright.
Large, elegant flowers on a robust, strong-growing plant; the sepals curve just a little upwards from the horizontal. Because of the long internodes should be stopped early and repeatedly. Flowers non-stop throughout the entire season.

'Groenekan's Glorie' (Steevens 1972, NL)
TUBE: salmon.
SEPALS: salmon-orange, green tips.
COROLLA: orange, single, large.
STAMENS: salmon and pink.
PISTIL: salmon and pink.
FOLIAGE: light green.
GROWTH: upright.
This cultivar has large, well-shaped flowers of brilliant orange. Care of the plant presents no problems. Early stopping leads to better branching. Tolerates and likes a lot of light and sun.

'Harry Gray' (Dunnett 1981, GB) No. 1607
('La Campanella' × 'Powder Puff')
TUBE: pink-striped, short.
SEPALS: white, slightly pink at the base, green tips.
COROLLA: white, a little pink at the base, double.
STAMENS: pink.
PISTIL: white.
FOLIAGE: dark green, small, red stalks.
GROWTH: lax-upright; will trail vigorously.
When a new cultivar becomes so popular in so short a time and is common, this must surely indicate special qualities. The plant branches naturally, so hardly needs to be stopped. Short internodes occasion a thick, bushy growth, over which the roundish, white flowers show up to perfection. Ideal show plant, especially and almost exclusively as a basket.

'Hathor' (Springer 1985, G)
('Buttercup' × 'Celia Smedley')
TUBE: white, green stripes, short and compact.

'Inferno'

'Hathor'

SEPALS: upperside white with pink, underside pink, green tips.
COROLLA: plate-shaped, salmon-pink (RHS 54^b), lighter at the base, single.
STAMENS: whitish-pink.
PISTIL: white, very long.
FOLIAGE: dark green, medium-sized, serrulate.
GROWTH: upright, well branched, short internodes.
This lovely new fuchsia with its conspicuous, spectacular flowers, which form a shallow plate when mature, while the sepals, perfectly upright, cloak the tube, will quickly win many friends. The plant, stopped once, develops very attractively and is particularly decorative as a pot plant.

'Heidi Ann' (Smith 1969, GB) No. 818
TUBE: crimson.
SEPALS: crimson.
COROLLA: pale lilac, red-veined, double.
STAMENS: cerise.
PISTIL: cerise.
FOLIAGE: dark green, red midrib.
GROWTH: upright.
A first-rate, profusely flowering cultivar which is fully self-branching and reacts particularly well to pinching. Flowers early and then throughout the whole season. 'White Ann' has the same flower shape and is a red and white sport of 'Heidi Ann'.

'Heinzelmännchen' (Hobgoblin) (Brembach 1911, G)
('Cupido' × 'James Lye')
TUBE: carmine-red.
SEPALS: carmine-red.
COROLLA: amethyst-violet, single to semi-double.
STAMENS: red.
PISTIL: pink.
FOLIAGE: dark green.
GROWTH: upright, low and bushy.
Profusely flowering, useful pot and bedding cultivar. This fuchsia is more common in Europe than in the UK.

'Henriette Ernst' (Curio 1907, G)
(unnamed seedling × 'Gertrude Pearson')
TUBE: bright blood-red.
SEPALS: bright blood-red.
COROLLA: beautiful blue, later reddish, single.
STAMENS: red.
PISTIL: red.
FOLIAGE: dark green.

GROWTH: straight upright, pyramid-shaped.
This cultivar, still readily cultivated today, with its decorative flowers carried tightly over the foliage, received a 1st Class award of the Flora Horticultural Society at Dresden shortly after its introduction. It is particularly good as a two-year-old plant.

'Heron' (Lemoine 1891, F)
TUBE: enamel-red, short.
SEPALS: enamel-red.
COROLLA: royal-blue, red-veined, single.
STAMENS: red.
PISTIL: pink.
FOLIAGE: dark green, glossy, red midrib.
GROWTH: upright.
Very good, old cultivar. The large, classic flowers are of good substance and last a long time. The plant is versatile in use, particularly anywhere where upright growth is required. Unfortunately the three very similar cultivars 'Royal Purple', 'Heron' and the much younger 'Schwabenland' are frequently confused with one another.

'Hidcote Beauty' (Webb 1949, GB)
TUBE: cream, waxy substance.
SEPALS: cream, waxy substance, green tips.
COROLLA: light salmon-pink, single.
STAMENS: light pink.
PISTIL: white.
FOLIAGE: light green.
GROWTH: upright and bushy and spreading.
An outstanding, versatile cultivar with delicately pastel-coloured flowers. A hanging basket with this is quickly grown over, and as a standard with broadly spreading head 'Hidcote Beauty' is unsurpassed in its beauty.

'High Peak' (Brough 1977, GB)
TUBE: white.
SEPALS: white.
COROLLA: white, slightly pink at the base, double.
STAMENS: white.
PISTIL: white.
FOLIAGE: mid-green, small.
GROWTH: lax-upright.
A recent white fuchsia. Whether the plant keeps the promise of its name has yet to be proven. It seems to grow decidedly slowly.

'Hindu Belle' (Munkner 1959, USA)
TUBE: wax-white.

SEPALS: wax-white outside, underside pink, broad, held high.
COROLLA: plum-blue, fading to red, large, single.
STAMENS: pink.
PISTIL: white.
FOLIAGE: dark green.
GROWTH: upright, well branched.
An incredibly floriferous and long-flowering cultivar which also forms a good standard.

'Hinnerike' (Bögemann 1984, G) No. 2045
(*F. cylindracea* × *F. magdalenae*)
(Bot. certificate of merit, Zeist 1985)
TUBE: enamel-red, longer than the corolla.
SEPALS: enamel-red, short and pointed.
COROLLA: orange-red, single.
STAMENS: orange, enclosed.
PISTIL: orange, conspicuously separated stigma.
FOLIAGE: dark green, glossy.
GROWTH: upright with long internodes.
The enamel-red 2-cm long flowers of the *Encliandra* type show up outstandingly against the beautiful glossy foliage. The vigorous plant grows effortlessly to 1 m tall in one season and therefore is particularly good in beds or large containers. Frequent stopping is advisable.

'Iceberg' (Mitchinson 1980, GB) No. 1538
TUBE: light red, darker striped.
SEPALS: white, slight red at the base, held upright.
COROLLA: white, single.
STAMENS: whitish-pink.
PISTIL: white.
FOLIAGE: dark green, denticulate.
GROWTH: lax-upright.
In a shady, cool position the medium-sized, beautifully shaped, white flowers on a plant which branches well and builds up to a bush are a real feast for the eyes.

'Iced Champagne' (Jennings 1968, GB)
TUBE: pale pink.
SEPALS: light pink.
COROLLA: pink with darker tinge, single.
STAMENS: pink.
PISTIL: white.
FOLIAGE: mid-green.
GROWTH: upright with short internodes.
Does not grow very tall and is therefore good to use as a pot plant. Because of the short internodes and the still relatively large leaves, the flowers are often hidden among the foliage. Less frequent pinching prevents this shortcoming. The flower is particularly beautiful in shape and colour.

'Igloo Maid' (Mrs E. Holmes 1972, GB)
TUBE: white.
SEPALS: white and broad.
COROLLA: white with a tinge of pink at the base, fully double.
STAMENS: pink.
PISTIL: white.
FOLIAGE: yellowish-green.
GROWTH: lax-upright, strong-growing.
Very good cultivar which is self-cleaning, i.e. it sheds the flower, which remains beautiful a very long time, together with the seed-pod. Like all white fuchsias, it prefers a shady position.

'Impudence' (Schnabel 1957, USA) No. 291
TUBE: light red.
SEPALS: light red, long and narrow.
COROLLA: white, slightly veined red, shallowly plate-shaped, single.
STAMENS: red.
PISTIL: red.
FOLIAGE: mid-green.
GROWTH: upright with long internodes.
The corolla, composed of four circular petals, which opens wide and flat, produces with the elegantly raised sepals a flower of absolute beauty. Early, frequent stopping is essential to get a well-balanced plant.

'Indian Maid' (Waltz 1962, USA) No. 524
TUBE: scarlet-red.
SEPALS: scarlet-red, long, held up and curved.
COROLLA: purest royal-blue, double.
STAMENS: light red.
PISTIL: pink.
FOLIAGE: dark green.
GROWTH: trailer.
The splendour of colour and the wealth of flowers of this cultivar cannot be beaten. Additional to this are the elegant, flexible growth and the completely problem-free cultivation. It is seldom that more advantages can be found together.

'Inferno' (Storvick 1983, USA) No. 1741
TUBE: light orange.
SEPALS: orange.
COROLLA: orange-red, lighter base, single.

STAMENS: orange, enclosed.
PISTIL: orange.
FOLIAGE: mid-green with red veins and stalks.
GROWTH: trailer.
This relatively new cultivar with exquisitely shaped, brilliant flowers does like a bright position but needs the coolness of shade. Blazing sun burns the flowers. Good for use as a hanging-basket plant.

'Ingram Maid' (Ryle 1976, GB) No. 1401
TUBE: white, thick.
SEPALS: white, pink base, underside pink, horizontal.
COROLLA: cream-white, single, remains closed and compact.
STAMENS: red.
PISTIL: red.
FOLIAGE: mid-green.
GROWTH: strong, upright and bushy.
Profusely flowering, robust fuchsia which has also proved itself good for training as a standard. The delicately coloured flowers are a surprise.

'Iris Amer' (Amer 1966, GB)
TUBE: white with pink tinge, short and thick.
SEPALS: whitish-pink, underside pink, green tips.
COROLLA: light red with carmine-red areas, orange base to outer petals, double.
STAMENS: light red.
PISTIL: whitish-pink.
FOLIAGE: dark green.
GROWTH: upright and bushy.
Early and incredibly profusely flowering cultivar with often four to six flowers in one leaf-axil. (Inherited from its parent 'Empress of Prussia'.) Reacts well to frequent stopping and quickly forms a standard with a well-branched head. Deservedly popular and sought after.

'Isidor Raffeiner' (Nutzinger 1971, A)
TUBE: scarlet-red.
SEPALS: scarlet-red.
COROLLA: white, red-veined, double.
STAMENS: red.
PISTIL: pink.
FOLIAGE: mid-green.
GROWTH: medium upright.
Because of the long internodes this cultivar must be stopped early and repeatedly and then a profuse and long-flowering shrub is obtained. The strong growth should also be sufficient for raising of standards or pyramids. This cultivar was named after an amiable

fuchsia-lover who has contributed much to the spread of fuchsias.

'Isle of Mull' (Tolley 1978, GB) No. 1455
TUBE: light magenta with darker veins.
SEPALS: light pink, firm, underside creped.
COROLLA: magenta-pink with metallic lustre, single.
STAMENS: magenta.
PISTIL: white.
FOLIAGE: dark green.
GROWTH: upright and bushy.
The abundant medium-sized flowers have the particularly pretty coolie's-hat shape.

'Jack Ackland' (Haag & Son 1952, USA)
TUBE: pink.
SEPALS: bright pink.
COROLLA: deep pink, later becoming lighter, single.
STAMENS: pink.
PISTIL: whitish-pink.
FOLIAGE: dark green with red veins.
GROWTH: lax and spreading.
This very popular cultivar has many good qualities. It flowers non-stop with large, classic flowers. The sepals are twice as long as the tube and elegantly raised. A very robust fuchsia, can be raised as a standard; makes an exceptional basket.

'Jack Shahan' (Tiret 1948, USA)
TUBE: Bengal-pink.
SEPALS: Bengal-pink.

'Kwintet'

'Joy Patmore'

COROLLA: Bengal-pink, single.
STAMENS: pink.
PISTIL: pink.
FOLIAGE: dark green.
GROWTH: lax bush, horizontal.

This and the previous cultivar are frequently confused with one another, even in nurserymen's catalogues. They can, however, be distinguished easily by the growth, for 'Jack Ackland' grows more rigidly and more upright and the pink of the flower is also lighter.

'Jamboree' (Reiter 1955, USA) No. 231
TUBE: pinkish-white.
SEPALS: salmon-pink, underside darker, white base.
COROLLA: salmon-pink to carmine-red, double.
STAMENS: pink.
PISTIL: white.
FOLIAGE: dark green, large and glossy.
GROWTH: upright and bushy.

'Frosted Flame'

Another cultivar that likes warmth and sun. The tough foliage seems not liked by pests. Very good as a bedding plant in the garden.

'Joan Gilbert' (Gilbert 1977, GB)
TUBE: neyson-rose.
SEPALS: neyson-rose, waxen, green tips.
COROLLA: blue and violet speckled and pervaded with salmon and pink, double.
STAMENS: pink.
PISTIL: pink.
FOLIAGE: dark green.
GROWTH: upright and bushy.
Characteristic of this cultivar are the petaloids grown together with the sepals. The more the sepals stand up, the wider the corolla unfolds. The short internodes and the natural branching are additional plus points of this versatile fuchsia which can be used as a bush or a standard.

'Joan Pacey' (Gadsby 1972, GB) No. 1067
TUBE: pink.
SEPALS: pink, underside darker, green tips.
COROLLA: pink with darker veining, single.
STAMENS: rose-red.
PISTIL: light pink.
FOLIAGE: mid-green.
GROWTH: upright.
The late Cliff Gadsby, the English hybridiser, has left us many outstanding fuchsia cultivars. 'Joan Pacey' is a good pot and bedding plant. In garden beds it tolerates full sun.

'Joy Patmore' (Turner 1961, GB)
TUBE: white.
SEPALS: white and waxen, raised.
COROLLA: bright carmine-red of distinctive shade, white at base, single.
STAMENS: pink.
PISTIL: white.
FOLIAGE: dark green.
GROWTH: upright and bushy.
A first-rate cultivar; as a bush does not grow very tall, but forms outstanding standards. The bright colours and the coolie's-hat-shape of the flowers are striking and very attractive.

'Juno' (Kennett 1966, USA) No. 677
TUBE: greenish and white.
SEPALS: white, green tips, completely upturned over tube.

COROLLA: dark red, later becoming lighter, white at the base, with white veins, single.
STAMENS: pink.
PISTIL: white.
FOLIAGE: large and light green.
GROWTH: trailer.
Very strong-growing cultivar with large and numerous leaves. One should not stimulate the almost too dense foliage growth with additional nitrogen otherwise the flowers are liable to get lost among the leaves. The flowers and also the elegant, long buds are enchanting. A plant for the edge of a large container.

'Jupiter 70' (R. Holmes 1970, GB) No. 1209
('Percy Holmes' × 'San Francisco')
TUBE: pale pink.
SEPALS: reddish-pink.
COROLLA: orange, single.
STAMENS: rose-red.
PISTIL: light pink.
FOLIAGE: mid-green.
GROWTH: upright.
One of the first fuchsias that flowers in spring. As an upright 'orange' it is particularly well suited as a bedding plant in full sun. The growth is thick and well branched and so one must watch out for *Botrytis*. In 1970 received a BFS Award of Merit at RHS London Show.

'Kathy Louise' (Antonelli 1963, USA) No. 558
TUBE: light red.
SEPALS: light red, green tips, underside creped.
COROLLA: soft pink and lavender, veined slightly darker, large, double.
STAMENS: pink.
PISTIL: pink.
FOLIAGE: dark green, glossy, rather small.
GROWTH: trailer, strong-growing.
Does not flower particularly early, but when it does is so profuse that a hanging basket planted with this cultivar becomes breathtakingly beautiful. Must be frequently stopped when young.

'Katrina' (Mrs E. Holmes 1968, GB)
TUBE: pink.
SEPALS: pink to almost red.
COROLLA: pale pink, round and double, fairly large.
STAMENS: pink.
PISTIL: pink.
FOLIAGE: dark green.

GROWTH: straight upright and bushy.

Owing to its upright growth this cultivar is very suitable for bed planting. It soon grows tall and flowers profusely.

'Kegworth Supreme' (H. Smith 1979, GB)
TUBE: empire-rose.
SEPALS: empire-rose, darker underside.
COROLLA: fuchsia-purple, single.
STAMENS: pink.
PISTIL: pink.
FOLIAGE: dark green.
GROWTH: upright and compact.
A relatively new fuchsia which with its strong growth and the many, medium-sized flowers can be used in a versatile way.

'Kentish Maid' (Ron Holmes 1976, GB) No. 1339
TUBE: Bengal-pink.
SEPALS: Bengal-pink, green tips, long and graceful.
COROLLA: fuchsia-purple, single.
STAMENS: Bengal-pink.
PISTIL: light pink.
FOLIAGE: mid-green.
GROWTH: lax-upright and bushy, well branching.
The classic flowers are carried well visible over the foliage, in large masses.

'Kernan Robson' (Tiret 1958, USA) No. 336
TUBE: white and green.
SEPALS: white, green tips.
COROLLA: salmon and pink, fully double.
STAMENS: pink.
PISTIL: pink.
FOLIAGE: dark green, glossy.
GROWTH: upright; good as a bush.
A fuchsia of exceptional quality, colour and flower size. As the corolla is partly fused with the sepals, when they open it becomes bigger and bigger. Succulent stalks require preventive measures against *Botrytis*.

'Keystone' (Haag 1945, USA)
TUBE: light pink.
SEPALS: light pink, green tips.
COROLLA: light pink, single.
STAMENS: light pink.
PISTIL: white.
FOLIAGE: mid-green.
GROWTH: upright and bushy.
Although this cultivar with its pastel-coloured, classic, medium-sized flowers is rewarding and profusely flowering, it is no longer often found in collections.

'Khada' (Roe 1973, GB)
TUBE: light red.
SEPALS: light red.
COROLLA: white, lightly veined red, single.
STAMENS: red.
PISTIL: red.
FOLIAGE: dark green, small.
GROWTH: upright and compact.
A small, natural bonsai fuchsia with delicate flowers held upright. With painstaking care—it is not easy to cultivate—this cultivar can make many friends.

'King of Hearts' (Fuchsia Forest 1965, USA) No. 627
TUBE: red.
SEPALS: red.
COROLLA: lavender, the outer petals pink and white, double.
STAMENS: pink.
PISTIL: pink.
FOLIAGE: dark green.
GROWTH: trailer.
This sport of 'Queen of Hearts' will in many cases form a very attractive hanging basket.

'King's Ransom' (Schnabel 1954, USA) No. 195
TUBE: snow-white.
SEPALS: snow-white, broad, crepe-like on the underside, held high.
COROLLA: deep purple, double.
STAMENS: pink.
PISTIL: pink.
FOLIAGE: dark green.
GROWTH: upright and bushy, strong-growing.
Compared with many difficult white and blue fuchsias this one is a good grower and problem-free. The flowers are of very good substance and the distinctive blue remains lovely for some time.

'Kiwi' (Tiret 1966, USA) No. 687
TUBE: greenish and white, long.
SEPALS: white, green tips, broad.
COROLLA: china-rose with lighter and darker petaloids, double.
STAMENS: light pink.
PISTIL: white.
FOLIAGE: mid-green.
GROWTH: lax-upright, strong stems.

'Joan Pacey'

'Oranje Boven'

Very large flowers which appear in relative abundance. Develops much foliage, among which the flowers are easily hidden. At its most beautiful in a wall basket.

'Kon-Tiki' (Tiret 1965, USA) No. 652
TUBE: pure white.
SEPALS: pure white.
COROLLA: medium-violet, white at the base, double.
STAMENS: pink.
PISTIL: white.
FOLIAGE: dark green, small.
GROWTH: trailer.
Lovely flowers, but the plant is not easy to keep. Special care is advisable with watering and also when repotting in larger pots, which should not be done too quickly.

'Kwintet' (van Wieringen 1970, NL)
TUBE: red, long and thick.
SEPALS: red, horizontal.
COROLLA: light red, single.
STAMENS: red.
PISTIL: whitish-pink.

FOLIAGE: mid-green with red veins, on red stalks.
GROWTH: upright and bushy.
There are not many good, plain red fuchsias with attractive flower shape and of good substance. 'Kwintet' is one of the best. Its cultivation is easy and it is unremittingly floriferous. Because it tolerates the sun well, it is used as a balcony fuchsia and bedding plant.

'La Bianca' (Tiret 1950, USA) No. 64
TUBE: greenish-white.
SEPALS: white with green stripes and green tips.
COROLLA: white, bell-shaped, single.
STAMENS: white.
PISTIL: white.
FOLIAGE: mid-green.
GROWTH: lax-upright; will trail.
A profusely flowering, white fuchsia which gives few problems. It must, though, be protected from *Botrytis* attack. Best results can be obtained in a shady position.

'La Campanella' (Blackwell, 1968, GB)
TUBE: white.

SEPALS: white with pink flush.
COROLLA: purple, semi-double.
STAMENS: pink.
PISTIL: white.
FOLIAGE: mid-green, small.
GROWTH: trailer and spreading.
Developed as a chance seedling at Blackwells of Swindon, this cultivar has proven itself an outstanding fuchsia in every respect. It is easy to propagate, easy to cultivate, not susceptible to pests or diseases, makes wonderful profusely flowering hanging baskets and is also suitable for the raising of standards or ornamental plants trained up on a cane. On top of that it easily and freely sets so many seeds that amateur hybridisers gladly use it as a female parent.

'Lace Petticoats' (Tiret 1952, USA) No. 145
TUBE: white.
SEPALS: white, green tips.
COROLLA: white, very slightly pink at base, double.
STAMENS: white to light pink.
PISTIL: white.
FOLIAGE: dark green.
GROWTH: lax-upright; will trail.
The white of the flowers remains clear for a long time even in very bright positions. The flowers should without fail, however, be protected from rain or spray water. Water with consideration and care. The plant is not all that robust and therefore must not be potted on too quickly and too often. The magnificent flowers in large numbers are, however, worth every effort.

'Lady Boothby' (Raffill 1939, GB)
TUBE: crimson.
SEPALS: crimson.
COROLLA: black and purple, single.
STAMENS: red.
PISTIL: red.
FOLIAGE: reddish-green.
GROWTH: upright, long internodes.
This fuchsia grows persistently upwards and can be restrained only as a climbing plant on a frame. The growth is extremely strong. Flowers in abundance, of an exceptionally dark, initially almost black-purple, fading to red.

'Lady Heytesbury' (Wheeler 1866, GB)
TUBE: white and waxen.
SEPALS: white, broad, horizontal.
COROLLA: coral-pink, lighter at the base, single.
STAMENS: pink.
PISTIL: white.
FOLIAGE: light green.
GROWTH: upright.
This is another of the ever good, well-tried, old cultivars. Easy to grow, strong-growing and particularly well suited for large forms such as a standard or pyramid.

'Lady Isobel Barnett' (Gadsby 1968, GB) No. 978
TUBE: rose-red.
SEPALS: rose-red.
COROLLA: pink and lavender to pinkish-lilac, open, single.

'Lucinda'

'Micky Goult'

STAMENS: light pink.
PISTIL: light pink.
FOLIAGE: mid-green.
GROWTH: upright.

The medium-sized, wide-open flowers are carried on strong stalks, facing sidewards to upwards over the foliage, and in incredible abundance. The plant is robust and branches naturally and well. The flowers present themselves to particular advantage on a pillar, which with the strong growth can easily be raised in a season.

'Lady Kathleen Spence' (Ryle 1974, GB) No. 1248
TUBE: cream-white.
SEPALS: cream-white outside, underside pale pink, green tips.
COROLLA: lavender-blue, veined light pink, single.
STAMENS: pink.
PISTIL: white.
FOLIAGE: dark green, small.
GROWTH: lax-upright and well branched.

Delicate colours like these demand a sheltered position so that wind and weather do not damage the flowers. The foliage is of soft, tender consistency and must be protected from attack by red spider. The plant is of attractive lax-upright growth and reacts well to repeated stopping. It received a gold Certificate of Merit in England in 1976, the only gold award given by the BFS.

'Lady Ramsey' (Goulding 1981, GB) No. 1647
TUBE: flesh-coloured, short.
SEPALS: flesh-coloured, held high.
COROLLA: violet, single.
STAMENS: whitish-pink.
PISTIL: white.
FOLIAGE: mid-green, matt upper surface.
GROWTH: upright and bushy.

The medium-sized, roundish flowers are very numerous. There are two, often three, in every leaf-axil. Branches naturally with great vigour and is versatile; can be used for larger plant forms.

'Lady Thumb' (Roe 1966, GB)
TUBE: red.
SEPALS: red.
COROLLA: white, slightly veined red.
STAMENS: red.
PISTIL: pink.
FOLIAGE: dark green, small.
GROWTH: upright and bushy.

This sport of 'Tom Thumb' located by George Roe is identical to the latter in foliage, growth and flower shape. Only the flower colour has changed. The sport seems also, however, to have lost something in robustness compared with the original cultivar.

'La Fiesta' (Kennett 1962, USA) No. 535
TUBE: white, long.
SEPALS: white, underside pink.
COROLLA: dark red to vinaceous-red with white streaks and white petaloids, double.
STAMENS: pink.
PISTIL: white.
FOLIAGE: dark green.
GROWTH: trailer, branches well.

There are not too many large-flowered, multi-coloured fuchsias that are profusely flowering like this one. It requires a sheltered position so that the flowers do not acquire brown spots from the rain.

'Lakeside' (Thornley 1967, GB) No. 1062
TUBE: rose-red.
SEPALS: rose-red, green tips.
COROLLA: bluish-violet, veined pink, single.
STAMENS: rose-red.
PISTIL: rose-red.
FOLIAGE: mid-green, small.
GROWTH: trailer.

One of the few cultivars that are self-cleaning. They shed the withered flowers together with the seed pods. With delicate flowers which decorate the plant in great masses, this means much labour saving. Attractive as a hanging basket or table standard.

'La Neige' (Tiret 1965, USA) No. 650
TUBE: white.
SEPALS: white, underside pale pink.
COROLLA: cream-white, double.
STAMENS: pale pink.
PISTIL: white.
FOLIAGE: dark green, large.
GROWTH: lax-upright; will trail.

Best results are obtained under glass or on a covered terrace in shade. The plant develops a lot of foliage among which the flowers conceal themselves. One should therefore be somewhat sparing with nitrogen feeds. If 'La Neige' is raised up on a stake and the side shoots are stopped once or twice, every flower is very visible in its full beauty. Also very attractive as a hanging-basket plant.

'Laura' (Martin 1968, USA) No. 774
(One of four cultivars with the same name)
TUBE: red.
SEPALS: red, shiny outside, underside creped, green tips.
COROLLA: sky-blue with pink streaks and red veins, double.
STAMENS: pink.
PISTIL: white to pink.
FOLIAGE: mid-green.
GROWTH: lax-upright; will trail.
The outer petals and petaloids are fused with the sepals so that, when these are raised up on bursting into blossom, the corolla is spread wide open and gives a loose, very restless impression. This is further emphasised by the lighter, almost white edge to each petal. An older cultivar with single white and pink flowers was also given the name 'Laura' by the hybridiser Niederholzer, 1946, USA, but it is apparently not in cultivation in Europe. As early as 1846 a pink and purple fuchsia by Youell came on to the market as 'Laura'.

'Laurie' (Antonelli 1963, USA) No. 557
TUBE: dark pink.
SEPALS: light pink, dark pink stripes, green tips.
COROLLA: pink when blossing out, later bright pink, double.
STAMENS: cerise.
PISTIL: pink.
FOLIAGE: dark green.
GROWTH: trailer.
A strong-growing, profusely flowering, pure weeping fuchsia with flowers of attractive shape which initially form a closed corolla and later throw out four larger petals from the centre. This gives the flower a very long and exquisite appearance.

'Le Berger' (de Graaff 1977, NL)
TUBE: white with pink tinge.
SEPALS: white, green tips.
COROLLA: white, just a little pink-veined, semi-double to double.
STAMENS: light pink.
PISTIL: white.
FOLIAGE: mid-green, small.
GROWTH: trailer.
As most of the white or even near-white fuchsias bear large to very large flowers, 'Le Berger' with its dainty, elegantly winged flowers is a real enrichment to the collection. It has been greeted with delight by the lovers of small-flowered fuchsias.

'Lena' (Bunney 1862, GB)
TUBE: cream to flesh-pink.
SEPALS: flesh-pink, underside rather darker, green tips.
COROLLA: purple, light pink at the base, semi-double.
STAMENS: light pink.
PISTIL: white.
FOLIAGE: mid-green.
GROWTH: lax bush; will trail.
A good, old, versatile cultivar with medium-sized flowers. Very similar in growth and flower colours are the cultivars 'Elsa', 'Eva Boerg' and 'Hapsburg'. It is difficult to be quite sure exactly which cultivar one is dealing with. The confusion became even greater when a German young plant operation abruptly turned the good old 'Lena' into 'Pink Ballet Girl'. The differences are minimal and vanish altogether in different growing conditions. A characteristic of 'Lena', however, is that it often develops flowers without petals in late autumn.

'Lena Dalton' (Reimers 1953, USA) No. 169
TUBE: pale pink.
SEPALS: pale pink, green tips.
COROLLA: lavender-blue, lightly veined red, double.
STAMENS: pink.
PISTIL: white.
FOLIAGE: dark green, on reddish stalks, small.
GROWTH: upright and bushy.
This cultivar with dainty, pastel-coloured flowers is often cultivated by fuchsia-lovers who exhibit at shows because it reacts so well to every pinch. The results are then cushion-shaped plants which are bedecked all over with flowers. In hot weather attention must be paid to red spider attack.

'Leonora' (Tiret 1960, USA) No. 434
(Certificate of Merit 1964)
TUBE: cream with pink stripes.
SEPALS: pink, green tips.
COROLLA: pink with a slight lilac tinge, faintly veined, single.
STAMENS: pink.
PISTIL: pink.
FOLIAGE: mid-green.
GROWTH: upright and bushy.
Still one of the best pink cultivars. The numerous, beautifully campanulate, medium-sized flowers

'Maori Pipes'

'Papillon'

'Lynn Ellen'

cause the plant to sparkle from a distance. Just the right fuchsia for the beginner, who must first gain experience and easily loses heart with difficult cultivars. 'Leonora' is of delicate substance and should be grown in a cool and shady situation.

Well suited for use as a bush or as a standard.

'Lilac Princess' (Handley 1979, GB) No. 1502
TUBE: short, thick, greenish-white.
SEPALS: greenish-white outside, underside light pink.
COROLLA: deep lilac, pink at the base, single.
STAMENS: pink.
PISTIL: pink.
FOLIAGE: dark green.
GROWTH: upright and bushy.
The medium-sized flowers stand on short stalks at right angles to the plant. Begins to flower early in the year, with four flowers in each leaf-axil.

'Lillibet' (Hodges 1954, USA)
TUBE: pinkish-white, long.
SEPALS: white, underside light pink, long and narrow.
COROLLA: rose-red and double.

'Peppermint Stick'

'Loeky'

'Machu Picchu'

'Orange Mirage'

STAMENS: pink.
PISTIL: pink.
FOLIAGE: mid-green.
GROWTH: trailer, with very long internodes.
Lovely fuchsia for large hanging baskets or the edge of a tub. It can also be raised up very decoratively on a support.

'Linda Goulding' (Goulding 1981, GB) No. 1648
TUBE: white, waxen, short.
SEPALS: whitish-pink, held high.
COROLLA: white, very slightly veined pink, single.
STAMENS: ruby-red.
PISTIL: ruby-red.
FOLIAGE: light green.
GROWTH: upright and bushy.
The relatively small but very numerous white flowers are bell-shaped and of good substance. The ruby-red stamens with their anthers make an unusual, very charming contrast to these. The plant, which is naturally self-branching, can be seen in England at every show as a bush or standard. That speaks for itself!

'Little Beauty' (unknown)
TUBE: light red.
SEPALS: light red.
COROLLA: lavender-blue, single.
STAMENS: pink.
PISTIL: pink.
FOLIAGE: mid-green, small.
GROWTH: upright and well branched.
Delicate flowers of clear blue cover the plant in incredible masses from May until the frosts. In shadow the little flowers are exceptionally brilliant. Good as a bed or balcony plant. A true beauty!

'Loeky' (de Graaff 1979, NL)
TUBE: rose-red.
SEPALS: rose-red, held above the horizontal.
COROLLA: pinkish-lilac with red veins, plate-shaped, horizontal, single.
STAMENS: rose-red.
PISTIL: pink.
FOLIAGE: small, mid-green leaves.
GROWTH: upright and well branched.
This new fuchsia with the relatively unusual, plate-shaped, particularly striking flowers originates from a cross between 'Joy Patmore' and 'Impudence'. Its care is easy and simple. Best results in the shade owing to the delicate substance. The future of this enchanting fuchsia seems assured.

'Lolita' (Tiret 1963, USA) No. 574
(AFS Certificate of Merit, 1967)
TUBE: whitish-pink.
SEPALS: whitish-pink, underside rose-red, green tips.
COROLLA: lilac and blue, lightly veined red, double.
STAMENS: pink.
PISTIL: whitish-pink.
FOLIAGE: light green, small, denticulate.
GROWTH: trailer.
Although a cultivar with delicate porcelain colours, it endures rain and damp well. A certain disadvantage lies in the fact that the plant becomes woody very early. Thus one must attempt frequent stopping early in the year to obtain many flower shoots, and regular feeding to keep it in growth. A wall basket is the right place for 'Lolita'.

'Lord Lonsdale' (unknown)
TUBE: pale pink.
SEPALS: salmon-pink with large green tips, drooping (divergent).
COROLLA: orange with salmon-pink, single.

STAMENS: salmon-pink.
PISTIL: pale pink.
FOLIAGE: light green, strongly undulated or rolled up.
GROWTH: upright.
The rolled leaves of 'Lord Lonsdale' are characteristic of the cultivar and do not in any way indicate a disease of the leaves. The succulent stalks are prone to *Botrytis*. Like all orange fuchsias it likes the sun and warmth. The harmony of light-coloured foliage and pastel flowers is enchanting.

'Lottie Hobby' (Edwards 1839, GB)
TUBE: cherry-red.
SEPALS: cherry-red.
COROLLA: scarlet-red, single.
STAMENS: red.
PISTIL: red.
FOLIAGE: mid-green, small.
GROWTH: upright.
An early *Encliandra* hybrid of dwarf growth with the typical small, fern-like *Encliandra* foliage and delicate bright red little flowers.

'Lucinda' (Mitchinson 1981, GB) No. 1654
('Baby Pink' × 'Norman Mitchinson')
TUBE: pink.
SEPALS: white, pink tips.
COROLLA: pink and lilac, semi-double.
STAMENS: light pink.
PISTIL: white.
FOLIAGE: mid-green, serrulate margin.
GROWTH: lax-upright.
The large flowers develop their best colours in a shady position. The plant is vigorous and strong-growing.

'Lydia Götz' (Götz 1958)
('Beacon' × 'Henriette Ernst')
TUBE: light red.
SEPALS: red.
COROLLA: blue, later reddish, single.
STAMENS: red.
PISTIL: light red.
FOLIAGE: dark green.
GROWTH: strong and upright.
This cultivar has inherited the strength of growth and prolificness of flowering from 'Beacon' and the beautiful blue of the corolla from 'Henriette Ernst'.

'Lye's Unique' (Lye 1886, GB)
TUBE: white, waxen.

SEPALS: white, waxen.
COROLLA: salmon-orange, single.
STAMENS: pink.
PISTIL: whitish-pink.
FOLIAGE: dark green.
GROWTH: upright, strong-growing.
The hallmark of the English hybridiser James Lye is the ivory-cream, very firm tube and sepals of many of his fuchsias. This is one of his best cultivars with long flowers of great beauty and durability.

'Lynn Ellen' (Erikson 1962, USA) No. 541
TUBE: pink.
SEPALS: deeper pink.
COROLLA: rose-red, fading lighter, double.
STAMENS: pink.
PISTIL: white.
FOLIAGE: mid-green.
GROWTH: upright.
A profusely and continuously flowering cultivar. The large flowers open wide and somewhat untidily. No problems to propagate or to grow.

'Machu Picchu' (de Graaff 1976, NL)
TUBE: salmon-orange.
SEPALS: salmon-orange.
COROLLA: somewhat darker orange, single.
STAMENS: pink.
PISTIL: yellowish.
FOLIAGE: grey-green, slightly pilose.
GROWTH: lax-upright; will trail.
Is a seedling from 'Speciosa', which in turn is a hybrid of *F. splendens* × *F. fulgens*. The flowers appear in clusters at the end of the shoots. It is very effective raised as a hanging basket. Also, raised up 80 cm on a support and all side shoots left in place, it flowered on all shoots at the same time, abundantly and non-stop and was a real gem. Considering these parent plants, it likes naturally warm conditions and is very tolerant of the sun.

'Magic Flute' (Handley 1975, GB) No. 1275
TUBE: wax-white, long and thin.
SEPALS: white, green tips, narrow.
COROLLA: coral-pink, white at the base, single.
STAMENS: whitish-pink.
PISTIL: white.
FOLIAGE: mid-green.
GROWTH: trailer.
The long, funnel-shaped flowers appear very early. A plant with a harmonious effect.

'Magic Lantern' (Handley 1976, GB) No. 1369
TUBE: salmon-pink, long and thin.
SEPALS: salmon-pink, underside orange, upright.
COROLLA: orange with darker edge, single.
STAMENS: salmon-pink.
PISTIL: whitish-pink.
FOLIAGE: dark green, medium-sized.
GROWTH: upright, strong-growing.
Good bush or shrub fuchsia for bed planting in the garden, including in sunny positions.

'Major Heaphy' (unknown, GB)
TUBE: orange-red.
SEPALS: orange-red, green tips.
COROLLA: brick-red, single.
STAMENS: red.
PISTIL: pink.
FOLIAGE: mid-green.
GROWTH: upright.
Well branched, upright growth and bright flower colours, which sparkle in the sun, make this profusely flowering cultivar a good bedding plant. Also very handsome as a table standard. As it drops buds and flowers in dry air conditions, it is not suitable for shows.

'Mandarin' (Schnabel 1963, USA) No. 582
TUBE: light salmon-pink with darker stripes.
SEPALS: light salmon-pink, darker underside, green tips.
COROLLA: carmine and orange, semi-double.
STAMENS: pink.
PISTIL: light pink.
FOLIAGE: dark green.
GROWTH: trailer.
A large, beautifully coloured flower of exceptionally good substance. The flowers show to good effect as a hanging-basket plant or when raised up on a support. Pests seem to shun the firm foliage.

'Maori Pipes' (de Graaf 1985, NL) No. 2048
(*F. excorticata* × *F. triphylla*)
TUBE: magenta, long.
SEPALS: magenta.
COROLLA: blood-red, single.
STAMENS: red.
PISTIL: red.
FOLIAGE: dark green, large.
GROWTH: upright, must be stopped frequently.
This new *triphylla* hybrid received the botanical merit certificate at Zeist NL in 1985 for primary hybrids.

'Party Frock'

'Margery Blake' (Wood 1950, GB)
TUBE: red.
SEPALS: red.
COROLLA: red and violet, single.
STAMENS: pink.
PISTIL: pink.
FOLIAGE: mid-green, small.
GROWTH: upright, rather horizontal, bushy.
Charming, small-flowered cultivar. Exceedingly profuse and incessant in flowering. The growth is rather horizontally spreading and remains low. Bonsailovers should try it with this cultivar.

'Marin Glow' (Reedstrom 1954, USA) No. 204
TUBE: white.
SEPALS: white, green tips.
COROLLA: dark violet, pink at the base, single.
STAMENS: pink.
PISTIL: white.
FOLIAGE: dark green.
GROWTH: upright and bushy.
A cultivar that is often to be seen at fuchsia shows and frequently wins prizes. Through regular stopping, after every second pair of leaves, incredibly floriferous specimens obtained. A standard with these medium-sized leaves is also very impressive. Best results are obtained in a sheltered position or in the greenhouse.

'Marinka' (Rozain-Boucharlat 1902, F)
TUBE: red.
SEPALS: red.
COROLLA: somewhat darker red, single.

'Postiljon'

'Pink Galore'

STAMENS: red.
PISTIL: red.
FOLIAGE: dark green with red midrib.
GROWTH: trailer.
One of the best-known weeping fuchsias, which has been in cultivation for over 80 years. It is robust and profusely flowering, with exquisite flower shape. On cool nights in spring or in autumn the foliage acquires dark patches, but these are harmless and as soon as it gets warmer they disappear again.

'Masquerade' (Kennett 1961, USA) No. 590
TUBE: green and white.
SEPALS: pink and white with green tips.
COROLLA: dark purple, later reddish, with pink areas on the outer petals, double.
STAMENS: pink.
PISTIL: white to pink.
FOLIAGE: dark green.
GROWTH: trailer, spreading.
Conspicuous, very large, yet easy to cultivate. It is best kept sheltered, in the greenhouse or under cover.

'Mazda' (Reiter 1947, USA)
TUBE: light orange-pink.
SEPALS: light orange-pink.
COROLLA: red-orange, base lighter, single.
STAMENS: pink.
PISTIL: pink.
FOLIAGE: dark green.
GROWTH: upright and bushy.
A strong-growing, sun-tolerant, versatile, proven cultivar. Frequent stopping improves the growth structure.

'Menna' (Bögemann 1982, G) No. 2204
('Leverkusen' ×)
TUBE: salmon, compact, cylindrical.
SEPALS: salmon, green tips.
COROLLA: orange, single.
STAMENS: orange.
PISTIL: light salmon.
FOLIAGE: dark green.
GROWTH: upright, broadly spreading.
'Menna', a strong-growing *triphylla* type, fascinates because of the great wealth of its brilliant flowers. It can be used as a bedding or tub plant in sunny positions.

'Mephisto' (Reiter 1941, USA)
TUBE: scarlet-red.

SEPALS: scarlet-red.
COROLLA: crimson-red, single.
STAMENS: cerise.
PISTIL: pink.
FOLIAGE: mid-green.
GROWTH: upright and bushy.
The classic, beautifully shaped, almost uniformly red flowers on an attractively structured large plant are very decorative in garden beds or larger containers. 'Mephisto' is hardy in most districts.

'Micky Goult' (Roe 1981, GB)
('Bobby Shaftoe' × 'Lustre')
TUBE: white to pale pink, short.
SEPALS: whitish-pink, underside pink, horizontal.
COROLLA: pink with a lilac-pink lustre, single.
STAMENS: pink.
PISTIL: whitish-pink.
FOLIAGE: mid-green, small, denticulate.
GROWTH: upright, well branched.
This relatively new cultivar is impressive for its harmonious, well-proportioned structure. The medium-sized, pastel-coloured flowers of classic shape are clearly visible. The profuse and continuous flowering commends itself for show purposes.

'Miss California' (Hodges 1950, USA)
TUBE: pinkish-red.
SEPALS: pinkish-red, underside darker, held above the horizontal.
COROLLA: white, veined pink, semi-double.
STAMENS: pink.
PISTIL: pink.
FOLIAGE: mid-green.
GROWTH: lax-upright.
A cultivar which definitely needs a shady position. The pretty flowers are of delicate substance and rapidly fade in the sun. The tender foliage is liable to attack by red spider in hot conditions.

'Mission Bells' (Walker & Jones 1948, USA)
TUBE: scarlet-red.
SEPALS: scarlet-red and lustrous (shiny).
COROLLA: bright purple, red at the base, single and large-flowered.
STAMENS: red.
PISTIL: red.
FOLIAGE: dark green.
GROWTH: upright and bushy.
A delightful cultivar which should be grown in every collection. It is easy to propagate, strong-growing

and carries the bright, eye-catching, bell-shaped flowers in rich profusion. As an older standard it should definitely be given a wind-sheltered position, for older wood is very brittle. Rather late in flowering.

'Miss Leucadia' (Stubbs 1971, USA) No. 999
TUBE: pink.
SEPALS: pink, green tips.
COROLLA: soft pink, double.
STAMENS: pink.
PISTIL: pink.
FOLIAGE: dark green.
GROWTH: trailer.
This good cultivar with its very large, wide-opening flowers—each petal has a toothed edge—is an outstanding hanging-basket plant for a sheltered position. The delicately coloured flowers are very susceptible to rain.

'Miss Vallejo' (Tiret 1958, USA) No. 334
TUBE: light pink.
SEPALS: light pink, green tips.
COROLLA: dark pink, slightly veined, double.
STAMENS: pink.
PISTIL: white.
FOLIAGE: dark green.
GROWTH: lax-upright; will trail with weight.
Because of the large, spherical, heavy flowers this cultivar must be supported and tied. It likes a sheltered position which should be positively bright but not sunny.

'Molesworth' (Lemoine 1903, F)
TUBE: bright cherry-red.
SEPALS: bright cherry-red.
COROLLA: cream-white, veined cherry-red, double.
STAMENS: red.
PISTIL: whitish-pink.
FOLIAGE: dark green.
GROWTH: lax-upright. Suitable for any type of growth.
This versatile, well-tried cultivar is well suited for the raising of larger plants such as standards, pyramids or pillars. Among the many red and white cultivars it can immediately be recognised by the handsome, particularly exact flower shape.

'Moonraker' (Clitheroe 1979, GB)
('Northumbrian Belle' × 'Blush of Dawn')
TUBE: whitish-pink, long and thin.
SEPALS: whitish-pink with green tips.

COROLLA: light blue, pink at the base, double.
STAMENS: pink.
PISTIL: white, very long.
FOLIAGE: mid-green, serrulate margin.
GROWTH: upright and bushy.
Even the lovely photograph is able only imperfectly to reflect the charm of the pastel-coloured flowers of 'Moonraker'. Each petal in the loosely double corolla is undulate and crimped. Thus an elegant, lively impression is created. A position should be chosen in half shade. Because of the heavy abundance of flowers support must be provided at the right time.

'Morning Light' (Waltz 1960, USA) No. 441
TUBE: coral-pink.
SEPALS: base, coral pink; white with green tips, broad, underside pink.
COROLLA: lavender, slightly spotted pink, double.
STAMENS: pink.
PISTIL: white.
FOLIAGE: yellow and green.
GROWTH: lax bush; will trail.
An enchanting, very colourful cultivar. Good like all cultivars of the hybridiser Waltz. The subtle colours produce the most beautiful effect under glass or protected from rain and weather in some other way.

'Mosedale Hall' (Thornley 1974, GB) No. 1216
('Silverdale' × 'Silverdale')
TUBE: short, cream-coloured, tinged green.
SEPALS: cream, underside pink.
COROLLA: violet, small single flowers.
STAMENS: cream.
PISTIL: cream.
FOLIAGE: dark green.
GROWTH: upright.
From the point of view of origin a very interesting cultivar which should in fact be hardy in most climates. This plant with its fine-looking foliage and overwhelming profusion of dainty, beautifully coloured flowers is very decorative in a pot as well as in a garden bed. The delicate foliage is unfortunately susceptible to red spider.

'Mrs Lovell Swisher' (Evans & Reeves 1942, USA)
TUBE: pink to dark pink.
SEPALS: white, underside pink, green tips.
COROLLA: dark pink to almost red, lighter at the base, small and dainty, single.
STAMENS: dark pink.
PISTIL: pink.

FOLIAGE: mid-green.
GROWTH: upright.
A cultivar with no great pretensions, equally good as pot or bedding plant. Raised as a standard it forms a nice thick head and produces its delicate flowers in scarcely imaginable abundance from June until the frosts. It must be fed well in order to sustain the masses of flowers. The head will take an annual pruning back to the old wood.

'Mrs Marshall' (Jones, date unknown, GB)
TUBE: creamy-white.
SEPALS: creamy-white.
COROLLA: cerise, medium-sized, single.
STAMENS: pink.
PISTIL: white.
FOLIAGE: grass-green and glossy.
GROWTH: upright and bushy.
A good, old cultivar which can be used in a versatile way. In 1929 it gained an award from the RHS. Particularly good standard fuchsia.

'Mrs Victor Reiter' (Reiter 1940, USA)
('Amy Lye' × 'Mrs W. Rundle')
TUBE: snow-white.
SEPALS: snow-white and of waxy substance.
COROLLA: carmine-red, long, single.
STAMENS: pale pink.
PISTIL: white.
FOLIAGE: light green, slightly pilose.
GROWTH: lax-upright.
The bright colours and the elegant flower shape are impressive. As the plant grows relatively slowly and also does not overwinter that well, some cuttings should always be made in the autumn. Very good as a perennial plant if cultivated through. The flowering is then especially profuse.

'Mrs W. P. Wood' (Wood 1949, GB)
TUBE: pale pink, almost white.
SEPALS: pale pink.
COROLLA: white, single.
STAMENS: pale pink.
PISTIL: white.
FOLIAGE: light green and small.
GROWTH: upright and bushy.
Is a seedling of 'Margaret' with *F. magellanica* var. *molinae* origin. The flowers, however, are a clear improvement both in colour and also in number. Planted out in a garden bed, preferably not in full sun, the dainty flowers on a low bush show up

particularly well against the light foliage. In England it is very hardy.

'Mrs W. Rundle' (Rundle 1883, GB)
TUBE: flesh-pink.
SEPALS: flesh-pink with green tips.
COROLLA: orange, long flowers, single.
STAMENS: pink.
PISTIL: pink.
FOLIAGE: light green.
GROWTH: lax bush; will trail.
This old, renowned and, because of its subtle beauty, very popular cultivar does not branch all that readily. It must therefore be repeatedly stopped as a young plant and, if an upright bush is desired, also supported. 'Mrs W. Rundle' develops its full beauty as a standard. Somebody has described it as a true embodiment of grace and charm and that really is the case, too. It likes a sunny or at least really bright place. The flowers, though, show their full beauty best under glass.

'Nancy Lou' (Stubbs 1971, USA) No. 998
TUBE: pale pink.
SEPALS: pink, turned right back almost hiding the tube.
COROLLA: brilliant white, large round flowers of perfect shape, double.
STAMENS: bright pink.
PISTIL: pale pink.
FOLIAGE: mid-green.
GROWTH: upright and compact.
Eileen Saunders justifiably calls it a superstar of the fuchsia world with the whitest of white which the washing-powder advertisements commend to us. The plant is in addition unassuming and easy to look after.

'Native Dancer' (Tiret 1965, USA) No. 648
TUBE: red.
SEPALS: red, shiny.
COROLLA: deep purple, double.
STAMENS: red.
PISTIL: red.
FOLIAGE: dark green.
GROWTH: lax-upright; will trail.
The large flowers appear in fair profusion on a beautiful plant.

'Nellie Nuttall' (G. Roe 1977, GB)
('Khada' × 'Icecap')

TUBE: red.

SEPALS: red.

COROLLA: snow-white, slightly veined, single.

STAMENS: red.

PISTIL: red.

FOLIAGE: mid-green, small.

GROWTH: upright, very bushy with short internodes. The medium-sized flowers appear in profuse abundance and are of the 'upward look' type, facing sideways and upwards. An exceptionally good cultivar which easily eclipses many older red and white cultivars. This gem was introduced by the Markham Grange Nursery in Doncaster.

'Neue Welt' (Mahnke 1912, G)

TUBE: red.

SEPALS: red and shiny.

COROLLA: violet.

STAMENS: red.

PISTIL: red.

FOLIAGE: dark green.

GROWTH: upright, strong-growing and well branched.

A first-rate, older German variety which ought to be much better known. A standard is quickly raised and becomes more beautiful from year to year without any problems.

'Nicola' (Daglish 1964, GB)

('Swanley Gem' × 'Citation')

TUBE: cerise.

SEPALS: cerise, fully reflexed hiding the tube.

COROLLA: violet and purple, lighter at the base, veined pink, single.

STAMENS: cerise.

PISTIL: cerise.

FOLIAGE: glossy dark green with red leaf veins and stalks.

GROWTH: upright and bushy.

This enlarged version of 'Swanley Gem' has the same charming, plate-shaped flowers. The upswept sepals completely hide the tube.

'Nicolaas Aalhuizen' (Steevens 1973, NL)

TUBE: red.

SEPALS: red.

COROLLA: purple, single.

STAMENS: red.

PISTIL: red.

FOLIAGE: mid-green, small.

GROWTH: upright and well branched.

This seedling of 'Peter Pan' with its dainty flowers

was named after the long-standing, deserving president of the Dutch fuchsia society and is impressive for its profusion of flower.

'Nicola Jane' (Dawson 1959, GB)

TUBE: cerise.

SEPALS: cerise, upright, underside creped.

COROLLA: light pink with pink veining, double.

STAMENS: cerise.

PISTIL: cerise.

FOLIAGE: dark green with red veining and red stalks.

GROWTH: upright and bushy.

This profusely flowering cultivar is well suited for bed planting and is hardy in England.

'Nightingale' (Waltz 1960, USA) No. 442

TUBE: white, short.

SEPALS: white, flushed pink.

COROLLA: deep purple inside, pink outside, white and coral-coloured, double, very large.

STAMENS: pink.

PISTIL: pale pink.

FOLIAGE: dark green.

GROWTH: trailer.

The large, tricoloured flowers, wide open on blossoming out, are of exceptionally good substance and remain beautiful for a long time. It is particularly handsome as a hanging basket.

'Nina Wills' (Wills-Atkinson 1961, GB) No. 1129

TUBE: pink.

SEPALS: pink.

COROLLA: light pink, single.

STAMENS: pink.

PISTIL: pale pink.

FOLIAGE: light green, glossy.

GROWTH: upright and bushy.

This pink sport of 'Forget-Me-Not' is outstandingly well suited for bed planting. The delicately coloured flowers stand out well from other colours.

'Normandy Bell' (Martin 1961, USA) No. 465

TUBE: light pink.

SEPALS: light pink.

COROLLA: orchid-blue and pink, lightly veined, single.

STAMENS: pale pink.

PISTIL: whitish-pink.

FOLIAGE: mid-green.

GROWTH: lax-upright; if supported also as bush.

This descendant of 'Citation' has the same perfect,

bell-shaped flowers and also makes the same demands for cultivation. A well-cultivated hanging basket planted with this cultivar will always cause a sensation.

'Norman Mitchinson' (Dr Ryle 1976, GB) No. 1477
TUBE: whitish-pink.
SEPALS: waxen-white, green tips, pink base.
COROLLA: deep purple, sometimes pink and white marked, single.
STAMENS: pink.
PISTIL: pink.
FOLIAGE: green, slightly variegated.
GROWTH: upright.
Very good newer cultivar which was awarded a BFS silver Certificate of Merit in Manchester in 1976.

'Northumbrian Belle' (Dr Ryle 1973, GB) No. 1115
('Lena Dalton' × 'Citation')
TUBE: short, thick, pink.
SEPALS: pink.
COROLLA: deep bluish-violet, veined pink, single to semi-double.
STAMENS: cerise.
PISTIL: pink.
FOLIAGE: dark green with red midrib and red stalks.
GROWTH: upright, well branched.
One of the best cultivars of M. Ryle. With its bushy growth and the persistent profuse flowering is particularly well suited for pot cultivation.

'Northway' (Golics 1976, GB)
('La Campanella' × 'Howlett's Hardy')
TUBE: light pink, short and compact.
SEPALS: light pink.
COROLLA: cerise, single.
STAMENS: pink.
PISTIL: pink.
FOLIAGE: light green.
GROWTH: lax bush; will trail.
Unremittingly floriferous cultivar with beautiful colours. The dainty flowers are held sideways and upwards on strong stalks and are clearly visible over the foliage. The plant requires special care with feeding. Nitrogen deficiency is recognised by paler foliage.

'Novella' (Tiret 1968, USA) No. 796
TUBE: flesh-pink, very long.
SEPALS: rosy-pink, green tips.
COROLLA: smoky-orange, double.

STAMENS: pale pink.
PISTIL: pale pink.
FOLIAGE: mid-green, dentate.
GROWTH: trailer, spreading.
The beautiful flowers develop particularly good colours in full sun.

'Orange Crush' (Handley 1972, GB) No. 1057
TUBE: salmon-orange.
SEPALS: salmon-orange.
COROLLA: brilliant orange, lighter at base, single.
STAMENS: pink.
PISTIL: light pink.
FOLIAGE: light green.
GROWTH: straight upright.
Unlike 'Orange Flair', the sepals are carried horizontally. In other respects the two cultivars are similar. Both like the sun and are good bedding plants but also form good standards.

'Orange Drops' (Martin 1963, USA) No. 572
TUBE: orange, waxen and thick.
SEPALS: orange, horizontal, green tips.
COROLLA: orange, single.
STAMENS: orange.
PISTIL: orange.
FOLIAGE: mid-green, large.
GROWTH: horizontal, lax bush; will trail.
From the point of view of flower colour one of the best orange-coloured cultivars, if only the plant had a somewhat more elegant growth. Early, frequent stopping is definitely essential. Perhaps it should just be tried as a weeping standard? Nevertheless, it gained an AFS award in 1967.

'Orange Flair' (Handley 1972, GB) No. 1058
TUBE: salmon-orange, thick and waxen.
SEPALS: salmon-orange, underside creped, upswept, also hiding the tube.
COROLLA: orange, lighter at the base, single.
STAMENS: orange.
PISTIL: orange.
FOLIAGE: mid-green.
GROWTH: upright.
This cultivar produces side shoots only if frequently pinched. Sun, the more the better, makes the orange radiant. The single flower is well shaped and long-lasting.

'Orange Mirage' (Tiret 1970, USA) No. 896
TUBE: salmon-pink.

SEPALS: salmon-pink, underside orange, green tips.
COROLLA: orange, single, large-flowered.
STAMENS: pink.
PISTIL: pink.
FOLIAGE: mid-green, red midrib and red stalks.
GROWTH: lax-upright.
As in many cultivars with this colour arrangement, the orange of the corolla often looks somewhat burnt. The flowers are exquisitely shaped and of good substance.

'Oranje Boven' (de Graaff 1980, NL) No. 1874
(Award of the VKC at Apeldoorn, 1980)
TUBE: salmon-orange, long and thin.
SEPALS: salmon and orange, narrow, large green tips.
COROLLA: strong smoky-orange, single.
STAMENS: light salmon.
PISTIL: light salmon.
FOLIAGE: large, light green.
GROWTH: strong, upright.
A strong-growing plant with long internodes which grows very tall in a relatively short time. The flowers are long and narrow, very elegant and of beautiful, delicate colour which stands out particularly well against the light-coloured foliage. Raisers even recommend it as a climbing fuchsia on a trellis.

'Oranje van Os' (van Os pre-1970, NL)
TUBE: salmon-pink, long.
SEPALS: salmon-pink, long, with green tips, held horizontally.
COROLLA: bright orange, single.
STAMENS: salmon-pink.
PISTIL: salmon-orange.
FOLIAGE: light green, large.
GROWTH: straight upright.
If the young plant is stopped more frequently so as to balance out the rather stiff growth, a beautiful large bush with numerous bright, elegant flowers is quickly obtained. A sun- and warmth-loving cultivar, which J. van Os, who discovered it some years ago in Venlo in the Netherlands, suspected was of German origin.

'Ortenburger Festival' (Töpperwein 1973, G) No. 1432
TUBE: red, short and thick.
SEPALS: deep red, held horizontally.
COROLLA: bluish-violet, later wine-red, single.
STAMENS: red.
PISTIL: red.
FOLIAGE: dark green.

GROWTH: upright and well branched.
This 'Bodethal' × 'Beacon' seedling has somewhat larger flowers than its ancestors and is an excellent bedding plant which has quickly acquired a wide distribution. Registered in 1977 by the Fuchsiarama nursery of Fort Bragg, USA.

'Other Fellow' (Hazard and Hazard 1946, USA)
TUBE: white and waxen, long.
SEPALS: white and waxen, green tips.
COROLLA: coral-pink, white at the base, single.
STAMENS: white.
PISTIL: white.
FOLIAGE: mid-green, denticulate.
GROWTH: upright and bushy.
The small, dainty flowers appear in such abundance that every bush or standard becomes a striking eye-catcher. A gem and yet robust and suitable for any intended purpose.

'Ovation' (Stubbs 1981, USA) No. 1614
('Pepi' × 'Applause')
TUBE: ivory, long, thin.
SEPALS: ivory to pink, long, broad.
COROLLA: dark red, spotted orange, double.
STAMENS: light pink.
PISTIL: cream.
FOLIAGE: mid-green, large, dentate margin.
GROWTH: trailer and spreading.
This cultivar prefers a cool and shady position; certainly bright, but the sunlight should be filtered. So that the flowers are not hidden by the large leaves, it is best raised in a hanging basket or at the edge of larger containers.

'Pacific Queen' (Waltz 1963, USA) No. 587
TUBE: whitish-pink.
SEPALS: pink, white tips.
COROLLA: rose-red, double, of good substance.
STAMENS: pink.
PISTIL: pale pink.
FOLIAGE: dark green, red midrib.
GROWTH: upright.
Strong and tall-growing with many large, very beautifully shaped flowers. With good cultivation an eye-catcher of great impact, as well as completely problem-free.

'Pacquesa' (Clyne 1974, GB) No. 1286
TUBE: red, short, waxen.
SEPALS: deep red, shiny, creped underside.

COROLLA: snow-white with a little red veining, single.
STAMENS: red.
PISTIL: red.
FOLIAGE: grass-green, glossy.
GROWTH: upright, well branched.
The substance and durability of the medium-sized, classic flowers is outstanding. There are many kinds of red and white fuchsias; this is an improvement on the older ones with radiant flowers in great abundance.

'Padre Pio' (Boullemier 1987, GB) No. 2198
('Fascination' × 'Mission Bells')
TUBE: light red faintly streaked darker red.
SEPALS: bright red, creped, bright red underneath with reflexed tips.
COROLLA: opens dark blue-violet, maturing to violet heavily veined red, semi-double.
STAMENS: red.
PISTIL: red.
FOLIAGE: light to medium green with serrulate edges.
GROWTH: upright inclined to be lax under glass.
Very unusual shaped red and violet blooms with broad pointed sepals sweeping over the tube without hiding it. Classic shaped blooms holding colour over long period, deeper in colour than other 'red/purples'. Raised by the compiler of the world-wide acknowledged *Fuchsia Checklist*. Named after the famous Italian priest after having received miraculous cure for serious illness.

'Papa Bleuss' (Tiret 1956, USA) No. 253
TUBE: greenish-white.
SEPALS: white, underside pink, creped.
COROLLA: very dark violet, fading to red, double.
STAMENS: pink.
PISTIL: white.
FOLIAGE: mid-green, red midrib.
GROWTH: lax-upright; will trail.
Because of the unusually large and heavy flowers every single shoot must be supported in time. The flowers are lovely, only one should not expect all that many of them at once. As for the rest, what has been said earlier about white and blue fuchsias applies.

'Papillon' (v. d. Post 1985, NL) No. 2052
Certificate of Merit, Zeist
TUBE: peach-coloured.
SEPALS: light pink with darker underside.
COROLLA: light pink in various shades, single.

STAMENS: pink.
PISTIL: white.
FOLIAGE: mid-green.
GROWTH: upright.
A plant which can be easily shaped. The large single flowers are reminiscent of a butterfly.

'Party Frock' (Walker & Jones 1953, USA)
TUBE: rose-red.
SEPALS: rose-red, long, upturned and upright, green tips.
COROLLA: lilac-lavender, outer petals pervaded with pink, single to semi-double.
STAMENS: pink.
PISTIL: pale pink.
FOLIAGE: dark green.
GROWTH: upright, well branched and strong-growing.
An outstanding cultivar, good as a bush or standard. The pastel-coloured, well-shaped flowers are lovely.

'Paul Cambon' (Lemoine 1909, F)
TUBE: scarlet-red, short and thick.
SEPALS: scarlet-red, broad and upswept.
COROLLA: Parma-violet, double.
STAMENS: scarlet-red.
PISTIL: scarlet-red, no longer than the stamens.
FOLIAGE: mid-green with red midrib, strongly dentate.
GROWTH: medium upright.
An old, lovely cultivar with a perfect, rosette-shaped corolla of striking colour. The plant is slow-growing, though, and difficult to bring into a good shape. It likes cool and shady conditions and is best cultivated under glass.

'Peloria' (Martin 1961, USA) No. 466
TUBE: enamel-red.
SEPALS: enamel-red, underside creped, partly fused with the petals.
COROLLA: inside purple-blue, outside streaked and variegated pink, double.
STAMENS: red.
PISTIL: red.
FOLIAGE: dark green, veined red, on red stalks.
GROWTH: upright and strong.
Very large, star-shaped flowers on a strong and naturally very orderly growing plant. On a plant several years old the wealth of flowers is enormous and the flowers are good and long-lasting.

'Pennine' (Mitchinson 1981, GB) No. 1655
('Norman Mitchinson' × 'Eden Lady')
TUBE: red with dark stripes.
SEPALS: white, a little red at the base.
COROLLA: violet and blue, single.
STAMENS: pink.
PISTIL: whitish-pink.
FOLIAGE: dark green, small, serrated margin.
GROWTH: upright and bushy.
Compared with many older blue and white fuchsias, which are all somewhat difficult to grow, here we are dealing with a strong-growing, problem-free cultivar. The plant is naturally self-branching and makes a good bush or, with our assistance, even a standard.

'Pepi' (Tiret 1963, USA) No. 578
TUBE: white to pink.
SEPALS: white with pink tinge, underside pink.
COROLLA: cerise, mottled orange, orange petaloids, double.
STAMENS: cerise.
PISTIL: pink.
FOLIAGE: mid-green, red midrib.
GROWTH: upright; will trail with weights.
Very large flowers of good substance. Because of the heaviness of the flowers a good bush shape cannot be achieved even with support. It is best planted in a hanging basket, then it flowers profusely and beautifully.

'Peppermint Stick' (Garson 1951, USA)
TUBE: light red.
SEPALS: light red, pinkish-red at the tips.
COROLLA: purple, with red and pink streaks, double.
STAMENS: pink.
PISTIL: pink.
FOLIAGE: mid-green.
GROWTH: upright.
One of the first fuchsias with tricoloured flowers. Unlike many newer cultivars of this kind, it is robust and floriferous. Under glass, flowers early in the year and is easy to care for.

'Phenomenal' (Lemoine 1869, F)
TUBE: scarlet-red.
SEPALS: scarlet-red, very broad.
COROLLA: indigo-blue, lighter at the base, slightly veined red, double.
STAMENS: red.
PISTIL: red.
FOLIAGE: dark green, red midrib.

GROWTH: upright and bushy.
Very large, distinctively shaped flowers. Even the really strong growth of this cultivar is not sufficient to bear the heavy flowers without support. If the conditions where it is placed are not optimum many flowers do not open. A cool, shady position is recommended.

'Pinch Me' (Tiret 1969, USA) No. 831
TUBE: snow-white.
SEPALS: snow-white.
COROLLA: lilac-blue to purple, double.
STAMENS: pink.
PISTIL: white.
FOLIAGE: light green, attractively dentate, red stalks and red midrib.
GROWTH: trailer.
A strong-growing, very decorative hanging-basket plant. There are many difficult, fastidious fuchsias in this colour combination. 'Pinch Me' on the other hand is rewarding and presents no problems in growing. Stopping several times leads to good branching. Also good as an espalier. In Holland this cultivar has at times been sold as 'Phoenix', which has led to some confusion.

'Pink Bon Accord' (Thorne 1959, GB)
TUBE: pale pink.
SEPALS: pale pink, underside darker, green tips.
COROLLA: bright coral-pink, single.
STAMENS: coral-pink.
PISTIL: pale pink.
FOLIAGE: grass-green, attractively dentate.
GROWTH: upright and bushy.
The medium-sized flowers of brilliant colour are held more sideways on the tips of the shoots, and thus not quite so upright as in 'Bon Accord', of which this cultivar is said to be a mutation or a seedling. Very tolerant of the sun and therefore particularly good as a bedding plant.

'Pink Cloud' (Walker 1953, USA) No. 269
TUBE: pink.
SEPALS: pink, underside darker.
COROLLA: pale pink, darker, single.
STAMENS: dark pink.
PISTIL: light pink.
FOLIAGE: mid-green.
GROWTH: upright.
An unusually large, beautifully shaped flower with gaily rolled-up sepals but poor substance. If fre-

quently stopped as a young plant it quickly makes a large bush. The growing strength is also sufficient for standard or pyramid forms. The position should, however, always be chosen in as cool and shady a place as possible.

'Pink Darling' (Machedo 1961, USA)
TUBE: dark pink.
SEPALS: pale pink, underside darker.
COROLLA: soft lilac and pink.
STAMENS: pink.
PISTIL: white.
FOLIAGE: dark green, small.
GROWTH: straight upright.
Unlike the preceding cultivar, the flowers are small and dainty and are carried sideways-upwards on strong stalks. Early, frequent stopping makes the plant bushy and gives it many shoots. It then produces flowers in unbelievable amounts throughout the entire summer. An excellent cultivar in every way.

'Pink Flamingo' (Castro 1961, USA) No. 470
(AFS Certificate of Merit 1964)
TUBE: pink.
SEPALS: dark pink, green tips which curl into various shapes, hence the name.
COROLLA: whitish-pink, with red veins at the base.
STAMENS: pale pink.
PISTIL: white.
FOLIAGE: dark green, the new growth is bronze.
GROWTH: lax bush with very long internodes, but flexible branches.
A distinguishing mark of this cultivar is the curiously rolled sepals on the long flower, which were probably also the reason for the choice of name. Early stopping is essential. A wall basket is the best place to present this fuchsia. Propagation and cultivation are problem-free. The plant does not, though, grow very old. It is always advisable to make a cutting in autumn to be on the safe side.

'Pink Galore' (Fuchsia-La 1958, USA) No. 469
(AFS Certificate of Merit 1958)
TUBE: pink, long, rather darker than the corolla.
SEPALS: pink, broad and upswept.
COROLLA: pink, double.
STAMENS: light pink.
PISTIL: light pink.
FOLIAGE: dark green and glossy, the young growth is flushed pink.

GROWTH: trailer.
This is without doubt the fuchsia with the purest pink and very beautiful flowers if only it were not so troublesome as a plant. To get an attractive, uniformly grown hanging basket at least five plants should be used. The growth is also sufficient for a small standard. It is best kept constantly under glass, where the breathtaking flowers last for a very long time. As 'Pink Galore' does not overwinter well, it should be raised anew every year from autumn cuttings.

'Pink Marshmallow' (Stubbs 1971, USA) No. 996
TUBE: pinkish-white.
SEPALS: white, underside rosy, green tips.
COROLLA: white, slightly veined pink, double.
STAMENS: pale pink.
PISTIL: white.
FOLIAGE: light green and large, often 11–12 cm long.
GROWTH: trailer and spreading.
One of the best cultivars of Annabella Stubbs. The cultivar is nearly 20 years old and is famous for its gigantic flowers. For lovers of large-flowered fuchsias it is an absolute must. The flowers reach their full size and beauty in the greenhouse. Here they are up to 8.5 cm long, excluding seed-vessel and stamens. This cultivar is not fastidious and even in a sheltered place outdoors it flowers very profusely. The individual flower, though, is then smaller. The almost round buds are also striking.

'Pink Pearl' (Bright 1919, GB)
TUBE: pale pink.
SEPALS: pale pink, underside darker and creped, green tips.
COROLLA: dark pink, slight veining, semi-double to double.
STAMENS: pale pink.
PISTIL: light pink.
FOLIAGE: dark, small and pointed, reddish stalks and branches.
GROWTH: upright and bushy.
One of the irrepressible old cultivars. It was bred by Lye's son-in-law, who was renowned for growing huge pyramids. The exquisite flower shape, the roundish corolla which is surrounded by roundish sepals, stands out conspicuously against many others. The plant is robust and problem-free. It flowers extravagantly, especially on overwintered plants.

'Pink Quartet' (Walker & Jones 1949, USA)
TUBE: pink.
SEPALS: dark pink, upswept.
COROLLA: whitish-pink, semi-double.
STAMENS: pink.
PISTIL: pink.
FOLIAGE: dark green.
GROWTH: upright, rather rigid.
Like a quartet the petals are very neatly curled into four rolls. This gives the flower a distinctive shape and good substance. Early stopping leads to better branching.

'Pink Temptation' (Wills 1966, GB)
TUBE: cream-white.
SEPALS: cream-white, underside pink, green tips, horizontal.
COROLLA: Tyrian-pink, with whiter base, single.
STAMENS: pink.
PISTIL: whitish-pink.
FOLIAGE: dark green, undulate at the margins.
GROWTH: lax-upright, flexible, very dense and branched.
This sport of 'Temptation' has all the good qualities of the original cultivar. The flexible branches enable planting of boxes in exposed places. A standard of this cultivar develops a particularly thick, profusely flowering head.

'Pinup' (Kennett 1968, USA) No. 775
TUBE: pure white, long.
SEPALS: pure white, long and narrow.
COROLLA: bright pink, semi-double.
STAMENS: pale pink.
PISTIL: whitish-pink.
FOLIAGE: dark green.
GROWTH: trailer.
In a wall basket the charming, pastel-coloured, medium-sized flowers produce a lovely effect.

'Playboy' (Homan 1969, GB)
('Phyllis' × 'Fascination')
TUBE: cerise.
SEPALS: cerise, creped, held above the horizontal.
COROLLA: pink, veined and mottled red, double.
STAMENS: cerise.
PISTIL: cerise.
FOLIAGE: dark green.
GROWTH: upright and bushy.
An extravagantly flowering cultivar which is versatile in use. Particularly good and literally brilliant as a balcony or bedding plant in full sun.

'Plenty' (Gadsby 1974, GB) No. 1223
('Cloverdale' × 'Lady Isobel Barnett')
TUBE: carmine-red.
SEPALS: deep carmine, underside lighter, slightly curled at the tip.
COROLLA: violet and purple, pink base, bell-shaped, single.
STAMENS: carmine-red, varying in length.
PISTIL: pink.
FOLIAGE: dark green, large.
GROWTH: upright and bushy.
One of the best cultivars from Cliff Gadsby, aptly named. The flowers stand sideways on short stalks as in 'Lady Isobel Barnett'. Very beautiful as a large, ornamental show plant, but even small plants are literally covered with flowers.

'Poseidon' (Travis 1980, GB) No. 1584
TUBE: slender and long (92 mm), apricot-coloured.
SEPALS: long and narrow, apricot-coloured.
COROLLA: small, short, apricot-coloured, single.
STAMENS: apricot-coloured, enclosed.
PISTIL: apricot-coloured.
FOLIAGE: sage-green, large.
GROWTH: upright and strong.
Seedling of *F. fulgens* var. *rubra grandiflora*, with same qualities but lighter flower colour.

'Postiljon' (von der Post 1975, NL)
TUBE: white with pink tinge.
SEPALS: cream-white with green tips.
COROLLA: reddish-violet, white at the base, single.
STAMENS: white.
PISTIL: white.
FOLIAGE: mid-green, small.
GROWTH: trailer; branches very well.
'La Campanella' descendant with very good qualities. This cultivar flowers without a break from May to October and in the greenhouse even right through the winter.

'Prelude' (Kennett 1958, USA) No. 348
TUBE: whitish-pink.
SEPALS: whitish-pink.
COROLLA: large lilac petals in the centre, surrounded by white and pink mottled petaloids, double.
STAMENS: pink.
PISTIL: pinkish-white.
FOLIAGE: mid-green.
GROWTH: trailer.
For all enthusiasts who place a lovely flower above all

'Royal Purple'

else, this is the right fuchsia. The growth, however, is difficult to control. It is best to stop the young plant once or twice and then let nature run its course. In a hanging basket, at eye-level, the flowers with their singular beauty are an enchanting sight. There is a second fuchsia with the name 'Prelude', having single red and magenta flowers (Blackwell 1957, GB).

'President' (Standish 1841, GB)
('Formosa Elegans' × *F. corymbiflora*)
TUBE: bright red.
SEPALS: bright red.
COROLLA: rosy and magenta, red at base, single.
STAMENS: red.

PISTIL: red.
FOLIAGE: dark green with new growth red.
GROWTH: upright and bushy.
This very old, early-flowering cultivar is still a match for many modern fuchsias of the same colour arrangement. 'President' has been hardy over several years in a sheltered position.

'President B. W. Rawlins' (Thorne 1966, GB)
TUBE: light pink.
SEPALS: light pink, underside orange-pink, green tips.
COROLLA: carmine-red, pervaded with orange, lighter at the base, single.
STAMENS: pink.
PISTIL: pale pink.
FOLIAGE: mid-green.
GROWTH: trailer.
Beautifully shaped, large flowers with half-raised sepals creped on underside. The growth is strong and healthy and tends to be hanging. Very good for large hanging baskets. This cultivar was named after a former president of the BFS.

'President Leo Boullemier' (Burns 1983, GB)
('Joy Patmore' × 'Cloverdale Pearl')
TUBE: short fluted tube streaked magenta.
SEPALS: white flared sepals sweeping up to angle of 45 degrees, held well away from tube, pointed.
COROLLA: bell-shaped, magenta-blue maturing to bluish-pink, single.
STAMENS: bluish-pink.
PISTIL: white.

'Stanley Cash'

FOLIAGE: dark-green, pointed with prominent serrated edges.

GROWTH: upright and bushy, vigorous.

This cultivar is extremely vigorous, producing masses of shoots after early pinching. Most attractive single flowers, extremely floriferous, short-jointed and well in the exhibition category, inherits the colour of 'Joy Patmore' and the habit and shape of 'Cloverdale Pearl'. Named after a former President of the British Fuchsia Society and prolific writer.

'President Margaret Slater' (Taylor 1972, GB) No. 1119

('Cascade' × 'Taffy')

TUBE: white, thin and long.

SEPALS: outside whitish-pink, underside orange, long and narrow, green tips, elegantly curled.

COROLLA: mauve-pink with orange tones, single.

STAMENS: pink.

PISTIL: light pink.

FOLIAGE: mid-green, veined red, denticulate.

GROWTH: trailer.

From the female parent 'Cascade' comes the incredible wealth of flower and the growth, which immediately at the edge of the pot heads downwards. Particularly decorative as a hanging basket. Named after a former president of the BFS.

'Preston Guild' (Thornley 1971, GB) No. 1010

TUBE: pure white, long and thin.

SEPALS: pure white, slightly curled, held above the horizontal.

COROLLA: bluish-violet, white at the base, single.

STAMENS: white.

PISTIL: white.

FOLIAGE: mid-green with red midrib, on red stalks.

GROWTH: upright, well branched.

The dainty flowers excite enthusiasm everywhere. If the bright colours are to remain beautiful for any time, a shady place sheltered from the rain is certainly necessary.

'Prosperity' (Gadsby 1974, GB) No. 1224

TUBE: dark red.

SEPALS: dark red.

COROLLA: pale pink, veined and spotted red, double.

STAMENS: rose-red.

PISTIL: pink.

FOLIAGE: dark green with red veining.

GROWTH: rigidly upright.

A cultivar that grows very tall and branches poorly even with frequent stopping. In the background of a garden bed the many flowers stand out at their most beautiful. One of the very few double hardy cultivars.

'Purple Heart' (Walker and Jones 1950, USA)

TUBE: bright red.

SEPALS: red, long, waxen.

COROLLA: inner petals violet-blue, outer petals rose-red, edged red, double.

STAMENS: red.

PISTIL: red.

FOLIAGE: dark green, red veins.

GROWTH: medium upright.

Lovely flowers, unfortunately only a few of them at the same time on a strongly growing plant, which can be cultivated without any great problems. Early, repeated stopping is beneficial.

'Queen Victoria' (unknown)

TUBE: wax-white.

SEPALS: wax-white, pink tinge, green tips.

COROLLA: dark lavender-blue, pink base, double.

STAMENS: pink.

PISTIL: light pink.

FOLIAGE: mid-green.

GROWTH: upright and bushy.

Delightful cultivar, completely problem-free, makes a large, profusely flowering plant from a January cutting. Not to be confused with the famous fuchsia of the same name from Story 1855, which possessed the first red and white double flowers.

'Radings Gerda' (Reimann 1984, NL) No. 1932

(F_2 of *F. paniculata* × *F. arborescens* × *F.* × *bacillaris*)

(Certificate of Merit Aalsmer 1985)

TUBE: reddish-purple, 10 mm long.

SEPALS: reddish-purple, reflexed tips.

COROLLA: lilac-coloured, edges undulate, single.

STAMENS: pink-lilac, enclosed.

PISTIL: reddish-purple, projects 5 mm outside the corolla.

FOLIAGE: dark green, small, 25 × 12 mm.

GROWTH: upright and bushy.

Attractively shaped, upright little shrub which, with its dainty flowers, is well suited for pot cultivation. Named after Gerda Manthey during her period of office as editor of the *Fuchsia Courier* of the German Fuchsia Society.

'Radings Inge' (Reimann-Dietiker 1980, NL)

(*F.* × *bacillaris* seedling)

(Award at Apeldoorn in 1980)
TUBE: rose-red.
SEPALS: cream.
COROLLA: orange, single.
STAMENS: orange.
PISTIL: red.
FOLIAGE: small, fern-like.
GROWTH: upright, many-branched.
Flowers about 12 mm long by 8 mm lower width.

'Radings Karin' (Reimann-Dietiker 1981, NL)
(*F.* × *bacillaris* seedling)
TUBE: rose-red.
SEPALS: rose-red.
COROLLA: orange-red, single.
PISTIL: red.
FOLIAGE: small, fern-like.
GROWTH: upright and bushy.
Dainty flowers, 13 mm long by 10 mm lower width.

'Radings Marjorie' (Reimann-Dietiker 1980, NL)
No. 1935
(*F.* × *bacillaris* seedling)
(Award at Apeldoorn in 1980)
TUBE: white.
SEPALS: light Bordeaux red.
COROLLA: light pink, single.
PISTIL: red.
FOLIAGE: small and delicate.
GROWTH: upright.
The flowers are 13 mm long by 9 mm lower width.

'Radings Michelle' (Reimann-Dietiker 1980, NL)
No. 1936
(*F.* × *bacillaris* seedling)
(Award at Apeldoorn in 1980)
TUBE: pink.
SEPALS: whitish-pink.
COROLLA: light pink, single.
PISTIL: red.
FOLIAGE: small, fern-like.
GROWTH: upright and many-branched.
Flowers dainty, 12 mm long by 8 mm lower width.
Beautiful black berries in autumn.

'RAF' (Garson 1942, USA)
TUBE: cherry-red.
SEPALS: cherry-red.
COROLLA: pink, light veins and spots, double.
STAMENS: cherry-red.

PISTIL: cherry-red.
FOLIAGE: mid-green, veined red.
GROWTH: lax bush; will trail.
The profusion of flowers of this cultivar is unimaginable. If they are not allowed regular feeding, the later flowers become clearly smaller. Flowering begins particularly early in the year and lasts without interruption up to the first frost.

'Razzle Dazzle' (Martin 1965, USA) No. 630
TUBE: pale pink.
SEPALS: pale pink, underside darker, broad, creped.
COROLLA: mid-blue, pink at the base with pink petaloids, double.
STAMENS: pink.
PISTIL: light pink.
FOLIAGE: mid-green.
GROWTH: trailer.
The flowers of this cultivar are a phenomenon. At the beginning they appear rather small, but very fully double. It is days before the many petals and petaloids have unfolded and the thick sepals roll up completely into bizarre horns. At the end the flower is twice as large and hangs from an unusually long pedicel.

'Rebecca' (Singleton 1980, GB) No. 1580
TUBE: pale green, short and thick.
SEPALS: white, slightly upright.
COROLLA: white, single.
STAMENS: white.
PISTIL: white.
FOLIAGE: dark green.
GROWTH: medium upright.
This seedling from 'Ting-a-Ling' has beautiful plate-shaped flowers and is well suited for all growth forms, including larger ones. Best colour in the shade.

'Red Jacket' (Waltz 1961, USA) No. 356
TUBE: scarlet-red.
SEPALS: scarlet-red, long, upright.
COROLLA: snow-white, large, double.
STAMENS: red.
PISTIL: red.
FOLIAGE: mid-green, red veins and stalks.
GROWTH: natural trailer.
A striking vision with its long red buds and the large, wide-open, exquisitely shaped flowers. This cultivar is very popular as a hanging basket and should become even more widespread.

'Red Ribbon' (Martin 1959, USA) No. 371
TUBE: red.
SEPALS: red, very long and thin.
COROLLA: snow-white with red veins, double.
STAMENS: red, do not protrude much from sepals.
PISTIL: whitish-pink.
FOLIAGE: mid-green, medium-sized.
GROWTH: lax bush or trailer.
The long, narrow sepals, which often turn elegantly around the tube, are a distinguishing mark of this strong-growing and robust hanging-basket plant. Good care and repeated stopping are rewarded by richer abundance of flowers.

'Red Spider' (Reiter 1946, USA)
(AFS Certificate of Merit 1948)
TUBE: long, thin, carmine-red.
SEPALS: crimson-red, long, narrow and reflexed.
COROLLA: somewhat darker red, single.
STAMENS: light red.
PISTIL: light red.
FOLIAGE: mid-green, very thick.
GROWTH: natural trailer, strong-growing.
The fabulously rich abundance of flowers which 'Red Spider' produces over a long period can only be dreamt of in many other fuchsias. A hanging basket, however, should be pinched early and often so that the flowers are not only present on the long-drooping shoots but are distributed uniformly over the whole plant. Also very good for cultivation in larger containers. In hot positions the very thick foliage must be protected from attack by red spider.

'Reichards Sämling' (Teupel 1931, G)
TUBE: white, waxen, short and compact.
SEPALS: white, waxen, green tips, reflexed.
COROLLA: pink with somewhat darker edges, white base, single.
STAMENS: light pink.
PISTIL: white.
FOLIAGE: mid-green, small.
GROWTH: upright, self-branching.
Dainty, delicately coloured flowers of very good substance and consequently very good weather resistance on a bushy plant. Early and profusely flowering cultivar. The botanic gardens in Berlin has saved it from being lost over the last 50 years, though there it was cultivated under the name of 'Reichsminister Semmler'.

'Reverend Dr Brown' (Taylor 1973, GB) No. 1118
('Sophisticated Lady' × 'Citation')
TUBE: pale pink, short and thick.
SEPALS: pale pink outside, inside deep pink, green tips, upswept almost hiding the tube.
COROLLA: white, slightly veined pink, double.
STAMENS: pink.
PISTIL: pinkish-white.
FOLIAGE: mid-green.
GROWTH: upright and well branched.
Very profusely flowering, delicate-looking and yet robust cultivar which grows quickly and strongly and is easy to cultivate. It is named after one of the founder members and later president of the BFS.

'Ridestar' (Blackwell 1965, GB)
TUBE: scarlet-red.
SEPALS: scarlet-red.
COROLLA: deep, pure blue, with pink veins, rosy-lavender when faded, double.
STAMENS: red.
PISTIL: red.
FOLIAGE: dark green.
GROWTH: upright.
Large flowers in masses on a strong-growing plant, which also forms a good standard.

'Rolla' (Lemoine 1913, F)
TUBE: pale pink.
SEPALS: pale pink.
COROLLA: cream-white, pink at the base, double.
STAMENS: whitish-pink.
PISTIL: whitish-pink.
FOLIAGE: mid-green.
GROWTH: upright.
A very good old cultivar which has lost something of its popularity. It has been much used in hybridising, particularly in America. As well as 'Flying Cloud' there are many other cultivars which have 'Rolla' in their genealogical tree.

'Rose of Castille' (Banks 1855, GB)
TUBE: waxen-white, thick, roundish.
SEPALS: waxen-white, green tips, very slight tinge of pink.
COROLLA: bluish-purple, white at the base, single.
STAMENS: pale pink.
PISTIL: white.
FOLIAGE: light green.
GROWTH: stiffly upright, bushy.
One of the very good, much-loved cultivars with

'Reverend Dr Brown'

'Rose of Castille'

medium-sized, sideways-upwards held, very pretty flowers of great luminosity. Flowers very early and profusely without a break until the frost.

'Rose of Castille Improved' (Lane 1871, GB)
TUBE: flesh-pink.
SEPALS: flesh-pink.
COROLLA: violet-purple, single.
STAMENS: pink.
PISTIL: white.
FOLIAGE: light green.
GROWTH: upright.
Very different from 'Rose of Castille'. Strong-growing and versatile like the latter, but in no way an improvement.

'Rosy Frills' (Handley 1979, GB) No. 1503
TUBE: greenish-white.
SEPALS: outside whitish-pink, inside pale pink, yellowish-green tips, broad.
COROLLA: rose-red, with red edges, outer petals streaked salmon, double.
STAMENS: pink.
PISTIL: white.

FOLIAGE: dark green with red stalks.
GROWTH: lax bush; will trail.
Early and profusely flowering cultivar.

'Rough Silk' (Baker 1970, GB)
TUBE: pale pink, long.
SEPALS: pale pink, green tips, long and narrow.
COROLLA: wine-red, pink at the base, single.
STAMENS: pink.
PISTIL: pink.
FOLIAGE: light green.
GROWTH: trailer, vigorous.
Originally this cultivar was named 'Baker's Boy' and later renamed. The elegant, large flowers show up best in a wall basket.

'Royal Purple' (Lemoine 1896, F)
TUBE: deep red, shiny.
SEPALS: deep red, waxen, underside lighter.
COROLLA: royal blue, lighter at base, veined red, single.
STAMENS: cherry-red.
PISTIL: cherry-red.
FOLIAGE: mid-green, glossy.

GROWTH: upright and bushy.

Attractive structure, large and beautifully shaped flowers of good substance and brilliant colours. Versatile as tub plant or in garden bed, also very good as standard and pyramid, even as climbing plant. What is offered in Germany under 'Heron' or 'Schwabenland' often turns out to be 'Royal Purple'.

'Royal Touch' (Tiret 1964, USA) No. 597
TUBE: rose-red.
SEPALS: rose-red.
COROLLA: royal blue, double.
STAMENS: pink.
PISTIL: pink.
FOLIAGE: dark green.
GROWTH: trailer.
Of the many red and blue fuchsias this cultivar stands out through its particularly beautiful blue. Strong-growing and problem-free; also attractive as a weeping standard.

'Royal Velvet' (Waltz 1962, USA) No. 526
TUBE: crimson-red.
SEPALS: crimson-red, broad, underside creped.
COROLLA: deep purple-blue, base spotted red, double.
STAMENS: red.
PISTIL: red.
FOLIAGE: mid-green, veined red, red stalks.
GROWTH: lax and bushy.
Among the many cultivars with strongly double, purple-blue corolla and red tube and sepals 'Royal Velvet' is one of the very best. On blossoming out the corolla opens wide and reveals a red centre. The red stamens and the long red pistil further emphasise its beauty. Frequent stopping produces a strong bush which gets along with a little supporting. Also very good as a standard.

'Ruffled Petticoat' (Foster 1974, USA) No. 1173
TUBE: wine-red.
SEPALS: wine-red.
COROLLA: white, flushed wine-red, double.
STAMENS: pink.
PISTIL: pink.
FOLIAGE: light green, denticulate.
GROWTH: upright and bushy.
Large, widely opened flowers with pleated petals. Prolific and long-flowering, of exquisite beauty.

'Rufus' (Nelson 1952, USA) No. 177
TUBE: red.

SEPALS: red.
COROLLA: red, single.
STAMENS: red.
PISTIL: red.
FOLIAGE: light green.
GROWTH: upright, strong-growing.
Always affectionately known as 'Rufus the Red'. A cultivar for the beginner, completely problem-free. The medium-sized flowers appear in great number and without a break throughout the whole season. Also very attractive as a standard.

'Ruth King' (Tiret 1967, USA) No. 736
TUBE: white.
SEPALS: white, green tips.
COROLLA: lilac and pink, outer petals mottled white, double.
STAMENS: pink.
PISTIL: light pink.
FOLIAGE: dark green.
GROWTH: trailer.
A strong-growing hanging-basket cultivar with conspicuous large flowers. No particular problems with its care; well-fed plants are very floriferous.

'Sahara' (Kennett 1966, USA) No. 679
TUBE: pink.
SEPALS: pink with green tips.
COROLLA: the middle petals are purple, the outer ones pink with orange petaloids, double.
STAMENS: pink.
PISTIL: pale pink.
FOLIAGE: mid-green.
GROWTH: upright.
For a fuchsia with such large, striking, beautifully coloured flowers it is easy to cultivate and quickly grows into a bushy plant. The full beauty of the flowers, though, develops only under glass. In the open the flowers remain smaller.

'Salmon Glow' (Handley 1978, GB) No. 1454
TUBE: quite pale salmon-pink, long and thin, waxen.
SEPALS: salmon-pink, with green tips, horizontal.
COROLLA: salmon-orange, single, each petal on its own little stalk.
STAMENS: salmon-pink, enclosed.
PISTIL: whitish-pink.
FOLIAGE: light green.
GROWTH: lax-upright; will trail.
Long, elegant flowers which look very good against the light foliage are produced in masses and are of

'Sleigh Bells'

'Seventh Heaven'

outstanding substance. This cultivar is strong-growing enough to fill a hanging basket quickly. A weeping standard, as it were a hanging basket on a stem, is also soon raised.

'Santa Cruz' (Tiret 1947, USA)
TUBE: red.
SEPALS: red.
COROLLA: carmine-red, semi-double or double.
STAMENS: red.
PISTIL: red.
FOLIAGE: mid-green, serrated margin.
GROWTH: upright and bushy.
A strong-growing, well-proven cultivar for many purposes. Very good as a freely planted-out bedding cultivar of relatively good hardiness. The large flowers appear in great number and without a break.

'Sarah Jane' (Putley 1974, GB)
TUBE: pink, very short.
SEPALS: rose-red, lighter tips.
COROLLA: lilac, darker at the base, double.
STAMENS: pink.
PISTIL: pink.

FOLIAGE: dark green.
GROWTH: upright and bushy.
Extremely profusely flowering with small, rosette-like flowers of lovely shape. The plant is strong-growing and problem-free for cultivation.

'Satellite' (Kennett 1963, USA) No. 642
TUBE: greenish-white.
SEPALS: white, green tips.
COROLLA: dark red, light red with white longitudinal stripes, single.
STAMENS: pink.
PISTIL: white.
FOLIAGE: mid-green.
GROWTH: upright.
Very beautiful, large-flowered cultivar with bright colours. The succulent branches must be protected against *Botrytis*. Early stopping produces correct growth.

'Schneewittchen' (Klein 1878, G)
TUBE: red, short and thick.
SEPALS: red, waxen, horizontal.
COROLLA: white, veined red, double.
STAMENS: red.
PISTIL: pink.
FOLIAGE: dark green, small.
GROWTH: upright and bushy.
The relatively small, compact flowers are of very good substance and therefore weather-resistant. With its upright and good self-branching growth, this long-tried, old German cultivar is particularly suitable for bed planting in the garden or park. The

flowers also have a good effect from a distance.

The deep pink and light purple single cultivar distributed in Britain is not the true 'Schneewittchen'.

'Sensation' (Munkner 1962, USA) No. 545
TUBE: pale pink, waxen, long.
SEPALS: pink, underside darker, green tips, very long and narrow.
COROLLA: violet, pink at the base, veined red, semi-double.
STAMENS: cerise.
PISTIL: whitish-pink, extremely long.
FOLIAGE: mid-green, red midrib.
GROWTH: trailer.
This cultivar may with justification be called sensational. The elegantly curled sepals measure 10–12 cm from one end to the other. Each petal is handsomely curved and undulate at the lower edge. The whole together results in an exceptionally large and beautiful flower whose charm it is difficult to translate into words. It should not be forgotten, however, that the plant really needs optimal growing conditions to develop its full beauty. But it is worth providing it with these.

'Seventh Heaven' (Stubbs 1981, USA) No. 1620
('Pepi' × 'Applause')
TUBE: white, medium-long, thick.
SEPALS: white with pink tinge, creped.
COROLLA: orange-red, white streaks at the base, double.
STAMENS: pink.
PISTIL: white.
FOLIAGE: dark green, red midrib and stalk.
GROWTH: lax-upright, also upright if supported; will trail with weights.
A vigorous plant with very large flowers of intense colour. Because some sepals are fused firmly with the petals, during its development the flower is pulled wide apart. Good hanging basket which after the first, profuse flowering takes a brief rest.

'Shanley' (unknown, USA)
TUBE: long, pale salmon-orange.
SEPALS: salmon-orange with green tips.
COROLLA: short, orange, single.
STAMENS: salmon-pink.
PISTIL: salmon-pink.
FOLIAGE: light green, with bronze cast, large.
GROWTH: lax-upright.

Like all fuchsias of this colour arrangement it likes sun and warmth. Strong-growing and problem-free, yet charming and continuously prolific in flowering. It is particularly suitable for balcony boxes in a sunny position. The similarity to 'Swanley Yellow' is very great.

'Shuna Lindsay' (Travis 1980, GB) No. 1585
TUBE: red and thick, long.
SEPALS: red with green tips.
COROLLA: orange-red, single.
STAMENS: red.
PISTIL: red.
FOLIAGE: dark green.
GROWTH: upright.
This new cultivar, one of the last that the late James Travis had registered, can best be described as a dwarf-like *F. denticulata*.

'Sierra Blue' (Waltz 1957, USA) No. 313
TUBE: white, short.
SEPALS: white, pale pink at base and edge, green tips.
COROLLA: silvery-blue, white at the base, veined pink, double.
STAMENS: pale pink.
PISTIL: white.
FOLIAGE: dark green.
GROWTH: trailer.
The beautiful, delicate blue and waxen white of the flowers are a feast for the eyes. Everything that has repeatedly been said about the cultivation of white and blue fuchsias must be borne in mind, particularly here if one wishes to gain the sheer delight of this beauty.

'Sipke Arjen' (Reiman-Dietiker 1979, NL)
(*F.* × *bacillaris* seedling)
TUBE: white.
SEPALS: white.
COROLLA: white, single.
FLOWERS: dainty, about 10 mm long by 10 mm lower width.
FOLIAGE: small, fern-like.
GROWTH: upright and well branched.
Beautiful black berries in autumn.

'Sleigh Bells' (Schnabel 1954, USA) No. 196
TUBE: white and long.
SEPALS: white, long and narrow, upturned with green tips.
COROLLA: white, large, single.

STAMENS: white.
PISTIL: white.
FOLIAGE: dark green.
GROWTH: medium upright.
One of the best white cultivars. The flowers have a perfect bell shape; sufficient growth for larger forms. Best results in the shade.

'Snowcap' (Henderson, GB)
TUBE: scarlet-red.
SEPALS: scarlet-red.
COROLLA: white, veined red, semi-double.
STAMENS: pink.
PISTIL: pink.
FOLIAGE: dark green, small.
GROWTH: upright and bushy.
Because of its great abundance of flower, and its strong growth with beautiful structure, this old cultivar is still popular in England as a show plant. The date of its introduction is not known, but it was mentioned in the literature as long ago as 1880.

'Snowfire' (Stubbs 1978, USA) No. 1442
('Pink Marshmallow' × 'Fan Tan')
TUBE: whitish-pink.
SEPALS: white, pink at the base, green tips.
COROLLA: coral-pink, marked with white, double.
STAMENS: whitish-pink.
PISTIL: whitish-pink.
FOLIAGE: dark green, large, red stalks.
GROWTH: upright.
Striking, very beautiful colour combination of the large flowers. After the first flowering the plant takes a break of a few weeks. Used as hanging basket or in pot (with stakes).

'So Big' (Waltz 1955, USA) No. 228
TUBE: pink.
SEPALS: pink, darker at the base, green tips.
COROLLA: cream-white, double.
STAMENS: pink.
PISTIL: pale pink.
FOLIAGE: light green, very large.
GROWTH: natural trailer.
A very big, elongate flower of lovely shape. Even the long, narrow buds are decorative. The plant is also robust and strong-growing. Should be used only as a hanging plant in balcony boxes or better still in a hanging basket in a cool, shady position. Even using stakes it cannot be shaped into an upright bush.

'Sonata' (Tiret 1960, USA) No. 437
TUBE: greenish-white.
SEPALS: pink, green tips.
COROLLA: white, veined pink, double.
STAMENS: pale pink.
PISTIL: pale pink.
FOLIAGE: mid-green.
GROWTH: lax-upright.
The growth is extremely rigid and brittle. Because of the weight of the large flowers every single branch must be well supported. Particularly good results under glass or in other sheltered places.

'Sophisticated Lady' (Martin 1964, USA) No. 609
TUBE: pink.
SEPALS: pink, lighter towards the tip, green tips.
COROLLA: cream-white, short, double.
STAMENS: light pink.
PISTIL: light pink.
FOLIAGE: mid-green, red midrib.
GROWTH: trailer.
Characteristic are the broad sepals not quite reaching up to the horizontal. The plant is not very easy to grow. It likes cool and airy conditions. In greater warmth or dryness of the air the buds do not open at all or do so only partially.

'South Gate' (Walker and Jones 1951, USA)
TUBE: pale pink.
SEPALS: pale pink, green tips.
COROLLA: light pink, veined darker, double.
STAMENS: light pink.
PISTIL: white.
FOLIAGE: dark green, red stalks.
GROWTH: lax-upright; will trail.
Without the protection of a greenhouse many double pink fuchsias are difficult to bring to optimum development. 'South Gate' on the other hand is easy and problem-free to cultivate. Strong-growing and profusely flowering with beautifully shaped flowers. Each stopping is necessary, though. Also very good as a standard.

'Space Shuttle' (de Graaff 1981, NL)
TUBE: long, about 2 cm, scarlet-red.
SEPALS: short, pointed, green.
COROLLA: orange with yellow edge, inside white and yellow, single.
STAMENS: white.
PISTIL: white, long.
FOLIAGE: grey-green, creped and pilose.

'Snowfire'

'Waxen Beauty'

GROWTH: lax-upright.

This seedling, which earlier went under the number 105, was awarded a distinction in April 1981 in Aalsmeer. The large, velvety leaves are indicative of a *F. splendens* or 'Speciosa' origin. The flowers are very exquisite.

'Spring Bells' (Kooijman 1972, NL)
TUBE: red.
SEPALS: red.
COROLLA: white, red veins, semi-double.
STAMENS: pink.
PISTIL: pink.
FOLIAGE: dark green.
GROWTH: upright.

It is assumed that this cultivar arose as a mutation of 'Snowcap'. The flowers are somewhat larger and have one or two petals more; otherwise all good qualities of the original cultivar.

'Stanley Cash' (Pennisi 1970, USA) No. 905
TUBE: white.
SEPALS: white, green tips.
COROLLA: royal blue, double.
STAMENS: light pink.
PISTIL: white.
FOLIAGE: dark green.
GROWTH: trailer.

This is a rather more robust white and blue fuchsia with very large, well-shaped, somewhat angular flowers. The snow-white, thick, almost round buds are also very handsome. After the first profuse and early flowering the plant takes a brief rest and then forms further buds. It must be frequently pinched so that more flower shoots emerge.

'Starlite' (Waltz 1961, USA) No. 493
TUBE: dark pink.
SEPALS: pink, underside dark pink, green tips.
COROLLA: lilac-blue with pink patches, double.
STAMENS: pink.
PISTIL: pink.
FOLIAGE: mid-green, large.
GROWTH: lax-upright, somewhat stiff; will trail.

The attractive, star-shaped interior of the large, flat flower with its particularly long pistil stands out best in a hanging basket, at eye-level. The robust plant is easy to grow.

'Strawberry Fizz' (Stubbs 1971, USA) No. 997
TUBE: pink.
SEPALS: pink, rolled back.
COROLLA: dark pink, petals denticulate, double.
STAMENS: pink.
PISTIL: light pink.
FOLIAGE: dark green.
GROWTH: trailer.

A large-flowered, profusely flowering hanging-basket fuchsia of good shape. As in all Stubbs hybrids, the flowers are of outstanding substance. Best results in a shady, sheltered position.

'Strawberry Sundae' (Kennett 1958, USA) No. 350
TUBE: greenish-white, long.
SEPALS: white with green tips.

COROLLA: delicate lilac-pink, double.

STAMENS: pink.

PISTIL: white.

FOLIAGE: mid-green.

GROWTH: lax bush or trailer.

Another of the few fussy cultivars which only grow well in a bright but cool greenhouse. Water with care and do not repot into a larger pot too soon. Whitefly and red spider like the tender foliage of the pastel-coloured fuchsias. One should therefore spray as a preventive against pests. Once all these difficulties have been mastered, the flowers of 'Strawberry Sundae' are a well-deserved reward.

'Sugar Blues' (Martin 1964, USA) No. 610

TUBE: white.

SEPALS: white, underside pink.

COROLLA: dark blue, outer pearls mottled pink, double.

STAMENS: pink.

PISTIL: white.

FOLIAGE: dark green.

GROWTH: trailer.

The clear colour contrast of this cultivar is preserved for longer under glass or in a cool, shady position. In the sun, the tube and sepals become pink and the corolla fades more quickly to a still pretty violet. For a hanging basket three to four plants.

'Summer Snow' (Waltz 1956, USA) No. 272

TUBE: white, long.

SEPALS: white, green tips, reflexed.

COROLLA: cream-white, semi-double.

STAMENS: white.

PISTIL: white.

FOLIAGE: mid-green.

GROWTH: trailer; also upright if supported.

The flowers are very similar to those of 'Flying Cloud', but the plant is better branched, of stronger growth and easier to shape.

'Sunset' (Niederholzer 1938, USA)

('Rolla' × 'Aurora Superba')

TUBE: light pink.

SEPALS: light pink, green tips.

COROLLA: orange-red, single.

STAMENS: pink.

PISTIL: pink.

FOLIAGE: light green.

GROWTH: upright, strong-growing.

The numerous, medium-sized flowers display the

'Ting-a-Ling'

'Toos'

very popular, almost flat corolla. Very sun-tolerant; usable for all—even larger—forms.

'Susie Tandy' (Whitehouse-Fuchsiavale 1980, GB) No. 1537
TUBE: dark pink.
SEPALS: pink outside, darker underside, green tips.
COROLLA: cream with pink, small, compact, double.
STAMENS: pink.
PISTIL: whitish-pink.
FOLIAGE: mid-green, small and pointed, red midrib and red stalks.
GROWTH: natural trailer; thickly leaved with short internodes.
Hanging baskets planted with this cultivar are enchanting. The pretty, rather small flowers appear in astonishing multitude. The colours develop best in the shade. Raising a table standard should be worthwhile.

'Suzanna' (van der Grijp 1968, NL)
TUBE: rose-red, short.
SEPALS: red.
COROLLA: blue, veined red, single to semi-double.
STAMENS: red.
PISTIL: rose-red.
FOLIAGE: dark green.
GROWTH: upright, strong and bushy.
Small, beautifully shaped flowers of really brilliant colour cover the well-branched bush in incredible abundance. The flowering period begins in early May and does not finish until the first frost.

'Swanley Gem' (Cannell 1901, GB)
TUBE: scarlet-red.
SEPALS: bright scarlet-red.
COROLLA: blue and violet, lighter at the base, slightly veined red, single.
STAMENS: red.
PISTIL: red.
FOLIAGE: mid-green, small.
GROWTH: upright and bushy.
The medium-sized flowers are striking, not just because of the beautiful colour combination but even more so through the distinctive flower shape. The four roundish petals open up to a flat plate, which is borne handsomely over the delicate foliage and strikes everybody's fancy. There are only a few cultivars with this exquisite flower shape. The plant is not very strong-growing, but it is capable of reaching the height of a table standard (30 cm).

'Swanley Yellow' (Cannell 1900, GB)
TUBE: orange and pink, very long.
SEPALS: orange and pink, held horizontally.
COROLLA: bright yellow-orange, single.
STAMENS: pink.
PISTIL: pink.
FOLIAGE: bronze-green, large.
GROWTH: lax-upright.
The two 'Swanleys', although developed back at the turn of the century, have still lost nothing of their popularity and are even today still a credit to any fuchsia collection. Although we might expect a yellow flower from the name, this is not the case. But the orange does tend more to yellow than to red. 'Swanley Yellow' likes the sun and a sheltered place. The flowers appear at intervals in clusters at the end of the branches. With one stop a very good bedding plant is obtained.

'Sweet Leilani' (Tiret 1957, USA) No. 296
TUBE: pink.
SEPALS: pink, reflexed.
COROLLA: smoky-blue, double.
STAMENS: pink.
PISTIL: pink.
FOLIAGE: mid-green.
GROWTH: lax-upright.
On blossoming out the fully double flower becomes ever larger and broader. Good heat resistance and easy to cultivate. Because of the heavy flowers good support is necessary.

'Swingtime' (Tiret 1950, USA) No. 66
('Titanic' × 'Yuletide')
TUBE: short, shiny red.
SEPALS: outside shiny red, underside rose-red and creped.
COROLLA: milky-white, slightly veined red, strongly double.
STAMENS: red.
PISTIL: red.
FOLIAGE: dark green, red midrib.
GROWTH: lax-upright and bushy; will trail but may need weights.
A fuchsia collection without 'Swingtime' would not be complete. Among the many good red and white cultivars it assumes, now as ever, a central position. It is problem-free to grow and exceptionally weather-resistant, therefore very good as a bedding plant in the garden. A standard of considerable dimension is raised relatively quickly and tolerates pruning so well

that a compact head is retained over many years. It is also very effective raised as an espalier.

'Sylvia' (Veitch 1892, GB)
TUBE: scarlet-red.
SEPALS: scarlet-red.
COROLLA: white with cerise veining, double.
STAMENS: red.
PISTIL: red.
FOLIAGE: dark green.
GROWTH: lax-upright.
This profusely flowering old cultivar is still in circulation. It is particularly well suited for the raising of long-lasting standards. Regrettably it is sometimes mistakenly offered under the name of 'Schneewittchen'. These two old cultivars are, however, markedly and clearly distinguishable from one another in growth and flower shape. Not to be confused with 'Sylvia' of Curtis 1971, GB, which is rose-red and cream with bronze and green foliage.

'Taffeta Bow' (Stubbs 1974, USA) No. 1196
TUBE: dark pink.
SEPALS: dark pink, green tips, broad and long.
COROLLA: violet-purple, pink at the base, double.
STAMENS: pink.
PISTIL: whitish-pink.
FOLIAGE: mid-green with red midrib, large.
GROWTH: natural trailer.
Like all cultivars from Mrs Stubbs, outstanding. Strong-growing with good branching. The very big, beautifully coloured flowers appear in profuse abundance. It is very suitable as a hanging basket, but perhaps even better as an ornamental plant raised on a stake and the side shoots stopped once.

'Tangerine' (Tiret 1949, USA)
(*F. cordifolia* ×)
TUBE: greenish-orange, rather long and narrow.
SEPALS: light green with dark green tips, underside yellowish, not upswept.
COROLLA: light, pure orange, single, each petal ends in a point.
STAMENS: pink-orange, very short.
PISTIL: white, short.
FOLIAGE: mid-green.
GROWTH: upright with long internodes.
This beautiful plant is deservedly popular. Anybody planting a trio of this cultivar in a sunny place in the garden—it quickly grows to a metre tall—will be more than delighted with it. The initially soft and sappy shoots should be supported a little. In autumn it must be potted again. Alternatively, cuttings can be made.

'Tausendschön' (Nagel 1919, G)
TUBE: enamel-red.
SEPALS: enamel-red.
COROLLA: light pink, veined red, double.
STAMENS: red.
PISTIL: red.
FOLIAGE: mid-green, with red veining, on red stalks.
GROWTH: upright and bushy.
A free-flowering, profusely flowering and robust cultivar which is still, after more than 70 years, readily and often cultivated. Strong-growing, well branching and particularly suitable as a bedding and balcony fuchsia.

'Television' (Walker and Jones 1950, USA)
TUBE: white.
SEPALS: white, underside light pink.
COROLLA: plum-blue, marked with pink, double.
STAMENS: pink.
PISTIL: white.
FOLIAGE: dark green.
GROWTH: lax-upright.
A profusely flowering plant, for the impressive colour combination of white and blue even a robust one. Good to use in a hanging basket, but with the help of a few stakes can also be raised as a very decorative bush.

'Temptation' (Petersen 1959, USA) No. 376
TUBE: pinkish-white.
SEPALS: pinkish-white.
COROLLA: orange and pink, white at the base, single.
STAMENS: pink.
PISTIL: pale pink.
FOLIAGE: mid-green with undulate margins.
GROWTH: lax-upright with flexible branches.
As a bedding and pot plant flowers profusely and continuously. As a standard with a well-branched, thick head this cultivar is particularly long-lasting.

'Tennessee Waltz' (Walker and Jones 1951, USA)
Plate 15
TUBE: light red.
SEPALS: light red.
COROLLA: a mixture of mauve and pink, double.
STAMENS: pink.
PISTIL: pink.

FOLIAGE: mid-green.

GROWTH: strong and upright.

The somewhat angular flowers of exquisite shape are distributed nice and evenly over the whole plant. The bush is strong enough to bear the many, relatively large flowers without support. Also one of the cultivars for the beginner, completely problem-free, whether as bush or as standard. Every cutting roots in a short time. Frequent pinching produces show plants.

'Texas Longhorn' (Fuchsia-La 1960, USA)

TUBE: red and short.

SEPALS: red, extremely long.

COROLLA: white, veined red, semi-double to double.

STAMENS: red.

PISTIL: red.

FOLIAGE: dark green, veined red, large with long internodes.

GROWTH: cascading trailer.

This plant is difficult to train to a satisfactory shape. It gets its popularity solely from the enormous flowers. Even the exceptionally long buds (often up to 12 cm) are a sensation. When open, the horizontal sepals have a span of 15 cm and stand like windmill sails around the rather small, thick corolla. The large leaves with undulate margins often curl around the stem, fully enveloping the latter. A standard of 'Texas Longhorn' with more than 50 of the huge flowers was constantly surrounded by admiring people at the Chelsea Show in London some years ago. Mostly, however, hanging baskets are raised from this cultivar.

'The Aristocrat' (Waltz 1953, USA) No. 165

TUBE: pink.

SEPALS: pink, white tips, upswept.

COROLLA: cream-white, with red veins, double.

STAMENS: whitish-pink.

PISTIL: white.

FOLIAGE: mid-green.

GROWTH: upright and bushy.

The strongly double corolla is arranged somewhat loosely and each of the outer petals is denticulate. The beautiful white ages without the rusty spots which unfortunately appear in many white cultivars. Despite its thin stalks, the plant bears the numerous flowers without difficulty and flowers continuously until the frost.

'The Doctor' (unknown origin, GB)

TUBE: pale pink.

SEPALS: pale pink, darker underside.

COROLLA: orange-red, single.

STAMENS: pink.

PISTIL: pale pink, very long.

FOLIAGE: mid-green, large.

GROWTH: lax-upright.

This cultivar with the classically beautiful large flowers of outstanding substance has been in cultivation for a very long time. It is strong-growing and sun-tolerant. Even a beginner can easily succeed in raising a standard or even a pyramid from this cultivar.

'Ting-a-Ling' (Schnabel-Paskesen 1959, USA) No. 381

TUBE: white.

SEPALS: white, outside pale pink, green tips.

COROLLA: white, widely open, single.

STAMENS: pale pink.

PISTIL: white.

FOLIAGE: grey-green.

GROWTH: upright and bushy.

A good all-round fuchsia, as a bush as well as a standard. One of the best white fuchsias. Like all delicately coloured fuchsias it is easily prone to *Botrytis* and should be treated with a preventive fungicide, especially in damp years.

'Tinker Bell' (Hodges 1955, USA) No. 244

TUBE: whitish-pink, long.

SEPALS: whitish-pink outside, inside darker, tips red.

COROLLA: white, slightly veined pink, long, single.

STAMENS: white.

PISTIL: white.

FOLIAGE: dark green.

GROWTH: trailer.

Profuse and lengthy flowerer with elegant, long flowers. For planting a hanging basket at least five plants should be used.

'Tolling Bell' (Turner 1964, GB)

TUBE: scarlet-red.

SEPALS: scarlet-red.

COROLLA: snow-white, slightly veined red, single.

STAMENS: red.

PISTIL: red.

FOLIAGE: mid-green, veined red.

GROWTH: upright and bushy, strong-growing.

Because of the perfect large bell shape the name is well chosen. An autumn cutting, efficiently cultivated and stopped after each second pair of leaves, produces a real show plant of great beauty by the next June. Its resistance to heat, though, is not particularly great, so the position should be as cool and shady as possible.

'Toos' (van Suchtelen 1980, NL)
(Award of the VKC, Apeldoorn 1980)
TUBE: cream, shiny.
SEPALS: light pink, green tips.
COROLLA: light pink-lilac, slightly veined at the base, single.
STAMENS: light pink.
PISTIL: whitish-pink.
FOLIAGE: grey-green, small.
GROWTH: upright and bushy.
'Toos' was described by the hybridiser as a true pot plant which develops an attractive structure without needing much stopping. A standard can also be raised easily if it is started on in the autumn. Unfortunately it is somewhat susceptible to *Botrytis*. It flowers early, profusely and at length with flowers held sideways-upwards on strong stalks ('Bon Accord' ×).

'Torch' (Munkner 1963, USA) No. 566
TUBE: cream, flushed pink, waxen.

'Starlite'

'Television'

'Sugar Blues'

SEPALS: pink, broad.

COROLLA: rosy to red in the centre with apricot-orange petaloids, double.

STAMENS: pink.

PISTIL: whitish-pink.

FOLIAGE: light green.

GROWTH: stiffly upright, strong-growing.

Upright-growing, double flowering cultivars are not all that common. 'Torch' is admittedly rigid in structure, but with early stopping good as a bush or standard. Holds its own even in the garden in full sun.

'Tranquillity' (Soo Yun 1970, USA) No. 909

TUBE: white.

SEPALS: white, underside pink, green tips.

COROLLA: purple with pink, double.

STAMENS: pink.

PISTIL: pink.

FOLIAGE: dark green, veined red, red stalks.

GROWTH: trailer.

The sepals curl and roll elegantly and give the flower a very animated expression. Very beautiful hanging-basket plant with numerous large flowers.

'Traudl Böhm' (Nutzinger 1971, A)

TUBE: red.

SEPALS: red.

COROLLA: whitish-pink, single.

STAMENS: pink.

PISTIL: pink.

FOLIAGE: mid-green, small.

GROWTH: upright and bushy.

The dainty flowers stand like little trumpets on the many-branched plant. Very profusely flowering, robust bedding and balcony fuchsia.

'Troika' (de Graaff 1976, NL)

TUBE: rose-red.

SEPALS: white.

COROLLA: blue and lilac, fading to lilac and pink, semi-double.

STAMENS: rose-red.

PISTIL: white.

FOLIAGE: mid-green.

GROWTH: natural trailer.

'Troika' is a seedling of 'La Campanella' and has many qualities of the mother plant, unfortunately including the break in flowering. The colours and the larger flower are a distinct improvement. As it likes cool conditions, it is best in the autumn months; it then flowers until the first frosts.

'Twinkling Star' (Handley 1976, GB) No. 1373

TUBE: white, striped pink.

SEPALS: white, underside pink, green tips.

COROLLA: cerise.

STAMENS: cerise.

PISTIL: whitish-pink.

FOLIAGE: dark green, small.

GROWTH: upright.

The flowers are held sideways-upwards, four to six in each leaf-axil. The slightly crooked tube gives the flower something out of the ordinary. A compact, very early and profusely flowering pot plant. Watch out for the five sepals produced freely.

'UFO' (Handley 1972, GB) No. 1059

TUBE: white, short.

SEPALS: white, narrow and long, upright with green tips.

COROLLA: deep violet, white at the base, single, plate-shaped.

STAMENS: pale pink.

PISTIL: white to pink.

FOLIAGE: mid-green.

GROWTH: upright.

Looks like a flying-saucer. The flowers are of good substance, the plant is naturally self-branching. Forms a beautiful bush with many flowers and particularly elegant buds.

'Uncle Charley' (Tiret 1949, USA)

TUBE: light red.

SEPALS: light red, long, narrow and rolled.

COROLLA: beautiful, bright light blue, semi-double.

STAMENS: pink.

PISTIL: whitish-pink.

FOLIAGE: mid-green.

GROWTH: upright and bushy.

A very good and colourful cultivar which can be used for many purposes.

'Uncle Jules' (Reiter 1947, USA)

TUBE: red.

SEPALS: red.

COROLLA: campanula-blue, very double.

STAMENS: red.

PISTIL: pink.

FOLIAGE: mid-green.

GROWTH: natural trailer.

The enormous flowers are of beautiful shape and good substance, though not very numerous.

'Unique' (Haag & Son 1950, USA)
TUBE: white, short, thick, with red stripes.
SEPALS: white with slight pink tinge, green tips.
COROLLA: pink, single.
STAMENS: light pink.
PISTIL: white.
FOLIAGE: light green, large.
GROWTH: upright and strong-growing.
The flowers are waxen, very weather-resistant and durable, relatively small, but compact and compressed rather than dainty. As well as this cultivar there are two others of the same name: red and dark purple, brought out by Miller 1845, GB; and one with uniformly rose-red, single flowers by Hazard and Hazard, USA.

'Upward Look' (Gadsby 1968, GB) No. 870
('Bon Accord' × 'Athela')
TUBE: carmine-red, short.
SEPALS: carmine-red, broad, green tips.
COROLLA: pale purple to magenta, single.
STAMENS: pink.
PISTIL: pink.
FOLIAGE: mid-green.
GROWTH: upright and bushy.
With this profusely flowering seedling from an interesting cross Cliff Gadsby began a new breeding line. The fuchsias of this series all have more or less upward-held flowers on strong stalks.

'Vanessa' (Colville 1964, GB)
TUBE: pink.
SEPALS: pink, long and broad, curled.
COROLLA: pale lavender-blue, fully double.
STAMENS: pink.
PISTIL: pale pink.
FOLIAGE: light green.
GROWTH: upright.
A strong-growing cultivar with large leaves and succulent branches which can be trained to a good shape only with difficulty. The well-shaped, delicately coloured flowers are so beautiful, however, that any effort is justified. When it is hot the fully double buds open only poorly. 'Vanessa' likes a cool, shady position.

'Vanity Fair' (Schnabel-Paskesen 1962, USA) No. 534
TUBE: greenish-white, thick.
SEPALS: greenish-white, flushed pink, green tips, reflexed.

COROLLA: quite pale pink, very large and fully double.
STAMENS: pale pink.
PISTIL: white.
FOLIAGE: mid-green.
GROWTH: upright and strong-growing.
One of the almost white fuchsias which is comparatively easy to grow. Naturally it likes shelter from wind and weather. Owing to the extremely heavy flowers the branches must be well supported.

'Venus Victrix' (Gulliver 1840, GB)
TUBE: white.
SEPALS: white, green tips.
COROLLA: almost pure blue, slightly pink and white at the base of the petals, single.
STAMENS: light pink.
PISTIL: whitish-pink.
FOLIAGE: mid-green, denticulate, small.
GROWTH: upright; very weak grower.
This famous cultivar, developed as a chance seedling in an English rectory garden, exhibited for the first time in the growing history of the fuchsia with white tube and sepals. The delicate plant is difficult to grow. Even fuchsia experts only seldom succeed in keeping it over any lengthy period of time. Up to the present day the cultivar has been and still is used frequently as a cross-breeding parent. In almost all white and blue fuchsias its ancestry—even though diluted—is present. The ardent fuchsia collector will use every means possible to acquire this jewel for his collection. As none of the known fuchsia gardeners offers this rarity, however, one must often look long and wide for it, although it is now offered quite freely by the occasional British fuchsia nurseryman.

'Violet Bassett Burr' (Mrs E. Holmes 1972, GB)
TUBE: greenish-white.
SEPALS: white with green tips, underside pink, pink-edged.
COROLLA: light and lilac, paler at the base, double.
STAMENS: pink.
PISTIL: white.
FOLIAGE: dark green.
GROWTH: upright.
A particularly handsome flower in delicate pastel colours. The growth is strong and young plants should be repeatedly stopped. A place sheltered from wind and weather is essential. The flowers are at their best in a well-ventilated greenhouse. The plant does not overwinter very well in later years.

'White Spider'

'White King'

'Whirlaway'

'Violet Rosette' (Kuechler 1963, USA) No. 549
TUBE: scarlet-red, long and thin.
SEPALS: scarlet-red, shiny, underside creped and reflexed.
COROLLA: dark bluish-violet, with a little red at the base, double.
STAMENS: scarlet-red.
PISTIL: scarlet-red, very long.
FOLIAGE: mid-green.
GROWTH: lax-upright.
Particularly attractive and thickly developed, rosette-shaped flowers of good substance. For the size of the flower also comparatively profusely flowering. Young plants should be repeatedly stopped and each individual shoot well supported.

'Viva Ireland' (Ireland 1956, USA)
TUBE: pale pink.
SEPALS: pink, long and narrow, curled.
COROLLA: soft lavender-blue, single.
STAMENS: pink.
PISTIL: whitish-pink.
FOLIAGE: mid-green.
GROWTH: lax-upright, flexible.

A lovely cultivar. The overall impression is light and buoyant. Four to six plants are needed to obtain a well-filled hanging basket.

'Vobeglo' (De Groot, NL)
(('Frau Henriette Ernst' × *F. regia typica*) × 'Bon Accord')
TUBE: salmon-pink.
SEPALS: salmon-pink.
COROLLA: lilac, single.
STAMENS: pink.
PISTIL: light pink.
FOLIAGE: small, dark green.
GROWTH: upright, compact, with short internodes.
One of the few fuchsias whose lineage is known. 'Vobeglo' is best as a pot plant under glass, when it flowers profusely without a break up to autumn. In full flower it looks like an azalea with its upward-held flowers. The raiser advises raising it afresh each year from cuttings and giving it a bright position. It has inherited from 'Bon Accord' a certain susceptibility to *Botrytis*.

'Voodoo' (Tiret 1953, USA) No. 157
TUBE: dark red, short.
SEPALS: dark red, reflexed.
COROLLA: very dark purplish-violet, fully double.
STAMENS: red.
PISTIL: red.
FOLIAGE: dark green.
GROWTH: upright.
Because of the large, heavy flowers it must be supported early and well. The flowers appear rather scattered and last for a long time.

'Waldfee' (Travis 1973, GB) No. 1150
(*F. michoacanesis* ×)
TUBE: long and narrow, lilac-pink.
SEPALS: lilac and pink, relatively broad.
COROLLA: lilac and pink, single.
STAMENS: white and pink, enclosed.
PISTIL: white and pink.
FOLIAGE: small and narrow.
GROWTH: upright and very strong.
Tiny, elongate little flowers of the *Encliandra* type. For the lovers of small-flowered, distinctive fuchsias a rarity. Particularly attractive is the almost transparent, long tube, which allows the stamens and pistil to show through.

'Walsingham' (Clithero 1979, GB)
('Northumbrian Belle' × 'Blush of Dawn')

TUBE: almost white.
SEPALS: white, flushed pink, horizontal.
COROLLA: quite light lilac, semi-double, bell-shaped.
STAMENS: red.
PISTIL: pale pink.
FOLIAGE: emerald-green, attractively dentate and tapering to a point.
GROWTH: lax-upright and well branched; will trail.
This new cultivar is named after the famous pilgrims' shrine in Norfolk. The well-shaped, pastel-coloured flowers appear in masses.

'War Paint' (Kennett 1960, USA) No. 431
TUBE: greenish-white.
SEPALS: white, underside pink.
COROLLA: carnation-red, mottled pink, double.
STAMENS: pink.
PISTIL: white.
FOLIAGE: mid-green, red midrib.
GROWTH: upright.
Succulent, fragile branches and large leaves on a plant which is just difficult to keep in shape. The flowers are enchanting and of good substance, but appear rather sparsely and always in pairs.

'Waxen Beauty' (Clyne 1975, GB) No. 1287
TUBE: white with red tinge.
SEPALS: white, green tips.
COROLLA: white, somewhat pink at the base, double.
STAMENS: pinkish-white.
PISTIL: white.
FOLIAGE: mid-green.
GROWTH: upright.
Forms a well-branched bush with many flowers. Like all white cultivars it should be given a sheltered, shady position. Good show plant.

'Wedgewood' (Schnabel 1951, USA) No. 82
TUBE: white.
SEPALS: white, shiny, long and narrow.
COROLLA: bluish-violet, widely open, double.
STAMENS: pink.
PISTIL: white.
FOLIAGE: mid-green.
GROWTH: upright.
Delightful, elegant flowers which adorn a well-grown plant in large numbers. Early pinching is advisable.

'Westergeest' (de Graaff 1979, NL)
TUBE: light orange.

SEPALS: salmon and orange, with green tips, held horizontal, often five and more sepals.
COROLLA: salmon-pink, dark pink at the edges, single.
STAMENS: pink.
PISTIL: pale pink.
FOLIAGE: light green.
GROWTH: upright and well branched.
This dainty, small-flowered cultivar, which flowers very profusely and for a long time, is one of the new varieties from Holland which have really enriched the existing assembly of fuchsias.

'Whirlaway' (Waltz 1964, USA) No. 494
TUBE: greenish-white.
SEPALS: white, very long and narrow, twisting and reflexing on maturity.
COROLLA: white, single, occasionally semi-double.
STAMENS: pale pink.
PISTIL: pale pink.
FOLIAGE: dark green.
GROWTH: trailer.
A very popular, lovely white cultivar. The flowers are particularly attractive in an early stage, when the sepals divide at the top and at the tip still stay together, thus forming a Chinese lantern. To raise a larger plant, e.g. for a show, planting must be done in the autumn of the previous year.

'White King' (Pennisi 1968, USA) No. 753
TUBE: white, with green stripes.
SEPALS: white.
COROLLA: white, extremely big, double.
STAMENS: white.
PISTIL: white.
FOLIAGE: dark green.
GROWTH: lax-upright; spreading; will trail.
Very strong-growing and easy to cultivate. If one wishes to raise it as a bush, it must be stopped early and often. The beautifully shaped, extremely large flowers appear continuously and are carried on very long pedicels. Unlike other white fuchsias it is not particularly susceptible to *Botrytis*, assuming good growing conditions.

'White Queen' (Doyle 1899, GB)
TUBE: cream-white.
SEPALS: cream-white, pure white underside.
COROLLA: salmon-orange, each petal has the beginnings of a lengthways pleat, single.
STAMENS: pale pink.
PISTIL: white.

FOLIAGE: mid-green.
GROWTH: lax-upright.
Is often confused with 'Amy Lye'. The foliage of 'Amy Lye', however, is bronze-coloured in new growth. Strong-growing, profusely flowering, old cultivar.

'White Spider' (Haag 1951, USA)
TUBE: whitish-pink.
SEPALS: pink, green tips, long, narrow, elegantly curled.
COROLLA: white, slightly veined pink, single.
STAMENS: white.
PISTIL: white.
FOLIAGE: mid-green.
GROWTH: lax bush, flexible.
The name is somewhat misleading, for the tube and sepals in this cultivar are always pink, even in a shady position. The elegant flowers show up best on a standard and radiate a charm all of their own.

'Wings of Song' (Blackwell 1968, GB)
TUBE: rose-red, shiny.
SEPALS: rose-red, shiny.
COROLLA: lavender-blue, pink veining, double.
STAMENS: pink.
PISTIL: pink.
FOLIAGE: mid-green, red midrib.
GROWTH: trailer.
Like all large-flowered, delicately coloured fuchsias this cultivar should be given a position sheltered from wind and rain. For the rest, it is strong-growing, branches well and is best presented in a hanging basket.

'Winston Churchill' (Garson 1942, USA)
TUBE: pink, long.
SEPALS: pink, broad, reflexed, green tips.
COROLLA: lavender-blue, veined red, double.
STAMENS: cerise.
PISTIL: cerise.
FOLIAGE: mid-green.
GROWTH: upright, very strong.
This profusely flowering cultivar is, owing to its upright growth, well suited for bed planting. Unfortunately, in a sunny position it is very susceptible to red spider and should of course be sprayed as a preventive measure. It does not overwinter readily. Anyone who would not like to lose it must make cuttings in the autumn.

'Wood Violet' (Schmidt 1946, USA)
TUBE: red.
SEPALS: red.
COROLLA: violet-blue, semi-double.
STAMENS: red.
PISTIL: pink.
FOLIAGE: dark green, veined red.
GROWTH: upright and compact.
Dainty, well-shaped flowers in bright colours. The uniform, many-branched growth is suitable for the planting of small bowls or in the garden bed.

'Yonder Blue' (Tiret 1954, USA) No. 210
TUBE: rosy-red.
SEPALS: rosy-red, broad, reflexed.
COROLLA: mid-blue, fully double, firm and round.
STAMENS: pink.
PISTIL: pink.
FOLIAGE: mid-green.
GROWTH: lax-upright.

A Certificate of Merit of the AFS speaks for the quality of this plant. The flowers are of good substance and with frequent pinching also numerous.

'Ziegfield Girl' (Fuchsia Forest 1966, USA) No. 671
TUBE: pink.
SEPALS: pink, underside darker, green tips, broad and creped.
COROLLA: very beautiful, clear pink, double.
STAMENS: pink.
PISTIL: pale pink.
FOLIAGE: dark green, red midrib.
GROWTH: trailer.
These thrillingly beautiful, rosette-shaped, roundish flowers—the buds are also round and thick—are fastidious where position and cultivation are concerned. The flowers develop to their most beautiful in a cool greenhouse. In a hot atmosphere and a sunny position they do not open.

INCORRECTLY NAMED SPECIES

(after John O. Wright)

In order to remove misunderstandings in the naming of fuchsias,
some fuchsia species which are currently on the market under
incorrect names are given below with their correct names.

INCORRECT NAME	CORRECT NAME
F. aprica	Cultivated plants are mostly *F. × bacillaris*, rarely *F. microphylla* var. *aprica*.
F. coccinea	Pure species are no longer in cultivation. Plants on offer are *F. magellanica* or hybrids of this species.
F. colimae	Cultivated plants are all *F. × bacillaris*.
F. cordifolia	Cultivated plants are all *F. splendens* or hybrids of this species.
F. corymbiflora	Cultivated plants are all *F. boliviana* var. *luxurians*.
F. corymbiflora alba	Correct name is *F. boliviana* var. *luxurians* 'Alba'.
F. cylindracea	Cultivated plants are all *F. × bacillaris*.
F. encliandra	Cultivated plants are all *F. × bacillaris*.
F. hemsleyana	Cultivated plants are all *F. × bacillaris*.
F. kirkii	Male form of *F. procumbens*.
F. loxensis	Cultivated plants are hybrids of *F. splendens × F. fulgens*.
F. lycioides	Cultivated plants are all hybrids of *F. magellanica*.
F. mexiae	Cultivated plants are all *F. × bacillaris*.

INCORRECT NAME	CORRECT NAME
F. michoacanensis	Cultivated plants are all *F. microphylla* var. *aprica*.
F. microphylla	Cultivated plants are mostly *F. × bacillaris*, rarely *F. microphylla* var. *aprica*.
F. minimiflora	Cultivated plants are all *F. × bacillaris*.
F. minutiflora	Cultivated plants are all *F. × bacillaris*.
F. mixta	Cultivated plants are all *F. × bacillaris*.
F. pringlei	Cultivated plants are all *F. × bacillaris*.
F. riccartonii	Not a pure species but a hybrid of *F. magellanica*. Correct name as a cultivar is 'Riccartonii'.
F. serratifolia	Synonym for *F. denticulata*.
F. skutchiana	Cultivated plants are all *F. × bacillaris*.
F. speciosa	Hybrid of *F. splendens × F. fulgens*.
F. striolata	Cultivated plants are all *F. × bacillaris*.
F. tacanensis	Cultivated plants are all *F. × bacillaris*.
F. tetradactyla	Cultivated plants are all *F. × bacillaris*.
F. thymifolia	Cultivated plants are mostly *F. × bacillaris*, rarely *F. thymifolia* var. *thymifolia*.

FUCHSIA GARDENS AND DISPLAYS

Collections of specimen fuchsias can be seen in flower at the following establishments during the summer months, mainly from June to September.

The Royal Horticultural Society Gardens at Wisley in Surrey probably house the best collection in their temperate house. The RHS sometimes exhibit some of their spectacular specimens at their Annual Show at Chelsea in May. Several specialist nurserymen also have trade exhibits at Chelsea.

Lechlade Fuchsia Centre is a commercial enterprise at Lechlade, near Swindon, Wiltshire, where a large collection of both species and cultivars, originally founded by John Wright and totalling over 800, is displayed under glass but under conditions as close to the natural habitat as possible.

The Dingle, a sunken garden in the main park at Shrewsbury, displays many fuchsias bedded out during the summer, featuring many standards.

Chester Zoo, in the North West of England, features both animals and fuchsias. Hundreds of fuchsias are bedded out each summer, mainly full or half-standards.

Bristol Zoo, in the South West of England, also features fuchsias during the summer months and these are quite spectacular.

The Harlow Carr Gardens of the Northern Horticultural Society at Harrogate bed out sizeable trials of hardy fuchsias each year on behalf of the British Fuchsia Society.

By far the best fuchsias, however, are to be seen at the various national regional shows organised by the British Fuchsia Society during the months of July, August and September. The most important venues are at London, Manchester, Harrogate, Felixstowe, Midlands, West Country, Wales and Scotland.

The Botanic Gardens at Kew, Edinburgh, Glasgow, Oxford, Birmingham and Cambridge all house some fuchsias, mainly species under glass.

FUCHSIA SOCIETIES

GREAT BRITAIN

British Fuchsia Society
Ron Ewart
29 Princes Crescent
Dollar
Clackmannanshire FK14 7BW

Contact with fuchsia-lovers in other countries can very much enrich this hobby. Some addresses of foreign fuchsia societies are:

AUSTRALIA

Australian Fuchsia Society
PO Box 97
Norwood
South Australia 5067

AUSTRIA

Österreichische Fuchsienfreunde of the Österreichische Gartenbaugesellschaft
Elisabeth Schnedl
Wiener Str. 216
A-8051 Graz

BELGIUM

De Vlaamse Fuchsiavrienden vzw
O. Defeu, President
Hoge Akker 25
2130 Brasschaat

Dr Vrije Fuchsiavrienden
Erna Van Wiele, Correspondent
Lijkveldestraat 92
2778 St Pauwels

Les Amis du Fuchsia
Mr Michel Cornet
Rue du Moulin 24
6239 Pont-à-Celles (B)

CANADA

British Columbia Fuchsia Society
Lorna Herchenson
President
2402 Swinburne Avenue
North Vancouver, BC V7H IL2

DENMARK

Dansk Fuchsia Klub
Merete Printz
Frugtparken 1
DK-2820 Gentofte

FRANCE

Société Nationale d'Horticulture de France
Section Fuchsias
84 rue de Grenelle
F-75007 Paris

GERMANY

Deutsche Fuchsien-Gesellschaft
Hans-Peter Peters
Pankratiusstr. 10
D-3208 Giesen

Deutsche Dahlien-, Fuchsien- und Gladiolengesellschaft
E. Göring
Drachenfelsstr. 9a
D-5300 Bonn 2

NETHERLANDS

Nederlandse Kring van Fuchsiavrienden
M. A. Rijkaart van Capellen
Mauritshoek 73
NL-2988 EC Ridderkerk

NEW ZEALAND

Canterbury Horticultural Society Fuchsia Circle
W. McNickel
100 Richardson Terrace
Opawa
Christchurch 2

New Zealand Fuchsia Society
E. D. Sweetman
18 Churton Drive
Churton Park
Wellington 4

NORWAY

Norsk Fuchsia Selskab
Joan Haugland
Lohrmannsgate 3
N-3000 Drammen

SWEDEN

Fuchsiasällskapet
Agneta Westin
Ostermalmsgatan 68
S-11450 Stockholm

SWITZERLAND

Schweizer Fuchsienverein
Cornelia Angst-van der Leek
CH-8196 Wil/Zürich

SOUTH AFRICA

South African Fuchsia Society
Jean Spurling
Box 193
Hilton 3245
Natal

UNITED STATES OF AMERICA

American Fuchsia Society
Hall of Flowers
9th Avenue & Lincoln Way
San Francisco, CA 94122

National Fuchsia Society
PO Box 4687
Downey, CA 90241

NORTH AMERICAN FUCHSIA SOCIETIES

America possesses two national bodies, each based in California. The American Fuchsia Society based in San Francisco was established in 1929 and today has a membership of approximately 1500. It is an organization that encourages fuchsia culture all over the world, grants scholarships and among other activities fosters scientific research. In addition the Society is the International Authority for the Registration and Nomenclature of the Fuchsia. Their monthly Bulletin serves as a clearing house for articles on culture and includes a colour cover, illustrating a different fuchsia every issue. Membership is automatically available to those who join one of its branches which include, Coos Bay – Fort Bragg – Fort Dick – Eureka – Healdsburg – Jose – Los Altos – Novato Pacifica – Petaluma – Pinole-Rohnert Park – Sacramento – Salem – San Bruno – San Francisco – San Mateo – San Rafael – San Rosa – Sebastopol – Vallejo and Yamhill. Information is available from the American Fuchsia Society, Hall of Flowers, 9th Avenue and Lincoln Way, San Francisco, California.

The other American Society is the National Fuchsia Society with a membership of around 1000 based in Southern California, with branches centred upon Costa Mesa – Downey – Garden Grove – Glendale – Long Beach – Oceanside – Palos Verdes – Redondo – San Diego – Renton Wa – Ventura and Whitter. This society also publishes a monthly 'Fuchsia Fan' with front coloured cover. Contact can be made at the National Fuchsia Society 2982 Crown View Drive, Rancho, Palos Verdes, California.

The enthusiasm in the North West of USA is based around the areas of Seattle and Puget Sound, Washington known as the Northwest Fuchsia Society. Formed in 1983, it has seven affiliated societies with a total membership of approximately 850. Contact address is P.O. Box 33785, Bitter Lake Station, Seattle, Washington 98133.

The interest in Canada is centred in Vancouver with the formation of the British Columbia Fuchsia Society in 1961. Their membership is around the 300 figure with regular publications and having recently celebrated their 25th anniversary. The current Correspondence Secretary is Lorna Herchenson, 2402 Swinburne Avenue, North Vancouver, B.C., V7H 1L2.

Another much smaller society, the Greater Victoria Fuchsia Society, was formed in 1979 and is based at Victoria B.C. The mailing address is P.O. Box 5266, Postal Station B, Victoria, B.C.

SOURCES

GREAT BRITAIN

B. & H. M. Baker (no mail order)
Bourne Brook Nurseries
Greenstead Green
Halstead
Essex

H. A. Brown
20 Chingford Mount Road
South Chingford
London E4

High Trees Nurseries (Steve Head)
Buckland, near Reigate
Surrey

Fuchsiavale Nurseries
Stanklyn Lane
Summerfield
Kidderminster
Worcs DY10 4HS

Fuchsia Specialists
R. & J. Pacey
Stathern
Melton Mowbray
Leicestershire

Fuchsias
C. S. Lockyer
'Lansbury'
70 Henfield Road
Coalpit Heath
Bristol BS17 2UZ

Jackson's Nurseries
Clifton Campville
near Tamworth
Staffordshire B79 0AP

GERMANY

Rudolf and Klara Baum
– Fuchsienkulteren –
Scheffelrain 1
7250 Leonberg 1

Gärtnerei
Manfred Behre
Salinenstr. 40
3003 Ronnenberg 3

Gartenbau
Heinrich Breuckmann
Leinschede 22
5970 Plettenberg 2

Gärtnerei
Hermann Ermel
Kurpfalzstrasse
6719 Zellertal 1

Gartenbaubetrieb
Reinhard Heinke
– Spezialkulturen –
Eichholzstr. 2
4600 Dortmund 41

NETHERLANDS

Gebr. Van't Westeinde
Kwekerij 'Westhof'
's-Heer Arendskerke NL

Kooyman Fuchsia's
Papeweg 32
Wassenaar NL

SWITZERLAND

E + C Angst van der Leek
CH-8196 Wil/Zürich

CONVERSION TABLES

All measurements are given in metric units. For readers more familiar with the imperial system, the accompanying tables are designed to facilitate quick conversion to imperial units. Bold figures in the central columns can be read as either metric or imperial: e.g. 1 kg = 2.20 lb or 1 lb = 0.45 kg.

mm		in	cm		in	m		yd
25.4	**1**	.039	2.54	**1**	0.39	0.91	**1**	1.09
50.8	**2**	.079	5.08	**2**	0.79	1.83	**2**	2.19
76.2	**3**	.118	7.62	**3**	1.18	2.74	**3**	3.28
101.6	**4**	.157	10.16	**4**	1.57	3.66	**4**	4.37
127.0	**5**	.197	12.70	**5**	1.97	4.57	**5**	5.47
152.4	**6**	.236	15.24	**6**	2.36	5.49	**6**	6.56
177.8	**7**	.276	17.78	**7**	2.76	6.40	**7**	7.66
203.2	**8**	.315	20.32	**8**	3.15	7.32	**8**	8.75
228.6	**9**	.354	22.86	**9**	3.54	8.23	**9**	9.84

g		oz	kg		lb	km		miles
28.35	**1**	.04	0.45	**1**	2.20	1.61	**1**	0.62
56.70	**2**	.07	0.91	**2**	4.41	3.22	**2**	1.24
85.05	**3**	.11	1.36	**3**	6.61	4.83	**3**	1.86
113.40	**4**	.14	1.81	**4**	8.82	6.44	**4**	2.48
141.75	**5**	.18	2.27	**5**	11.02	8.05	**5**	3.11
170.10	**6**	.21	2.72	**6**	13.23	9.65	**6**	3.73
198.45	**7**	.25	3.18	**7**	15.43	11.26	**7**	4.35
226.80	**8**	.28	3.63	**8**	17.64	12.87	**8**	4.97
255.15	**9**	.32	4.08	**9**	19.84	14.48	**9**	5.59

ha		acres
0.40	**1**	2.47
0.81	**2**	4.94
1.21	**3**	7.41
1.62	**4**	9.88
2.02	**5**	12.36
2.43	**6**	14.83
2.83	**7**	17.30
3.24	**8**	19.77
3.64	**9**	22.24

Metric to imperial conversion formulae

	multiply by
cm to inches	0.3937
m to feet	3.281
m to yards	1.094
km to miles	0.6214
km^2 to square miles	0.3861
ha to acres	2.471
g to ounces	0.03527
kg to pounds	2.205

BIBLIOGRAPHY

BERRY, DR P. E. 'Systematics of the Apetelous Fuchsias of South America *Fuchsia* Section *Hemsleyella*' (*Annals of the Missouri Botanical Garden*, 42-213-251, 1985)

—— 'Systematic Revision of *Fuchsia* Section *Quelusia*' (*Annals of the Missouri Botanical Garden*, vol. 76, no. 2, 1989)

BOULLEMIER, L. B. *Fascinating Fuchsias* (Northampton, 1973)

—— *A Check List of Species, Hybrids and Cultivars of the Genus Fuchsia* (Blandford Press, London, 1985)

—— *Growing and Showing Fuchsias* (David & Charles, Newton Abbot, 1985)

—— *Plantsman's Guide to Fuchsias* (Ward Lock Ltd., London, 1989)

BREEDLOVE, D. E. *The Systematics of Fuchsia Section Encliandra (Onagraceae)* (University of California Press, Berkeley, 1969)

CALIFORNIA FUCHSIA SOCIETY. *A to Z on Fuchsias* (1946)

CESAR, J. *Les Fuchsias* (Dargaud Editeur, Neuilly sur Seine, Cedex, 1981)

DREYER, G. *Mein Fuchsienbuch* (Pauli-Balleis, Nürnberg, 1986)

ESSIG, E. O. *A Check List of Fuchsias* (The American Fuchsia Society, San Francisco, 1936)

EWART, R. *Fuchsia Lexicon* (Blandford Press, Poole, 1982)

FESSLER, A. *Fuchsien für Haus und Garten* (Kosmos, Stuttgart, 1980)

GANSLMEIER, H. *Fuchsien* (Landwirtschaftskammer Rheinland, No. 16, Bonn, 1979)

GOULDING, E. J. *Fuchsias* (Bartholomew, Edinburgh, 1973)

JENNINGS, K. and MILLER, V. *Growing Fuchsias* (Croom Helm, London, 1979)

LAAN, J. E., van der. *Fuchsias het Hele Jaar door* (Thieme, Zutphen, 1974)

MUNZ, P. A. *A Revision of the Genus Fuchsia (Onagraceae)* (California Academy of Sciences, 1943)

PORCHER, F. *Le Fuchsia* (Librairie Centrale d'Agriculture et de Jardinage, 1874, 4th edition)

PROUDLEY, B. and V. *Fuchsias in Colour* (Blandford Press, Poole, 1975)

PUTTOCK, A. G., and GIFFORD, J. *Lovely Fuchsias* (London, 1959)

SAUNDERS, E. *Wagtail's Book of Fuchsias*, I, II, III, IV

THE NATIONAL FUCHSIA SOCIETY. *The New A to Z on Fuchsias* (1976)

THORNE, T. *Fuchsias for All Purposes* (Collingridge, London, 1959)

TOMLINSON, V. *Growing Fuchsias in Southern Africa* (Galaxie Press, Salisbury, 1987)

TRAVIS, J. *Fuchsia Culture* (Travis, Bamber Bridge, Preston)

WELLS, G. *Fuchsias* (Royal Horticultural Society, Wisley, 1985, 2nd edition)

WILSON, S. J. *Fuchsias* (Faber & Faber, London 1965)

WOOD, W. P. *A Fuchsia Survey* (Williams & Norgate, 1950)

The Fuchsia Annual, The British Fuchsia Society, various volumes.

American Fuchsia Society Bulletin, various volumes.

Fuchsiana, organ of the Nederlandse Kring van Fuchsiavriended, various volumes.

Gartenwelt, various older volumes.

Möllers Deutsche Gartenzeitung, various older volumes.

INDEX